THREE CHRONICLES
OF THE REIGN OF
EDWARD IV

THREE CHRONICLES

OF THE REIGN OF

EDWARD IV

With an Introduction by
Keith Dockray

ALAN SUTTON PUBLISHING
BRUNSWICK ROAD · GLOUCESTER · UK

ALAN SUTTON PUBLISHING INC
WOLFBORO · NEW HAMPSHIRE · USA

Copyright © In Introduction, Keith Dockray 1988

First published in this edition 1988

British Library Cataloguing in Publication Data
Three Chronicles of the reign of Edward IV
    1. England. Edward IV, King of England
    942.04′4′0924
    ISBN 0-86299-568-X

Library of Congress Cataloging Data applied for

Printed in Great Britain

CONTENTS

INTRODUCTION

The fifteenth century saw important changes both in the character of historical writing in England and in the nature of the reading public towards which historical works were directed. Most fundamentally, the monastic chronicle, after centuries of vigour, declined into virtual non-existence during the Yorkist era; while the tradition of historical composition in English for a wider and more popular audience, although clearly developing (especially in London), had yet to provide an adequate alternative. Humanist histories in the Italian mould, moreover, were only to emerge in early Tudor times. Charles Ross, the king's modern academic biographer, commented gloomily on the particular dearth of narrative sources available to the historian of Edward IV and his times:

> For no other reign in English history since Henry III do we possess less strictly contemporary information, save perhaps that of Henry VI. It is often far from easy to establish a precise sequence of events, especially when these took place far from London, like the Lancastrian resistance of 1461–4 or the northern rising of 1469. Still more difficult is any discussion of motive and the interplay of personality in politics, matters generally beyond the range of the unsophisticated and often ill-informed and parochial writers of the time.[1]

Indeed, it is the sheer paucity of alternative narratives that gives the three short chronicles reprinted in this volume a degree of importance for the historian of English politics and war that they would not otherwise possess.

Widest in scope is the *Chronicle of John Warkworth* covering, as it does, the first thirteen years of the reign of Edward IV (1461–1474). The chronicle derives its name from, and may well have been written by, a rather obscure Northumbrian scholar who became chaplain to William Grey bishop of Ely in the 1450s and rose, under Grey's patronage, to become Master of Peterhouse, Cambridge, in 1473 (a position he retained until his death in 1500). Written sometime after Clarence's demise in February 1478, it had certainly been completed by 1483 when Warkworth presented to his college a handwritten *Brut* containing, as a continuation, the sole surviving copy of the chronicle.[2] J.O. Halliwell's edition of the manuscript, a generally accurate transcription backed up by interesting and informative notes, was published by the Camden Society in 1839.[3]

Warkworth's Chronicle has received a mixed press from recent historians: on the one hand it has been described (by Antonia Gransden) as a 'well informed, contemporary and generally moderate account of the period'; on the other it has been criticised (by J.R. Lander) as compressed to the point of confusion and inaccuracy, its author a man writing without notes, whose memory is suspect and whose chronology is unreliable.[4] The chronicler certainly has a penchant for portents and astronomical phenomena (although in this respect he is not untypical of later medieval annalists and his occasional flights of fancy need not necessarily discredit his more serious and down-to-earth material): inevitably, the recently murdered corpse of Henry VI 'bledde one the pament' at St. Pauls in 1471 and again at 'the Blake Fryres' (p. 21); while 'a blasynge sterre' three foot high 'by estymacyone' appeared 'in the weste' in 1468, reappeared in 1470, and yet again in 1471 when 'some menne seyde that the blassynges of the seid sterre was of a myle length' (pp. 5, 9, 22). No less alarmingly, in 1473, 'ther was a voyce cryenge in the heyre betwyx Laicestere and Bambury' (p. 24), heard by forty men, 'and some menne saw that he that cryed soo was a hedles manne; and many other dyverse tokenes have be schewede in Englonde this yere, for amendynge of mennys lyvynge.' The eccentricities of the English climate, too, could certainly make an impression on commentators even half a millennium ago: in 1463, we are told, 'ther was ane fervent froste thrugh Englonde, and snowe, (and) a fervent colde'; while in 1473, by contrast, 'ther was a gret hote somere, bothe for manne and beste, by the whiche ther was gret dethe of menne and women' (pp. 3, 23). Nevertheless, the chronicle *is* of considerable value for the political historian, particularly in its treatment of the dramatic events of 1469–1471.

Unusually for a narrative composed during the reign of Edward IV, *Warkworth's Chronicle* not only displays considerable sympathy for Henry VI and his plight but also has a distinctly pro-Lancastrian tinge throughout. This is most marked when the chronicler describes the restoration of Henry VI to the throne in the autumn of 1470 (p. 11):

. . . the Bisshoppe of Wynchestere . . . went to the toure of Londone, where Kynge Herry was in presone by Kynge Edwardes commawndement, and there toke hyme from his kepers, whiche was not worschipfully arayed as a prince, and not so clenly kepte as schuld seme suche a Prynce; thei had hym oute, and newe arayed hym, and dyde to hyme grete reverens, and brought hyme to the palys of Westmynster, and so he was restorede to the crowne agayne . . .

Whereof alle his goode lovers were fulle gladde, and the more parte of peple.[5]

Warkworth firmly places the blame for Henry's earlier loss of the throne (in 1461) on the 'myscheves peple that were aboute the Kynge' who were 'so covetouse towarde them selff' and presided over the loss of English possessions in France (pp. 11–12):

And these were the causes, withe other, that made the peple to gruge ageyns hym, and alle bycause of his fals lordes, and nevere of hym . . .

Warkworth is certainly a major source for the events of 1470 and 1471, ranging from the Lincolnshire rebellion of March 1470 (where, he reports p. 8, the leaders 'gaderid alle the comons of the schyre' and 'cryed "Kynge Herry" and refused Kynge Edwarde') to the battle of Barnet in April 1471 (where the 'grete myste', p. 16, was instrumental in causing the confusion that enabled Edward IV to snatch victory from the jaws of defeat), the long-delayed arrival of Margaret of Anjou in the West Country, the battle of Tewkesbury (where, p. 18, 'ther was slayne in the felde, Prynce Edward, whiche cryede for socoure to his brother-in-lawe the Duke of Clarence') and the Bastard of Fauconberg's spirited if unsuccessful efforts to seize London for Lancaster (pp. 19–20). He is interesting, too, on the murder of Henry VI ('beynge thenne at the Toure the Duke of Gloucetre, brothere to Kynge Edwarde, and many other', p. 21), and provides unique coverage of the last vestiges of resistance to Edward IV 1471–1474 (including a detailed account, pp. 24–6, of the arrest of George Neville archbishop of York who, along with his brothers, had once 'hade the reule of the lande and hade gaderyde grete rychesse many yeres', and a splendid description of the Earl of Oxford's landing in

INTRODUCTION

Cornwall in 1473, his seizure of St. Michael's Mount, and his short-lived holding of that formidable fortress, pp. 26–7).

Warkworth not only has a negative sympathy for Lancastrianism: he also makes a series of positive criticisms of the Yorkist regime. Looking back over the first decade of Edward IV's reign, the chronicler declares (p. 12) that during these years:

> . . . the peple looked after alle the forseide prosperytes and peece, but it came not; but one batayle aftere another, and moche troble and grett losse of goodes amonge the comone peple; as fyrste, the xv. of alle there goodes, and thanne ane hole xv., at yett at every batell to come ferre oute there countreis at ther awne coste; and these and suche othere brought Englonde ryght lowe, and many menne seyd that Kynge Edwarde had myche blame for hurtynge marchandyse, for in his dayes thei were not in other londes, nore wíthein Englonde, take in suche reputacyone and credence as they were afore.

He identifies Edward IV's marriage to Elizabeth Woodville in 1464 as an early cause of dissatisfaction, particularly on the part of the Earl of Warwick who was 'gretely displesyd withe the Kynge' and thereafter 'rose grete discencyone evere more and more betwene the Kyng and hym' (p. 3). This was compounded in 1467 by Edward IV's dismissal of Warwick's brother George Neville from the chancellorship (pp. 3–4):

> After that the Erle of Warwyke toke to hyme in fee as many knyghtys, squyers, and gentylmenne as he myght, to be stronge; and Kyng Edwarde dide that he myght to feble the Erles powere. And yett thei were acorded diverse tymes: but they nevere loffyd togedere aftere.

Not that Warkworth had much sympathy for the Nevilles, or for the king's brother George duke of Clarence (p. 15). His greatest contempt was reserved, however, for the 'New Yorkist' John Tiptoft earl of Worcester. Tiptoft condemned the Earl of Oxford and his fellow Lancastrian conspirators in 1462 'by lawe padowe' to be beheaded on Tower hill 'that alle menne myght see: whereof the most peple were sorry' (p. 5). Worse still, following the Lincolnshire rebellion in 1470, he sentenced twenty gentlemen and yeomen to be 'hangede, drawne, and quartered, and hedede' at Southampton (p. 9):

> . . . and after that thei hanged uppe by the leggys, and a stake made scharpe at bothe endes, whereof one ende was putt in att bottokys, and the other ende ther heddes were putt uppe one; for the whiche the peple of the londe were gretely displesyd; and evere afterwarde the Erle of Worcestre was gretely behatede emonge the peple . . .

Certainly, Tiptoft's own execution by the Readeption government later in 1470, when he was 'juged by suche lawe as he dyde to other menne' (p. 13), seems to have been greeted by Londoners with every sign of enthusiasm! Perhaps the most frequently recurring theme in Warkworth's criticisms of Edward IV's government in the 1460s, however, was the intolerable burden of its financial demands. In 1463, he declares (p. 3), 'the peple grocchede sore' at parliamentary taxation; the king's coinage debasement of 1464 was 'to the grete harme of the comene peple' (p. 4); and the fifteenth levied in 1469 again 'noyed the peple, for thei had payed a lytelle before a gret taske' (p. 8).

In an age when most chroniclers concentrated on events in London and southern England, *Warkworth's Chronicle* is almost unique in the degree of its interest in the North.[6] Although frequently confused (and confusing!), the chronicler provides interesting (if infuriatingly brief)

INTRODUCTION

evidence of the nature and extent of Lancastrian resistance to the new Yorkist regime in the far north of England 1461–1464.[7] Much of this centred on the great Northumberland castles of Alnwick, Dunstanborough and Bamborough, and Edward IV was clearly hard-pressed to get permanent control of them. Even when, as in the vicinity of Alnwick at the beginning of 1463, a Yorkist force seemed to have the upper hand, victory proved difficult to clinch. Warkworth comments (p. 2) that on this occasion:

> . . . whenne Kynge Edwardes hooste had knowlege that Sere Perys le Brasille with the Scottesmenne were comynge, thei remewed from the sege and were affrayed; and the Scottesche hoost supposed it hade be doone for some gayne, and thei were affrayed; also thei durst not come neghe the castelle; for and thei hade comyne one boldly, thei myghte have takyne and distressit alle the lordes and comeners, for they had lye ther so longe in the felde, and were greved with colde and rayne, that thei hade no coreage to feght.

For the northern rebellions of 1469 and 1470 Warkworth, despite providing relatively slight and not always reliable coverage, must be regarded as a major source. For instance, he reports (p. 6) that in the summer of 1469, by the assignment of Warwick and Clarence, there was 'a grete insurreccyon in Yorkeschyre' led by 'William Conyars knyghte' who called himself 'Robyne of Riddesdale': the eventual outcome of this was the battle of Edgecote and the short-lived imprisonment of Edward IV by Warwick the Kingmaker.[8] The Lincolnshire rebellion of March 1470, he believed, likewise owed much to the inspiration of Warwick and Clarence (p. 8):

And the Duke of Clarence and the Erle of Warwyke causede alle this, like as thei dyde Robyne of Riddesdale to ryse afore that at Banbury felde.

Warkworth's knowledge of, and interest in, events in the North is perhaps most graphically demonstrated by his account of Edward IV's landing at Ravenspur in Holderness in March 1471 and the hostile reception he received there (pp. 13–14). So little support did he find in Yorkshire, indeed, that he declared 'he came thedere by the Erle of Northumberlondes avyse' and merely 'to claim the Duchery of Yorke'; while, on arriving at the city of York, 'afore alle peple he cryed "A! Kynge Herry! A! Kynge and Prynce Edwarde!" and wered ane estryche feder, Prynce Edwardes lyvery' (p. 14). Only after his successful restoration to the throne, and then largely thanks to the efforts of his brother Richard of Gloucester, did Edward IV at last win the loyalty of the North.

At no other time in his reign was Edward IV's authority so severely challenged as it was during the crisis of 1469–1471, and it is no coincidence that the only official chronicles written in the Yorkist interest belong to this period as well. Although official and semi-official histories became an established means of pro-Valois propaganda and communication in fifteenth-century France, the *Chronicle of the Rebellion in Lincolnshire* and the *Historie of the Arrivall of Edward IV* are virtually the only examples of the genre produced in England during the fifteenth century. The Yorkist lords had, indeed, recognised the potential of carefully slanted publicity on their own behalf as early as 1460/1, but detailed and skilfully written political tracts like these, put together very soon after the events they describe by well-informed authors and having very much the character of diaries of the behaviour and movements of the king and his entourage, were on an altogether more sophisticated scale.[9]

INTRODUCTION

The *Chronicle of the Rebellion in Lincolnshire*, covering events during three critical weeks in March 1470, was written by an anonymous royal servant (probably connected with the privy seal office in Chancery) soon after the completion of Edward IV's successful campaign. Clearly an official account designed to present the government's view of the causes, character and results of the rebellion, it also had the deliberate purpose of implicating George duke of Clarence (the King's brother) and Richard Neville earl of Warwick (Warwick the Kingmaker) right up to the hilt. The propagandist intent of the chronicle is made abundantly clear at the outset (p. 5):

> A Remembrance of suche actes and dedes as oure souveraigne lorde the king hadde doon in his journey begonne at London the vi. day of Marche (1470) for the repression and seting down of the rebellyon and insurreccion of his subgettes in the shire of Linccolne, commeaved by the subtile and fals conspiracie of his grete rebelles George duc of Clarence, Richarde erle of Warrewike, and othere.

Edward IV, 'a prince enclined to shew his mercy and pitie to his subgettes', is portrayed as traitorously deceived by rebels who 'falsly compassed, conspired, and ymagened the final destruccion of his most roiall personne' (p. 5): his vigorous and effective response to the threat is most emphatically presented as an admirable object-lesson in good kingship. The chronicler specifically cites confessions made by Sir Robert Welles and others as authorities in support of his contentions, and J.G. Nichols (who edited the text for the Camden Society in 1847) helpfully printed the *Confession of Sir Robert Welles* as well as the chronicle itself (pp. 21–23). Although, apparently, only a single copy of the chronicle now survives, its circulation on the Continent at the time (presumably in a

French translation) is indicated by the fact that the Burgundian chronicler Jean de Waurin made use of it in his *Recueil des Croniques et Anchiennes Istories de la Grant Bretaigne.* Moreover, despite its obviously partisan character, it does provide an extremely valuable account of the Lincolnshire rebellion, written very soon after it was over, persuasively argued, well-documented and splendidly detailed.[10]

Certainly, most recent discussions of the rebellion in Lincolnshire have drawn heavily on the official account.[11] Sir Robert Welles, the chronicler tells us, 'callyng hym self grete capteyn of the comons of Linccolnshire' caused proclamations to be made throughout the county on Sunday 4 March 'in the kinges name, the duc, erle, and his owne name' calling on 'everye man' to assemble near Lincoln on Tuesday 6 March 'to resist the king in comyng down into the saide shire, saying that his comyng thidre was to destroie the comons of the same shire' (p. 6). Edward IV, seemingly, received news of Welles' initiative in Essex on 7 March and rapidly marched north-westwards into Lincolnshire. On 12 March the so-called battle of Lose-Coat field was fought where, according to the chronicler, the complicity of Clarence and Warwick was only too apparent (p. 10):

. . . at suche tyme as the batailes were towardes joyning, the kyng with (his) oost seting uppon (the rebels), and they avaunsyng theymself, theire crye was, *A Clarence! a Clarence! a Warrewike!* that tyme beyng in the feelde divers persons in the duc of Clarence livery, and especially sir Robert Welles hymself, and a man of the dukes own, that aftre was slayne in the chase, and his casket taken, wherinne were founden many marvelous billes, conteining matter of the grete seduccion, and the verrey subversion of the king and the common wele of alle this lande, with the most abhominable treason that ever were seen or attempted withinne the same . . .

Moreover, when Sir Robert Welles and other rebel leaders were 'severally examyned of there free willes uncompelled, not for fere of dethe ne otherwyse stirred, (they) knowleged and confessed the saide duc and erle to be partiners and chef provocars of all theire treasons' and that 'theire porpos was to distroie the king and to have made the saide duc king' (p. 11). As to the 'commocion in meoving of people in Richemond shire by the stirring of the lorde Scrope and othere' (p. 12), when news of Edward IV's victory reached the Yorkshire rebels they soon dispersed. The king himself made his way northwards towards the city of York. En route, at Doncaster, Sir Robert Welles was executed 'afore the multitude of the kinges oost'; while, at York, he received the submission of Scrope and other northern insurgents who had 'laboured, specially provoced and stirred the people in thies parties' (p. 17) and, at last, fully accepted the fact of the treachery of Clarence and Warwick.

Although Edward IV emerged triumphant in the spring of 1470, the next initiative by Warwick and Clarence (now enjoying the explicit support of Louis XI of France and the no doubt calculated backing of Margaret of Anjou) resulted in the king's precipitate flight to Burgundy and the Readeption of Henry VI in the autumn of the same year. Edward's return to England in March 1471, and the action-packed campaign which followed, is the subject of the *Historie of the Arrivall of Edward IV*. Covering a period of less than three months, from 2 March (when Edward IV took ship from Burgundy for England) to 26 May (when Edward arrived in Canterbury following the defeat of the Bastard of Fauconberg), this is very clearly an official Yorkist version of events designed to record the king's recovery of the throne in the most flattering of terms and never missing an opportunity to praise his courage, piety and love of peace. The anonymous author (perhaps, as Antonia Gransden suggests, the same royal official who penned the *Chronicle of the Rebellion in Lincolnshire*) specifically tells us (p. 1) that he was:

> . . . a servaunt of the Kyngs, that presently saw in effect a great parte of his exploytes, and the resydewe knewe by true relation of them that were present at every tyme.

Despite its partisan character, however, this is a narrative of very high quality, intelligently written, and splendidly detailed: indeed, it has a good claim to be regarded as the best contemporary chronicle produced in England during the Wars of the Roses.[12] The medieval original of the manuscript edited by John Bruce for the Camden Society in 1838 has disappeared: Bruce, in fact, transcribed Harleian Manuscript 543, a document copied by John Stow in the sixteenth century from 'Mastar Flyghtwods boke' (an even earlier copy made by the recorder of London William Fleetwood). It is clear, too, that the Burgundian chronicler Jean de Waurin made extensive use of the chronicle in the early 1470s (though in a more complete version than Stow's transcript), suggesting the tract was circulating on the Continent very soon after the events it describes.[13] To further complicate the issue, there was composed in French a shorter and even earlier version (of which four manuscripts still survive), apparently used by the French chronicler Thomas Basin. This short French version of the *Arrival*, indeed, may well have been penned within days of Edward IV's final triumph, on the king's orders, for the purpose of rapidly disseminating news of his successful campaign on the Continent.[14]

From the very beginning, it is clear that the author of the *Arrival* was not only concerned to chart Edward IV's campaign 'to recover his realme' which had been 'usurpyd and occupied' by Henry VI 'by the traitorous meanes of his greate rebell Richard, Erle of Warwicke, and his complices' (p. 2): he wanted to explain as well *why* Edward acted as he did. Nor does he duck difficult issues. Thus, when describing the king's early days back in England following his landing in Holderness, he emphasises that 'there came but right few' of the county to him 'or almost none'; Hull refused to admit him; and he had to resort to the subterfuge of declaring 'his entent and purpos was only to claime to be Duke of Yorke' (pp. 3–4). The city of York only reluctantly admitted him, and he was fortunate that Warwick's brother John marquis Montagu 'in no wyse trowbled hym', while Henry Percy earl of Northumberland 'sat still' and thereby 'dyd the Kynge right gode and notable service' (pp. 5–6).[15] Only when he reached the Midlands did Edward IV's prospects begin to look distinctly promising, being joined by a substantial force of Hastings' retainers and, of course, by his now disillusioned brother Clarence (pp. 8–11).[16] Meanwhile, in London, the parading of Henry VI through the streets proved a pathetic and counter-productive strategy, for Edward received an enthusiastic welcome (pp. 15–17). Warwick the Kingmaker, having failed to halt the Yorkist king's march south, followed in his wake, perhaps naively hoping to take him by surprise while he 'kepte and observyd the solemptie of Estar' (pp. 17–18). Instead, Edward IV himself took the initiative, and the result was the battle of Barnet. The *Arrival* provides the most detailed and convincing account we have of this extraordinary fracas (pp. 18–21), as it does also of the manoeuvring that culminated in the battle of Tewkesbury soon afterwards (pp. 22–30).[17] Finally, the chronicler supplies a vigorous account of the Bastard of Fauconberg's abortive efforts on behalf of Lancaster (or more probably himself!) in the south-east, Edward IV's triumphant entry into London and his firm measures to repress disorder in Kent (pp. 35–9). Only the fate of Henry VI in the Tower of London defeated him: surely his claim that Henry 'late called Kyng' died 'of pure displeasure and melencoly' (p. 38) can have convinced hardly anybody? By contrast, the final paragraph of the chronicle is masterly in its projection of a compelling image of king and government (pp. 39–40):

> And thus (was) begon, finished and termined, the reentrie and perfecte recover of the iuste title and right of owr sayd soveraygne Lord Kynge Edward the Fowrthe, to his realme and crowne of England ... Whereby it apperithe (that) in short tyme he shall appeas his subgetes thrwghe all his royalme; that peace and tranquillitie shall growe and multiplye in the same, from day to day, to the honour and lovynge of Almyghty God, the encreace of his singuler and famows renowme, and to the great ioye and consolation of his frinds, alies, and well-willers, and to all his people, and to the great confusion of all his enemys and evyll wyllars.

Keith Dockray
Huddersfield Polytechnic, July 1988

Page references made in this Introduction relate to pages of the original Camden editions.

NOTES
1. C. Ross, *Edward IV* (1974), p. 429.
2. C.L. Kingsford, *English Historical Literature in the Fifteenth Century* (1913), pp. 171–2; A. Gransden, *Historical Writing in England II:c.1307 to the Early Sixteenth Century* (1982), pp. 257–8.
3. Some of the notes to the Camden edition were Halliwell's own; others were

INTRODUCTION

provided by J.G. Nichols. They include transcriptions of several associated manuscripts, most notably a College of Arms fragment relating to events in the North in May/June 1464 (pp. 36–9) and a letter/manifesto despatched from Calais by Clarence, Warwick and the archbishop of York on 12 July 1469 (pp. 46–51).

4. Gransden, *op.cit.*, p. 259; J.R. Lander, 'The Treason and Death of the Duke of Clarence', *Crown and Nobility 1450–1509* (1976), pp. 260–1. Lander is particularly critical of the very brief and inaccurate treatment of the first eight years of Edward IV's reign and the reliability of this 'jejune continuation of the *Brut*' concerning a supposed agreement in France in 1470 that, should the Lancastrian line fail, the succession to the throne would then pass to Clarence. He does admit, however, that the chronicle is of interest for Robin of Redesdale's rebellion in 1469 and 'of very considerable value for events in England in 1470 and 1471.'

5. There is a clear note of sympathy, too, in Warkworth's description of Henry VI's capture in Lancashire in 1465 and his subsequent journey to London 'on horse bake, and his lege bownde to the styrope' (p. 5).

6. This may well reflect the fact that the author was himself a northerner, perhaps deriving his name from the Northumberland village of Warkworth.

7. Reviewing the situation in 1463, he remarks (p. 3) that 'Kynge Edward was possessed of alle Englonde, except a castelle in Northe Wales called Harlake.'

8. Gransden, *op.cit.*, p. 260, considers Warkworth's account of the rebellion of Robin of Redesdale 'well informed'; for a more critical view, see K.R. Dockray, 'The Yorkshire Rebellions of 1469', *The Ricardian*, vol. vi no. 83 (December 1983), pp. 246–57.

9. Ross, *op.cit.*, pp. 429, 432–3, and 'Rumour, Propaganda and Public Opinion during the Wars of the Roses', *Patronage, the Crown and the Provinces in Later Medieval England*, ed. R.A. Griffiths (1981), pp. 23–4. Gransden suggests, indeed, that the *Chronicle of the Rebellion in Lincolnshire* and the *Arrival* may even have been written by the same royal servant.

10. Kingsford, *op.cit.*, pp. 173–4; Gransden, *op.cit.*, pp. 261–4; *Recueil des Croniques*

et Anchiennes Istories de la Grant Bretaigne par Jehan de Waurin, vol. 5 (1891), ed. W. and E. Hardy, pp. 587–602.

11. For instance, Charles Ross in his biography of *Edward IV* pp. 138–41, and A. Goodman, *The Wars of the Roses* (1981), pp. 71–3. R.L. Storey, however, in pressing the case for seeking the origins of the rebellion in a private feud in Lincolnshire between Thomas Burgh of Gainsborough (a Yorkist parvenu) on the one hand and the long-established Welles family on the other develops a suggestion put forward by *Warkworth's Chronicle* (p. 8): R.L. Storey, 'Lincolnshire and the Wars of the Roses', *Nottingham Medieval Studies*, xiv (1970), pp. 71–2.

12. Kingsford, *op.cit.*, pp. 174–6; Ross, *op.cit.*, pp. 162n, 432–3; Gransden, *op.cit.*, pp. 261–5, and 'Propaganda in English medieval historiography', *Journal of Medieval History*, 1 (1975), p. 375.

13. Waurin, *op.cit.*, pp. 640–75.

14. J.A.F. Thomson, '"The Arrivall of Edward IV" – The Development of the Text', *Speculum*, xlvi (1971), pp. 84–93; see also Kingsford, *op.cit.*, pp. 174–6, and Gransden, *Historical Writing*, pp. 264–5, 481, 487–9.

15. Montagu, it seems, had too few men to move against Edward IV alone, while the powerful earl of Northumberland had reason to feel grateful to a king who had restored him to his earldom the previous year.

16. The subtlety of the *Arrival*'s propaganda is nicely demonstrated by the story that, while Edward was attending a Palm Sunday service at Daventry, there was 'a fayre miracle, a goode pronostique of good aventure that aftar shuld befall unto the Kynge.' Apparently, the doors of a statue of St. Anne (which were 'shett, closed and clasped') suddenly opened with 'a great crak' revealing the alabaster image of the saint. 'The Kynge, this seinge, thanked and honoryd God, and Seint Anne, takynge it for a good signe, and token of good and prosperous aventure that God wold send hym in that he had to do' (pp. 13–14).

17. The *Arrival* certainly has a graphic account of the battle of Tewkesbury itself (particularly useful since other chronicles provide notably sparse information), including the interesting comment that 'Edward, called Prince, was taken, fleinge to the towne wards, and slayne, in the fielde' (p. 30).

A CHRONICLE

OF THE

FIRST THIRTEEN YEARS OF THE REIGN OF

KING EDWARD THE FOURTH

BY JOHN WARKWORTH, D.D.

Master of St. Peter's College, Cambridge

Edited by
James Orchard Halliwell, Esq. F.R.S., F.S.A.

First published for the Camden Society
1839

INTRODUCTION.

MR. HUNTER, in the Appendix to the last Report of the Record Commissioners,* was the first who noticed the existence of a singularly valuable and curious historical document preserved in the library of St. Peter's College, Cambridge, which had been extensively quoted by Leland in his Collectanea at the commencement of the sixteenth century. Leland extracts from a MS. volume of Chronicles given to the College by John Warkworth, who was then Master, the greater portion of which is a mere copy of Caxton's edition of the Brute Chronicle; and although, without the slightest notion of a judicious selection, that industrious transcriber has extracted as largely from the Brute as from the other part of the manuscript, yet his Collectanea has for three centuries been the only known receptacle † of a portion of the exceed-

* Fol. Lond. 1837, p. 336, col. 2.

† Previously, however, to Mr. Hunter's notice, the manuscript itself had been mentioned, but not for an historical purpose, in Mr. Hartshorne's Book Rarities of the University of Cambridge, p. 390.

3

ingly curious facts recorded in Warkworth's own Chronicle, and would, perhaps, have been for three centuries longer, had not the antiquarian diligence of Mr. Hunter discovered its latent resting-place, and added one more to the many instances of valuable documents rescued from oblivion by that zealous and able historian.

The following Chronicle comprises a history of the first thirteen years of the reign of Edward the Fourth. "This eventful period," well observes Sir Henry Ellis, "though removed from us scarcely more than three centuries, is still among the darkest on our annals. Its records are confused, mutilated, and disjointed. They who wrote history in it, had no talents for the task; and there was a ferocity abroad among the partizans of both the rival houses, which prevented many from even assembling the materials of history."* The paucity of documents illustrating this period has, indeed, long † been a matter of regret. To meet with one, then, so minute in particulars, abounding in new facts, and of indisputable authenticity, cannot but be a matter of congratulation to the historian.

It is quite unnecessary here to enlarge on the history of the period to which the following narrative relates. There is, however, one part of this diary, for in many

* Original Letters. Second Series, vol. i. p. 94.
† Gentleman's Magazine, 1791, vol. 61, Pt. i. p. 222.

instances it is sufficiently minute to be called an occasional one, which must necessarily arrest the attention of
every reader,—the account of the mysterious death of King
Henry, expressed in such decided terms, and with such
apparently perfect knowledge of every part of the transaction, as cannot fail to raise strong doubts of its authenticity. On a question of so dark a nature, no excuse will
be needed for another writer entering into the contro-
versy, with the aid of an additional auxiliary of powerful
evidence.

Before I proceed further, I will place before the reader
a few of the unpublished evidences I have collected relative to this transaction :—

1. "Obitus Regis Henrici Sexti, qui obiit *inter* vicesi-
mum primum diem Maii et xxij^m. diem Maii." MS. Bib.
Reg. 2 B. xv. fol. 1, r°.

2. "Rex Henricus Sextus in arce Londoñ ferro trans-
figitur et occiditur." MS. Cotton. Otho, B. xiv. fol.
221, v°.

3. "Et Henricus, nuper Rex, reponitur in Turrim
Londoñ, et, in vigilia Ascenscionis dormiente, ibidem
feliciter moriens, per Tamisiam navicula usque ad Ab-
bathiam de Cheltosye deductus, ibi sepultus est." MS.
Arundel, (College of Arms) No. 5, fol. 171, v°.

4. "Et in vigilia ascensionis moriebatur Rex Henricus
Sextus in turri Londoniarum, qui quidem sepultus erat

apud Chersey, et postea translatus per Regem Ricardum usque Wynsowerem." MS. Laud, 674. (B. 23) fol. 11, r°.

5. There is a Latin prophecy (written perhaps after the fulfilment of the predicted event) in MS. Digb. 196, that King Henry the Sixth shall die a violent death.

6. "Also upon ascencion evyn, Kyng Henry was brought from the tower thrugh Chepe unto Powlys upon a bere, and abowte the beere more glevys and stavys than torches; who was slayne, as it was said, by the Duke of Glowcetir; but howe he was deed [nobody knewe, but] thedir he was brought deed; and in the chirch the corps stode all nyght, and on the morue he was conveyed to Chertsey, where he was buryed.." MS. London Chronicle. Bibl. Cotton. Vitell. A. xvi. fol. 133, r°.

7. The following is taken from a metrical history of the reign of Edward the Fourth, by John Herd, M.D., a copy of which is in MS. Cotton. Jul. C. ii.

> " Interea Henricus Sextus, spoliatus avito
> Qui fuit imperio, vita spoliatur, in arce
> In Thamesis ripa vitreas que prospicit undas.
> Illum fama refert rigidum jugulasse Richardum,
> Gloucestrensis erat qui dux, vir sevus et audax,
> Post cujus cœdem sic insultasse refertur ;—
> ' Masculus, en ! hæres Edverdo a rege creatus,
> Tertius illius qui vixit nominis olim,
> Preter nos hodie respirat nemo superstes—
> Nos, Eboracensis quos gloria stirpis honorat !'
> Henrici corpus Pauli transfertur in ædem,
> Et jacet in feretro, vulgi ut videatur ocellis.

Parvulus est vicus, Chersei nomine notus,
In quo cœnobium, sacer Erchenwalde, locabas,
Londini fueras qui clarus episcopus olim ;
Huc delatus erat tumuloque Henricus opertus;
Post Vindessoram translatus, conditur æde
Que sacrata tibi celebratur, dive Georgi !
Octo et ter denos Henricus præfuit annos ;
Sex etiam menses post sceptra recepta regebat ;
Vitæ annos binos et quinquaginta peregit :
Edverdus princeps gnatus fuit unicus illi."

Fol. 170 vᵒ—171 rᵒ.

8. " Eodem die [mensis Maij xxjᵒ.] decessit Henricus Sextus, olim dictus Rex Anglie, apud Turrim Londoñ, et sepultus est in monasterio de Chertesey juxta Tamisiam Wintoñ dioces'. Et sic nemo relinquitur in humanis qui ex illo stirpite coronam petat." MS. Arundel, Mus. Brit. 28, fol. 25, vᵒ.

John Blakman*, after relating an anecdote of the patience of Henry, adds—"Consimilem etiam misericordiam cum pluribus aliis ostendit, specialiter autem duobus, mortem ei intendentibus, quorum unus collo suo grave vulnus inflixit, volens excerebrasse vel decolasse eum, quod tamen Rex patientissime tulit, dicens, *forsothe and forsothe, ye do fouly to smyte a kynge enoynted so ;*" and he afterwards proceeds to state—" Et tandem mortis ibi corporis violentiam sustinuit propter regnum, et tunc spe-

* De virtutibus et miraculis Regis Henrici, pp. 301 et 303.

7

rabatur, ab aliis pacifice possidendum." Little did the author of the following curious song imagine that his reigning sovereign would arrive at so tragical an end—

" Now grawnt him hit so be may—
Pray we that Lord is Lord of alle,
To save our Kyng, his reme ryalle,
And let never myschip uppon him falle,
Ne false traytoure him to betray.
I praye ʒoue, seris, of ʒour gentre,
Syng this carol reverently ;
Fore hit is mad of Kyng Herre,
Gret ned fore him we han to pray !
ʒif he fare wele, wele schul we be,
Or ellis we may be ful sore ;
Fore him schul wepe mone an e,
Thus prophecis the Blynd Awdlay."*

And " mone an e " doubtless did weep for the sainted Prince. The Croyland Continuator forcibly concludes his account with the following prayer : " may God grant time for repentance to the person, whoever he was, who laid his sacrilegious hands on the Lord's anointed."

* MS. Douce, Bib. Bodl. Oxon. No. 302, fol. 29, vᵒ, a. A folio volume on vellum containing poems by John Awdlay, the blind poet, and (fol. 22, vᵒ, b.) written in the Monastery of Haghmond in the year 1426. Mr. Hartshorne will use this MS. in his forthcoming Shropshire Glossary. I may refer here to four Latin verses on Henry the Sixth in MS. Bodl. 926. Laud, 670. E. 3. (Bern. 61.)

But to return from this digression. Mr. Bayley says "we have satisfactory testimony that Henry lived at least up to the twenty-fifth of May," and he quotes the *Fœdera* for his authority, thereby falling into an error which Sharon Turner made, in mistaking the day of the payment of certain monies for that on which they were incurred,—an error which Dr. Lingard was the first to point out, and which takes away entirely the only seeming substantial evidence that has been brought forward to show that Henry did not die between the 21st and the 22nd of May, as stated in the following Chronicle. Fleetwood's narrative affirms that Henry expired on the 23rd "of pure displeasure and melancholy," and this very palpable attempt at deception proves at any rate that the popular feeling and opinion was strong enough to induce the Yorkists to attempt to throw a veil over the important circumstantial fact that would render a murder probable, viz. that Henry died the very night Edward made his triumphal entry into the metropolis.* Indeed, the whole

* The catalogue of authorities for the murder of Henry VI. might be extended *ad libitum*, and do not show more than the popular opinion after all; it may be as well, however, to give a few references. L'Art de verifier les Dates, i. 816, col. i.; Harl. Miscell. i. 313; Life of Henry the Sixth (8vo. Lond. 1712), p. 58; Grafton's continuation of Harding's Chronicle, Sir Henry Ellis's edition, p. 460; "Rex Henricus occiditur clam in Turri," MS. Tanner, Bodl. II.

of the circumstantial evidence is in favour of the murder ; Edward made his triumphal entry into London on the 21st, and went into Kent with the Duke of Gloucester on the following day ; on the afternoon of the 22nd, Henry's body was brought to St. Paul's, and there, as we are informed by four good authorities, *bled afresh*—

> " O, gentlemen, see, see ! dead Henry's wounds
> Open their congealed mouths, and bleed afresh !—
> Blush, blush, thou lump of foul deformity ;
> For 'tis thy presence that exhales this blood
> From cold and empty veins, where no blood dwells ;
> Thy deed, inhuman and unnatural,
> Provokes this deluge most unnatural."

William Habington* remarks that " the death of King Henry was acted in the darke, so that it cannot be affirmed who was the executioner, only it is probable it was a resolution of the state. The care of the king's safety and the publicke quiet, in some sort making it,

---

fol. 104, vº. and fol. 56, rº ; Hist. Anglic. a M. H. 1640, p. 180 ; Cooper's Chronicle, p. 267 ; MS. Harl. 2408 ; Palmesii Continuatio Chron. Eusebiani, edit. 1483, fol. 160, rº ; Mémoires Olivier de la Marche, sub anno 1469 ; Lilii Chronicon Angliæ, edit. 1565, fol. 63, rº ; the Breviat Chronicle of the Kings of England, edit. Cant. 1553, aº. 1470 ; MS. Vinc. in Coll. Arm. 418.

* The Historie of Edward the Fourth. Lond. 1640, p. 104.

however cruell, yet necessary ;" and he adds, " at what time his body lay in Saint Paul's, and after in Blacke-fryers, a large quantity of blood issued from his nose— a most miraculous way of speaking the barbarisme of his murther, and giving tyrants to understand that the dead dare in their language tell the truth, and call even their actions to account." I make this extract for the purpose of remarking on Habington's political reason for the murder of Henry—an argument which Hume and all subsequent historians, with the exception of Dr. Lingard, have strangely underrated. If the life of Henry was of no importance, how was it that at Ludford the leader of the Yorkists considered it expedient to report his death, and actually cause mass to be celebrated for the repose of his soul, although he knew that the King was then alive and well*. Neither do I consider the argument alleged by Sir James Mackintosh † of much weight—*it is improbable that those who through so many scenes of blood had spared the Prince should at last incur the odium of destroying him.* Had not the most recent of Edward's misfortunes been owing to him? and, moreover, while the child was living,‡ so long as the heir apparent of the

* Rot. Parl. V. 348 ; Owen and Blakeway's History of Shrewsbury, vol. i. p. 229.

† History of England, vol. ii. p. 44.

‡ " And shortly after [his final defeat], to make that parte sure,

throne was in existence—if so, indeed, he could be called after the treaty made by his father—the life of Henry was not worth caring for in comparison with the danger of destroying him. But now the love of the people, stronger and more enthusiastic as the unfortunate Henry was overwhelmed with greater and increasing difficulties, tended towards, and, perhaps, would ultimately have accomplished, the ejection of his rival, a sovereign who was inclined to deal heavily with them, and who never could have been a general favourite.

Warkworth informs us that the Duke of Gloucester was at the Tower of London on the night of the murder of Henry. No certain evidence has transpired relative to the share that this prince had in the deed, nor is it to be expected that we could obtain any ; the voice of the people attributed the direct performance of the murder to him ; and his insatiable ambition, for his road was doubtless more open after Henry's decease, afforded a fair ground for the presumption. Philip de Comines says, " if what was told me be true, after the battle was over, the Duke of Gloucester slew this poor King Herry with

was deprived of his lief, havinge loste also Edward his sonne the Prynce before spoken of, the hope of all his posteritie, in the Battayle of Tewksbury." MS. Sloan. 3479. fol. 6, vº. See also MS. Arundel, Mus. Brit. 28. fol. 25, vº. which contains the only early authority for this view of the transaction.

his own hand, or caused him to be carried to some private place, and stood by himself, while he was killed." There must have been some reason for these rumours, and De Comines was contemporary; perhaps Gloucester might have had a double purpose in the death of the king—the accomplishment of his grand aim of ambition and the service of his brother. He appears to have been detected in his aim at sovereignty, for Lewis Glyn Cothi (Works, p. 47, l. 13.) in a poem written immediately after the death of Edward, seems to have had some presentiment that Richard would succeed to the throne, for he emphatically styles him *y brenin Risiart.*

In the perusal of the following narrative every one must be struck with the difference between the characters of the two rival princes; and although, perhaps, with the enthusiasm of a staunch Lancastrian, its author has coloured the vices of the one, yet in no place has he magnified the virtues of the other. Nothing can be fairer or more sensible than the view he gives of the state of popular feeling, after the resumption of the throne by Henry.—" These were the causes, among others, which caused the people to grumble against him; and the common people said if they could have another king, he would regain all his lost possessions, and amend every corruption in the state, and bring the realm of England into prosperity and peace; nevertheless, when King Edward reigned, the people expected all the aforesaid prosperity and peace, but it came not; but one battle after another, and much trouble and loss among the common people." Almost every change, expected by the people to produce great and immediate advantage to them, has failed at least in its incipient operation, and the above clearly accounts for the strong reaction in favour of Henry. Afterwards it acted as a much more powerful motive, and so deeply did the fortunes of the royal prisoner excite the general compassion of his subjects, that, after he was really deceased, no adulation was considered sufficient to sustain the well-merited reputation of his moral virtues. Of this we have a remarkable instance in the legendary life of him, written by a monk of Windsor about the year 1500, which opens with the following hymn,*—

> " Salve ! miles preciose,
> Rex Henrice generose,
>   Palmes vitis celice ;
> In radice caritatis
> Vernans flore sanctitatis,
>   Viteque angelice.
>
> " Salve ! flos nobilitatis,
> Laus et honor dignitatis,
>   Seu corone regie ;

* De miraculis Henrici Sexti, libri duo. MS. Harl. 423, fol.72, r⁰.

Pie pater orphanorum,
Vera salus populorum,
    Robur et ecclesie.

" Salve ! forma pietatis,
Exemplar humilitatis,
    Decus innocencie !
Vi oppressis vel turbatis,
Mestis atque desolatis,
    Scola paciencie.

" Salve ! fax superne lucis,
Per quam servi summi ducis
    Illustrantur undique :
Dum virtute lucis vere,
Meruisti prefulgere
    Tantis signis gratie.

" Salve ! quem Rex seculorum
Choris jungens angelorum
    Civem fecit patrie ;
Te laudare cupientes
Fac ut semper sint fruentes
    Tecum vita glorie !   Amen."

Henry the Seventh made an application to Pope
Alexander the Sixth for the canonization of Henry, but
his extreme penuriousness was the reason of its not being
carried into effect, as he was unwilling to incur the necessary expenses.

John Lidgate's well-known poem on the Kings of England concludes with the reign of Henry VI.; but one manuscript * contains an addition relating to Edward IV. which renders the entire stanzas on those two reigns worthy of insertion, because the contrast is most singular;—

" Sixt Henry brought forthe in al vertu,
By just title borne by enheritaunce,
Aforne providede by grace of Criste Jhesu,
To were ij. crownys in Ynglonde and in Fraunce ;
To whom Gode hathe yove soverayne suffisaunce
Of vertuous lyfe, and chose hym for his knyghte,
Longe to rejoyse and reigne in his righte.

" Comforthe al thristy and drynke with gladnes !
Rejoyse withe myrthe thoughe ye have nate to spende !
The tyme is come to avoyden yowre distres—
Edwarde the fourthe the olde wronges to amende
Is wele disposede in wille, and to defende
His londe and peple in dede, withe kynne and myghte ;
Goode lyf and longe I pray to God hym sende,
And that seynte George be withe hym in his righte."

It is evident that this latter part was written at the commencement of the reign of Edward IV.

The MS. which contains the Chronicle now printed

* MS. Harl. 2251, fol. 4, r⁰.

consists of a folio volume of 225 leaves of vellum, the last being pasted to the cover, and written not long after the last mentioned event, A.D. 1473. Leland errs in saying that the MS. is in Warkworth's handwriting, for it is evidently the work of a common scribe; we fortunately possess a note of presentation in Warkworth's autography, and the fac-simile of this, with a specimen of the scribe's calligraphy, will be found at the commencement of the volume. The sentence with which Warkworth opens his memoranda is curious; it is probable that he had two copies of Caxton's Chronicle, in one of which he had written his own continuation, beginning with the words " at the coronacyone of the forseyde Edward," and in the other, instead of making a second copy of the continuation, he simply made the reference " as for alle thynges that folowe, referre them to my copey, in whyche is wretyn a remanente [or continuation] lyke to this forseyd werke" [i. e. written in the same manner as Caxton's Chronicle.] The scribe, who made the transcript of Caxton now preserved at Peterhouse, had been directed to refer from one manuscript to the other for the con- tinuation, and in so doing he added Warkworth's note of reference by way of introduction to the new part, joining them together by means of the words " that is to wytt, that."

The scribe of the Brute Chronicle has exchanged Caxton's orthography for his own, as the reader may readily see by comparing the printed edition with the following conclusion :—

" And here I make ane ende of this lytelle werke as myche as I can fynde aftere the forme of the werke by-fore made by Ranulpd Monke of Chestere. And where ther is ony faughte I beseche them that schal rede it to correcte it. For yf I cowede have founde moo storyes I wolde have sett in itt moo ; but the substaunce that I can fynde and knowe I have schortely seett them in this boke, to the entent that suche thynges as have be done sithe deythe or ende of the same booke of Polycronycone be hade in rememberaunce and not putt in oblyvione, ne forgetynge prayenge alle them that schalle see this simple werke to pardone my symple and rude wrytynge. Endede the secunde day of Julij the xxij. yere of the regne of Kynge Edwarde the fourt, and of the incarnacyone of oure Lorde M^l. cccc. iiij. score and tweyne.

" *Finysched and ended after the copey of Caxtone then in Westmynster.*" Fol. 214, v°.

For the sake of the general reader it may be as well to give the note of presentation, lithographed at the commencement of this volume, in full :—

" Liber Collegii Sancti Petri in Cantebrigia, ex dono Magistri Johannis Warkeworthe, Magistri dicti Collegii, sub interminacione anathematis nullatenus a libraria ibidem alienandus."

From the style in which this is written, there can be no doubt that it is in Warkworth's own handwriting; and it is also evident from a comparison with several of his autographs still preserved in the library of the College.

I have been able to collect nothing relative to the personal history of Warkworth, except that he was Master of St. Peter's College from A.D. 1473 to A.D. 1498.* He appears to have been a man of moderate learning and ability, although his story about the *Wemere* partakes strongly of superstition, and a reliance upon mere hearsay; but, in some instances, his minuteness in particulars would lead us to believe that he was intimately acquainted with the political affairs of the period.

The account which he gives of Henry's death is certainly most singular. It would seem as if he had intended for every reader a certain assurance far from being voluntarily taken—

* In St. Peter's College there is an original picture of Warkeworthe, executed in 1498, in a clerical habit, holding an open book with both his hands. This was formerly in the curious room called the Stone Parlour, but is now, I believe, transferred to the library. There is the following distich underneath—

" Vives adoptata gaudeto prole; probato
Non cuicunque libet, progenuisse licet.''

In the ancient register of donations to the College is a list of

" Rede this treyte it may hym move—
And may hym teche lightly with awe."*

Be that as it may, Warkworth's narrative is supported by
the strongest collateral proof, and is therefore deserving
of the greatest consideration.

I may observe that much new matter to illustrate this
period may be found in the contemporary poems of Lewis
Glyn Cothi, a Welsh bard, part of whose works have lately
been published by the Royal Cymmrodorion Institution,
under the able editorship of my friend the Rev. John
Jones, M.A. (Tegid), of Christ Church, Oxford, and the
Rev. W. Davies. I have made more particular reference
to these spirited poems in the notes; but I take the opportunity here of pointing out to the general reader Mr.
Jones's Introductory Essay on the Wars of the Rival
Roses, which would have done ample credit to a work
professing far higher pretensions: I speak of it not as
the result of much research, or of any difficult research
whatever, but as being an admirable view of the facts of
the case, discussed with great judgment and ability, and

books given to the library by Warkeworthe, and from this it appears
that he presented his MS. Chronicle in the year 1483.

* MS. Bodl. 3692. Hyp. Bodl. 160. (226.) Tract. sep. ult. fol.
1, r°. *A miracle play of the Burial of Christ, of the fifteenth century.*
I quote this MS. for the purpose of pointing out a curious miracle-
play which does not appear to have been hitherto known.

well adapted to fulfil the purpose for which it was intended.

I gladly take the opportunity of expressing my respectful and grateful thanks to the Rev. William Hodgson, D.D., Master of St. Peter's College, and Vice-Chancellor of the University of Cambridge, for the readiness with which I have been favoured with every possible facility for rendering the text of the following document as correct as the MS. will allow.

I also beg leave to return my best thanks to Charles George Young, Esq., York Herald, for the extreme kindness and liberality with which he assisted some researches I found it expedient to make in the library of the College of Arms ; and to John Gough Nichols, Esq. for the communication of some valuable observations, which will be found introduced among the notes under his initials, and for the comprehensive index to the text and notes. The correctness of the printed text has been ensured by a careful collation made by Mr. Black, whose experience in these matters has rendered his assistance most valuable.

James O. Halliwell.

35, Alfred Place, Sept. 18th, 1839.

Facsimile from the first page of Warkworth's Chronicle.

Note on the cover of the Volume.

22

WARKWORTH'S CHRONICLE.

As FOR alle thynges that folowe, referre them to my copey, in whyche is wretyn a remanente lyke to this forseyd werke: that is to wytt, that, at the coronacyone of the forseyde Edwarde, he create and made dukes his two brythir, the eldere George Duke of Clarence, and his yongere brothir Richard Duke of Gloucetre; and the Lord Montagu, the Erle of Warwykes brothere, the Erle of Northumberlonde; and one William Stafford squiere, Lord Stafforde of Southwyke; and Sere Herbard, Lorde Herbard, and aftere Lorde Erle of Penbroke; and so the seide Lorde Stafforde was made Erle of Devynschire; the Lorde Gray Ryffyne, Erle of Kent; the Lorde Bourchyer, Erle of Essex; the Lorde Jhon of Bokyngham, the Erle of Wyltschyre; Sere Thomas Blount, knyghte, Lord Mont[joy]; Sere Jhon Hawarde, Lorde Hawarde; William Hastynges he made Lorde Hastynges and grete Chamberlayne; and the Lorde Ryvers; Denham squyere, Lorde Dynham; and worthy as is afore schewed; and othere of gentylmen and yomenne he made knyghtes and squyres, as thei hade desserved.

And also the fyrst yere of his regne he ordeyned a parleament, at whiche were atteynted Kynge Herry and all othere that fledde with hym into Scotlonde oute of Englonde; and for so moche as he

23

fande in tyme of nede grete comforth in his comyners, he ratyfied
and confermyd alle the ffraunsches yeve to citeis and townes, &c.
and graunted to many cyteis and tounes new fraunschesses more
than was graunted before, ryghte largly, and made chartours therof
to the entent to have the more good wille and love in his londe.

Also Quene Margrett, Herry Duke of Excetre, the Duke of Somersett, and other lordes that fleede Englonde, hade kepte certeyne
castelles in Northumberlond, as Awnwyk, Bambrught, Dunstone-
brught, and also Werworthe, whiche they hade vytaled and stuffed
bothe with Englischemenne, Frenschemenne, and Scottesmenne; by
the whiche castelle[s] thei hade the moste party of alle Northumberlond.   Kynge Edwarde and his counselle, thynkynge and un [der]
stondynge wat hurte myghte appene thereof, made commyssiones to
the sowthe and west cowntre, and hade of them gret money, wyth the
whiche menne made redy, and beseged the same castelle[s] in the
moneth of Decembre in the yere aforseide.   And Sere Peris le Brasylle, knyght, of Fraunce, and the best warrer of alle that tyme, was
in Scotlonde to helpe Quene Margaret; when he knew that the
castelles were besegede, he hade xx m[l]. of Scottesmenne, and came
toward Alnwyke and alle the other castels.   And whenne Kynge
Edwardes hooste had knowlege that Sere Perys le Brasille with the
Scottesmenne were comynge, thei remewed from the sege and were
affrayed; and the Scottesche hoost supposed it hade be doone for
some gayne, and thei were affrayed; also thei durst noȝt come
neghe the castelle; for and thei hade comyne one boldly, thei
myghte have takyne and distressit alle the lordes and comeners, for
thei hade lye ther so longe in the felde, and were greved with colde
and rayne, that thei hade no coreage to feght, &c.   Never the lattere
whenne thei that were in the castelle beseged saw that the sege was
withedraw for fere, and the Scottes host afferde, also thei came
oute of the castelle and lefte them opene, &c.; and so afterwarde
Kynge Edwardes hoost enterde into alle the hole castelle, and kept
it, &c.

And after that, the castelle of Bamburght was yoldene to the Kynge, by treyatte and apoyntment by Herry the Duke of Somersett that kept it, and came in to Kynge Edwardes grace, whiche graunted to hym a Mˡ. marke by yere, whereof he was not payede; the[r]for he departed oute of Englonde after halff yere into Scotlonde, &c. And so Kynge Edward was possessed of alle Englonde, excepte a castelle in Northe Wales called Harlake, whiche Sere Richard Tunstall kepte, the qwhiche was gotene afterwarde by the Lorde Harberde.

And in the thyrde yere of the reygne of Kynge Edwarde, and anno Domini M°.cccc.lxiij, ther was ane fervent froste thrugh Englonde, and snowe, that menne myght goo overe the yise, and a fervent colde. And also ther was holde a parleamente at Westmynster, in the whiche was graunted to the Kynge ane ayde, whiche was as moche money as the xv. parte of mennys goodes and ane halff so myche more, where of the peple grocchede sore.

Also the iiijͤ yere of Kynge Edwarde, the Erle of Warwyke was sent into Fraunce for a maryage for the Kynge, for one fayre ladye, suster-doughtere to the Kynge of Fraunce, whiche was concludede by the Erle of Warwyke. And whiles the seyde Erle of Warwyke was in Fraunce, the Kynge was wedded to Elisabethe Gray, wedow, the qwiche Sere Jhon Gray that was hyre housbonde was slayne at Yorke felde in Kynge Herry partye; and the same Elisabeth was doughtere to the Lorde Ryvers; and the weddynge was prevely in a secrete place, the fyrst day of Maye the yere above seide. And when the Erle of Warwyke come home and herde hereof, thenne was he gretely displesyd withe the Kyng; and after that rose grete discencyone evere more and more betwene the Kyng and hym, for that and other, &c. And thenne the Kyng put oute of the Chaunceler-schepp the Bysshope of Excetre, brother to the Erle of Warwyke, and made the Bysshoppe of Bathe Chaunceler of Englonde. After that the Erle of Warwyke toke to hyme in fee as many

knyghtys, squyers, and gentylmenne as he myght, to be stronge;
and Kyng Edwarde dide that he myght to feble the Erles powere.
And yett thei were acorded diverse tymes: but thei nevere loffyd
togedere aftere.

Also in the iiij^te yere of the Kynge Edwarde, the monethe of
Maij, the Duke of Somersett, the Lorde Roos, the Lorde Moleyns,
Talboys the Erle of Kyme, Sire Phylippe Wenterworth, Sire
Thomas Fynderne, gadred a grete peple of the northe contre. And
Sere Jhon Nevelle, that tyme beynge Erle of Northumberlonde,
with x. ml. men come uppon them, and there the comons fleede that
were with them, and ther the forseide lordes were takene and afterward behedede. But thenne the Lorde Montagu, the Erle of Warwykes brothere, whiche the Kynge had made Erle of Northumberlonde, was myghty and stronge by the same, &c. And for so moche
as the Kynge and his counselle thought that he wolde holde with his
Erle of Warwyke, therfor the Kyng and his counselle made the
countre to desire that thei myght have the ryghtfull heyre Percy,
sonne to Henry Percy that was slayne at Yorke Feld, to be the Erle
of Northumberlond; and so it was doone. And aftere this the Kynge
made Lorde Montagu, Marquyus Montagu, and made his sonne
Duke of Bedford, whiche schulde wedde the princesse, the Kynges
heldest doughter, whiche, by possibylite, schuld be Kynge of
Englonde; and so he hade many fayre wordys and no lorde-
schyppys, but alwey he promysed he wuld do, &c.

Also the same yere, and the yere of oure Lord ml.cccc.lxiiij. Kynge
Edwarde chaunged the coyne of Englonde, by whiche he hade grete
getynge; for he made of ane olde noble a ryall, the whiche was
commaundyde to goo for x.s.; nevere the latter the same ryolle was
put viij.d. of aley, and so weyed viij.d. more by delaynge; and
smote hym in to a newe prynte. Also he made of iij.d. a grote;
and also he [made] angelle noblys of vj.s. viij.d., and by diverse
coynes, to the grete harme of the comene peple.

Also the same yere, Kynge Herry was takene bysyde a howse
of religione in Lancaschyre, by the mene of a blacke monke of
Abyngtone, in a wode called Cletherwode, besyde Bungerly Hyppyngstones, by Thomas Talbott, sonne and heyre to Sere Edmunde
Talbot of Basshalle, and Jhon Talbott his cosyne of Colebry, withe
other moo; whiche disseyvide, beyngne at his dynere at Wadyngtone
Halle, and caryed to Londone on horse bake, and his lege bownde
to the styrope, and so brought thrugh Londone to the Toure, where
he was kepte longe tyme by two squyres and ij. yomen of the
crowne, and ther menne; and every manne was suffred to come
and speke withe hym, by licence of the kepers.

And in the vth yere of Kynge Edwarde, the Erle of Oxenforde,
the Lord Abrey his sonne, and Sere Thomas Todenam knyght,
were taken, and brought into the Toure of Londone, and there
was leyde to them hye tresone; and aftyrwarde thei were brought
before the Erle of Worscetre, and juged by lawe padowe that thei
schuld be hade to the Toure Hylle, where was made a scaffolde of
viij. fote hy3t, and ther was there hedes smyten of, that alle menne
myght see; whereof the moste peple were sory.

And in the vi. yere of Kynge Edwarde regne, the Lorde Hungerforde was takene and behedede for hye treasoune at Salisbury.
And in vij. yere of Kynge Edwarde, Sere Thomas Cooke, Sere
Jhon Plummere, knyght, and aldermenne of Londone, and Humfrey Haward and other aldermen were arested, and treasoune
surmysed uppone them, whereof thei were acquyte, but thei lost
grete goodes to the Kynge, to the valowe of xl. м[l]. marke or
more; and diverse tymes in dyverse places of Englonde, men
were arestede for treasoune, and some were putt to dethe, and
some scaped.

And the viij. yere of the regne of Kynge Edwarde, a lytelle before
Michaelmasse, there apperyde a blasynge sterre in the weste, a
iiij. fote hyghe by estymacyone, in evenynge, goynge fro the weste

towarde the northe, and so endurede v. or vj. wekes. And the
same yere Sere Thomas Hungerforde knyght, sonne to the Lorde
Hungerforde, and Herry Curteney, the Erle of Devynschyre of
right, were takene for treasoune and behedede at Salisbury; and
menne seyde the Lorde Stafforde of Southwyke was cause of the
seyde Herry Curtenayes dethe, for he wolde be the Erle of Devynschyre, and so the Kynge made hym afterwarde, and [he] hade it
noʒt halff a yere.

And in the ix. yere of the regne of Kynge Edwarde, at mysso-
mere, the Duke of Clarence passede the see to Caleis to the Erle
of Warwyke, and there weddede his doughter by the Archebysshoppe of Yorke the Erle of Warwyke brothere, and afterwarde
come overe ayene. And anone aftere that, by ther assig[n]ment,
there was a grete insurreccyon in Yorkeschyre, of dyvers knyghtes,
squyres, and comeners, to the nowmbere of xx^{ti} M^l.; and Sere
William Conyars knyghte was therre capteyne, whiche callede
hym self Robyne of Riddesdale; and agens them aroose, by the
Kynges commawndement, Lorde Harbarde, Erle of Penbroke,
withe xliij. M^l. of Walschemenne, the beste in Wales, and Humfray
Stafforde, with vij. M^l. of archers of the weste countre; and as
thei went togedere to mete the northemenne at a towne, there
felle in a varyaunce for ther logynge, and so the Erle of Deven-
schyre departed from the Erle of Penbroke withe alle his menne.
And Robyne of Riddesdale came uppone the Walschemenne in
a playne byyonde Banbury toune, and ther thei faughte strongly
togedere, and ther was the Erle of Penbroke takene, and his brother
withe hym, and two M^l. Walschmenne slayne, and so the Walsch-
men loste the felde the xxvj. day of Juylle the same yere. The
names of the gentylmen that were slayne of Walsche party in the
same batelle :—Sere Rogere Vaghan, knyght; Herry Organ sonne
and heyre; Thomas Aprossehere Vaghan, squyere; William Harbarde of Breknoke, squyere; Watkyn Thomas, sonne to Rogere

Vaghan ; Yvan ap Jhon of Merwyke; Davy ap Jankyn of Lym-
meryke; Harry Done ap Pikton; John Done of Kydwelle; Ryse
ap Morgon ap Ulston; Jankyn Perot ap Scottesburght; John
Eneand of Penbrokeschire ; and Jhon Contour of Herforde. And
of the north party ther was slayne Sere Herry Latymere, sonne and
heyre to the Lorde Latymere ; Sere Rogere Pygot, knyghte ; James
Conya[r]s, sonne and heyre to Sere Jhon Conya[r]s, knyght;
Olivere Audley, squyere; Thomas Wakes sonne and heyre; William
Mallerye, squyere ; and many othere comyners, &c. And at that
tyme was the Lorde Ryvers takene, and one of his sonnes, in the
forest of Dene, and brought to Northamtone, and the Erle of Penbroke a[nd] Sere Richard Herbarde his brother were behedede at
Northamtone, alle iiij. by the commawndement of the Duke of
Clarence and the Erle of Warwyke ; and Thomas Harbarde was
slayne at Brystow, &c. And at that same tyme was Stafford, that was
Erle of Devynschyre but half a yere, take at Bryggewatere by the
comons ther in Somersettschyre, and ther ryghte behedede. And
after that the Archebysschoppe of Yorke had understondynge that
Kynge Edwarde was in a vilage bysyde Northamptone, and alle his
peple he reysyd were fledde fro hym; by the avyse of the Duke
of Clarence and the Erle of Warwyke he rode with certeyne hors-
menne harneysed withe hym, and toke Kynge Edwarde, and had
hym unto Warwyke castelle a lytelle whyle, and afterwarde to Yorke
cite ; and ther, by fayre speche and promyse, the Kynge scaped
oute of the Bisshoppys handes, and came unto Londone, and dyd
what hym lykede. And the same yere, the xxix. day of Septembre,
Humfrey Nevylle, knyght, and Charles his brothere, were takene
by the Erle of Warwyke, and behedede at Yorke, the Kynge beynge
present. And in the same yere [was] made a proclamacyone at the
Kynges Benche in Westmynstere, and in the cyte of Londone, and
in alle Englond, a generalle pardone tylle alle manere of men for
alle manere insurreccyons and trespasses; and also a hole xv^{sim}.

schulde be gaderyd and payed that same yere at Martynmasse, and
at oure Lady-Day in Lent after ; whiche noyed the peple, for thei
had payed a lytelle before a gret taske, and the xv. parte of every
mannes good, &c.

And in the x. yere of Kynge Edwardes regne, in the moneth
of Marche, the Lorde Willowby, the Lorde Welles his sonne,
Thomas Delalond knyght, and Sere Thomas Dymmoke knyght,
the Kynges Champyon, droff oute of Lyncolneschyre Sere
Thomas à Burghe, a knyght of the Kynges howse, and pullede
downe his place, and toke alle his goodes and cataylle that thei
myghte fynde, and thei gaderid alle the comons of the schyre to
the nowmbre of xxx. Mˡ., and cryed " Kynge Herry," and refused
Kynge Edwarde.   And the Duke of Clarence and the Erle of
Warwyke causede alle this, lyke as thei dyde Robyne of Riddesdale to ryse afore that at Banbury felde.   And whenne Kÿnge Edwarde herde hereof, he made oute his commyssyons, and gaderyd a
grete peple of menne, and sent his pardone to the Lorde Wyllowby,
and a commaundement that thei schuld come to hym, and so he
dyd.   And whenne the Kynge was sure of hym, he and alle his oste
went towarde Lyncolneschyre, the Lord Welles, and alle the othere
peple were gaderd togedere, and commawndede Lorde Wyllowby to
sende a lettere to hys sonne and to alle the peple that he gaderyde,
that thei schulde yelde them to hym as to ther sovereyne Lorde, or
ellys he made a woue that the Lorde Willowby schuld lese his
hede ; and he wrote and sent his lettere forthe, but therfor they
wulde noȝt ceysse ; wherfor the Kynge comawndyde the Lorde
Wyllowhby hede for to be smytene of, notwithstondynge his pardone.   And so the Kynge toke his oste and went towarde his enemyes, and losyde his gonnys of his ordynaunce uppone them, and
faught with them, and anone the comons fledde away ; but ther was
many manne slayne of Lyncolneschyre, and the Lorde Wellys, Sere
Thomas Delalonde, and Sere Thomas Dymmoke, knyghtys, takene

and beheddede. And whenne the Duke of Clarence and the Earl of Warwike herde the felde was loste, and how there cownselle was dyscoverede, thei fledde westwarde to the see syde, and toke there here schippys, and sayled towarde Southamptone, and e[n]tendet there to have a grete schyppe of the seide Erle of Warwykes, callyde the Trinite; but the Lorde Scales, the Quenes brother, was sent thedere by the Kynges commawndement, and other withe hym, and faught with the seide Duke and Erle, and toke there dyverse schyppes of theres and many of ther men therein; so that the Duke and the Erle were fayne to flee to the Kynge of Fraunce, where thei were worschipfully receyved. And after this the Kynge Edwarde came to Southamptone, and commawndede the Erle of Worcetere to sitt and juge suche menne as were taken in the schyppes, and so xx. persones of gentylmen and yomenne were hangede, drawne, and quartered, and hedede; and after that thei hanged uppe by the leggys, and a stake made scharpe at bothe endes, whereof one ende was putt in att bottokys, and the other ende ther heddes were putt uppe one; for the whiche the peple of the londe were gretely displesyd; and evere afterwarde the Erle of Worcestre was gretely behatede emonge the peple, for ther dysordinate dethe that he used, contrarye to the lawe of the londe.

And whenne the seide Duke of Clarence and the Erle of Warwyke were in Fraunce, there apperede a blasynge sterre in the weste, and the flame therof lyke a spere hede, the whiche dyverse of the Kynges house sawe it, whereof thei were fulle sore adrede. And thanne in Fraunce whenne the seide lordes where, thei toke there counselle qwhat was beste for to do; and thei coude fynde no remedy but to sende to Quene Margaret, and to make a maryage betwex Prynce Edwarde, Kynge Herry sonne, and an other of the seid Erle of Warwikys doughters, whiche was concluded, and in Fraunce worschippfully wedded. And there it was apoyntede and acordede that Kynge Herry schuld rejoyse the kyngdome of

Englonde ageyne, and regne as welle as he dyd before, and after hym hys Prynce Edward and his heyres of his body lawfully begotyne; and if it appenede that he disceysed witheoute heyres of his body lawfully gotene, thenne schulde the kyngdome of Eng- londe, with the lordschyppes of Irlonde, remane unto George, the Duke of Clarence, and his heyre[s] for evere more. Also it was apoyncted and agreede that **Herry Duke of Excetre, Edmunde Duke of Somersett,** brother to Herry that was slayne at Hexham felde, the **Erle of Devynschire** called **Courtnay,** and alle othere knyghtes, squyers, and alle other that were putt oute and atayntede for Kynges Herry quarrelle, schulde come into Englonde ageyne, and every man to rejoyse his owne lyflode and inhabytauntes; whiche alle this poyntment aforeseide were wrytene, indentyde, and sealede, bytwixe the seide **Quene Margaret,** the **Prynce** hire sonne, in that one party, and the **Duke of Clarence,** and the **Erle of Warwik,** one that othere party. And moreovere, to make it sure, thei were sworne, and made grete othys eche to othere, wiche was done be alle Kynge of Fraunce counselle.

And in the same x. yere aforeseide, a lytelle before Michaelmesse, the Duke of Clarence and the Erle of Warwyke londede in the west countre, and gadered there a grete peple. The Lorde Markes Montagu hade gaderyd vi. Ml. men, by Kynge Edwardes commysyone and commaundement, to the entente to have re- cistede the seide Duke of Clarence, and the Erle of Warwyke. Nevere the lattere, the seide Markes Montagu hatyde the Kynge, and purposede to have taken hym; and whenne he was withein a myle of Kynge Edwarde, he declarede to the peple that was there gaderede with hym, how Kynge Edwarde hade fyrst yevyne to hym the erledome of Northumberlonde, and how he toke it from hym and gaff it Herry Percy, whos fadere was slayne at Yorke felde; and how of late tyme hade he made hym Markes of Montagu, and yaff a pyes neste to mayntene his astate withe: wherefor he yaff

knoleage to his peple that he wulde holde withe the Erle of Warwyke, his brothere, and take Kynge Edwarde if he myght, and alle
tho that wolde holde with hym. But anone one of the oste went
oute frome the fellawschippe, and tolde Kynge Edwarde alle manere
of thynge, and bade hym avoyde, for he was noȝt stronge enoghe
to gyff batayle to Markes Montagu; and then anone Kynge Edwarde
haysted hym in alle that he myght to the towne of Lynne, and ther
he toke schyppynge one Michaelmesse day, in the x. yere of his
regne, with Lorde Hastynges, that was the Kynges Chamberleyne,
Lorde Say, withe dyverse other knyghtes and squyers, passed and
saylede overe the see into Flaunders, to his brother-in-lawe the
Duke of Burgeyne, for socoure and helpe, &c.

Here is to knowe, that in the begynnynge of the moneth of Oc-
tobre, the yere of oure Lorde a M.cccc.lxx, the Bisshoppe of Wynchestere, be the assent of the Duke of Clarence and the Erle of
Warwyke, went to the toure of Londone, where Kynge Herry was
in presone by Kynge Edwardes commawndement, and there toke
hyme from his kepers, whiche was noȝt worschipfully arayed as a
prince, and noȝt so clenly kepte as schuld seme suche a Prynce;
thei hade hym oute, and newe arayed hym, and dyde to hyme grete
reverens, and brought hyme to the palys of Westmynster, and so
he was restorede to the crowne ageyne, and wrott in alle his lettres,
wryttes, and other recordes, the yere of his regne, *Anno regni Regis
Henrici Sexti quadragesimo nono, et readempcionis sue regie potes-
tatis primo.* Whereof alle his goode lovers were fulle gladde, and the
more parte of peple. Nevere the lattere, before that, at he was putt
oute of his reame by Kynge Edwarde, alle Englonde for the more
partye hatyd hym, and were fulle gladde to have a chounge; and the
cause was, the good Duke of Glouceter was put to dethe, and Jhon
Holonde, Duke of Excetre, poysond, and that the Duke of Suffolke,
the Lorde Say, Danyelle Trevyliane, and other myscheves pepie
that were aboute the Kynge, were so covetouse towarde them selff,

and dyde no force of the Kynges honour, ne of his wele, ne of the comone wele of the londe, where Kynge Herry trusted to them that thei schuld do, and labour in tyme of innocence evere for the comone wele, whiche thei dyde contrary to his wille; and also Fraunce, Normandy, Gasgoyne, and Guyane was lost in his tyme. And these were the causes, withe other, that made the peple to gruge ageyns hym, and alle bycause of his fals lordes, and nevere of hym; and the comon peple seyde, yf thei myghte have another Kynge, he schulde gett alle ageyne and amende alle manere of thynges that was amysse, and brynge the reame of Englond in grete prosperite and reste. Nevere the lattere, whenne Kynge Edwarde iiij[th] regnede, the peple looked after alle the forseide prosperytes and peece, but it came not; but one batayle aftere another, and moche troble and grett losse of goodes amonge the comone peple; as fyrste, the xv. of alle there goodes, and thanne ane hole xv., at yett at every batell to come ferre oute there countreis at ther awne coste; and these and suche othere brought Englonde ryght lowe, and many menne seyd that Kynge Edwarde hade myche blame for hurtynge marchandyse, for in his dayes thei were not in other londes, nore withein Englonde, take in suche reputacyone and credence as thei were afore, &c.

And xxvj. day of Novembre, Kynge Herry callede a parleament at Westmynster, beyngethere George the Archebysshoppeof Yorke, Chaunceler of Englonde, whiche [discussed] this proposicion before the Kynge and his Lordes and the comons of that same parleament assemblede, *Revertimini ad me filii revertentes, ego enim vir vester. Jeremie tercio, etc.* And in the moneth of Februarij after, Herry Duke of Excetre, Eadmunde Duke of Somersett, Lorde Jhon of Somersett his brothir, Erle of Ormond, Jasper Erle of Penbroke, brother to the Kynge Herry, and the Erle of Richmonde, with many other knyghtys, and squyres, gentilmen, and yomen, came into Englonde, and entered into ther lordschippys and londe, whiche at the parleament above seide and alle other attaynderes that were made in

Kynge Edwardys tyme were anullede, and Kynge Herry was amitted to his crowne and dignite ageyne, and alle his men to there enherytaunce. And thenne was takene the Erle of Worcetre, whiche was arested and areynede befor Sere Jhon Veere, the Erle of Oxenforde, sonne and heyre to the forseide Erle of Oxenforde whiche was behedede at the Toure Hille, as before wrytene; and so the Erle of Worcetre was juged be suche lawe as he dyde to other menne; and, whenne he was dede, his body and his hede was buryede togedyr at the Blacke Frerys in Londone, with alle the honoure and worschyppe that his frendes coude do. Also Quene Elisabeth, Kynge Edwardes wyf, wiche hade welle vetelede and fortifyed the Toure of Londone, when sche herde that here so-evereyne and husbonde was fledde, sche went secretly oute of the toure in to sanctuary at Westmynster, with alle here childrene, and sche hir selff was grete withe childe, and was delyverede ther ryght of a sonne that was callede Prynce Edwarde of Englonde; and ther sche abode stylle in grete troble, tylle Kynge Edwarde came in ageyne tylle hire.

And in the secunde weke of Marche, the xlix. yere of the regne of Kynge Herry the vj^{te}, and in the x. yere of the regne of Kynge Edwarde the iiij^{te}, the same Kynge Edwarde toke his schippynge in Flaunders, and hade withe hym the Lorde Hastynges and the Lorde Say, and ix. c. of Englismenne and three hundred of Flemmynges with hande-gonnes, and sailed toward Englonde, and hade grete troble uppon the see with stormys, and lost a schyppe withe horse; and purpost to have londede in Northfolke, and one of the Erle [of] Oxenfordes brother withe the comons of the cuntre arose up togedere, and put hym abake to the see ageyne. And after that, at he was so trobled in the see, that he was fayne to londe in Yorkeschyre at Ravenys-spore; and there rose ageyns hym alle the cuntre of Holdernes, whose capteyne was a preste, and a per-sone in the same cuntre called Sere Jhon Westerdale, whiche aftyr-warde for his abused disposycion was casten in presone in the

Marchalse at Londone by the same Kynge Edwarde : for the same preste mett Kynge Edwarde and askede the cause of his landynge; and he answeryde that he came thedere by the Erle of Northumberlondes avyse, and schewede the Erles lettere y-send to hym, &c. undere his seale; and also he came for to clayme the Duchery of Yorke, the whiche was his inherytaunce of ryght, and so passed forthe to the cite of Yorke, where Thomas Clyfford lete hym inne, and ther he was examynede ayenne; and he seyde to the mayre and aldermenne and to alle the comons of the cite, in likewyse as he was afore in Holdernes at his landyng : that was to sey, that [he] nevere wulde clayme no title, ne take uppone honde to be Kynge of Englonde, nor wulde have do afore that tyme, but be excitynge and sturing of the Erle of Warwyke; and therto afore alle peple, he cryed "A! Kynge Herry! A! Kynge and Prynce Edwarde!" and wered ane estryche feder, Prynce Edwardes lyvery. And after this he was sufferd to passe the cite, and so helde his wey southwarde, and no man lettyd hym ne hurtyde hym.

Afterwarde that, he came towarde Notyngham, and ther came to hym Sere William a Stanley with ccc. men, and Sere William Norys, and dyverse other menne and tenauntes of Lorde Hastynges, so that he hade M^l. M^l. menne and moo; and anone aftere he made his proclamacyone, and called hym self Kynge of Englonde and of Fraunce. Thenne toke he his wey to Leycetre, where were the Erle of Warwyke and the Lord Markes his brother with iiij. M^l. menne or moo. And Kynge Edwarde sent a messyngere to them, that yf thai wulde come oute, that he wulde feght withe them. But the Erle of Warwyke hade a letter from the Duke of Clarence, that he schulde not feght withe hym tylle he came hym self; and alle was to the distruccion of the Erle of Warwyke, as it happenede aftyrwarde. Yet so the Erle of Warwyke kept stille the gates of the toune schet, and suffrede Kynge Edwarde passe towarde Londone; and a litelle oute of Warwyke mett the Duke of Clarence with Kynge Edwarde, with vij. M^l. men, and ther thei were made acorde, and made a proclamacion forthe-withe in Kynge Edwardes name; and so alle covandes of fydelite, made betwyx the Duke of Clarence, and the Erle of Warwyke, Quene Margarete, Prince Edwarde hir sonne, bothe in Englonde and in Fraunce, were clerly brokene and forsakene of the seide Duke of Clarence; whiche, in conclusione, was distruccion bothe to hym and them: for perjury schall nevere have better ende, witheoute grete grace of God. *Vide finem, &c.*

Kyng Herry thenne was in Londone, and the Archebysshoppe of Yorke, withein the Bysschoppys of Londone palece. And on the wennysday next before Ester-day, Kynge Herry and the Arche-bysschoppe of Yorke with hym roode aboute Londone, and desirede the peple to be trew unto hym; and every manne seide thei wulde. Nevere the latter, Urswyke, recordere of Londone, and diverse alder-men, suche that hade reule of the cyte, commaundede alle the peple that were in harnes, kepynge the cite and Kynge Herry, every manne to goo home to dynere; and in dyner tyme Kynge Edwarde was late in, and so went forthe to the Bisshoppes of Londone palece, and ther toke Kynge Herry and the Archebisschoppe of Yorke, and put theme in warde, the thursday next before Ester-day. And the Archebysschoppe of Cawnterbury, the Erle of Essex, the Lorde Barnesse, and suche other as awyde Kynge Edwarde good wylle, as welle in Londone as in othere places, made as many menne as thei myghte in strengthynge the seide Kynge Edwarde; so then he was a vij. M^l. menne, and ther thei refresched welle them self alle that day, and good frydai. And upone Ester evyne, he and alle his oste went toward Barnett, and caryede Kynge Herry withe hym: for he hade understondyng that the Erle of Warwycke and the Duke of Excetre, the Lorde Markes Montagu, the Erle of Oxenforde, and many other knyghtes, squyers, and comons, to the nombre of xx. M^l., were gaderide togedere to feghte ageyne Kynge

37

Edwarde.   But it happenede that he withe his oste were en-
terede into the toune of Barnet, before the Erle of Warwyke and
his host. And so the Erle of Warwyke and his host lay witheoute
the towne alle nyght, and eche of them loosede gonnes at othere,
alle the nyght.   And on Ester day in the mornynge, the xiiij. day
of Apryl, ryght erly, eche of them came uppone othere; and ther
was suche a grete myste, that nether of them myght see othere
perfitely; ther thei faughte, from iiij. of clokke in the mornynge
unto x. of clokke the fore-none.   And dyverse tymes the Erle of
Warwyke party hade the victory, and supposede that thei hade
wonne the felde.   But it hapenede so, that the Erle of Oxenfordes
men hade uppon them ther lordes lyvery, bothe before and behynde,
which was a sterre withe stremys, wiche [was] myche lyke Kynge
Edwardes lyvery, the sunne with stremys; and the myste was so
thycke, that a manne myghte not profytely juge one thynge from
anothere; so the Erle of Warwikes menne schott and faughte ayens
the Erle of Oxenfordes menne, wetynge and supposynge that thei
hade bene Kynge Edwardes menne; and anone the Erle of Oxenforde and his menne cryed "treasoune! treasoune!" and fledde
awaye from the felde withe viij. c. menne.   The Lorde Markes
Montagu was agreyde and apoyntede with Kynge Edwarde, and put
uppone hym Kynge Edwardes lyvery; and a manne of the Erles of
Warwyke sawe that, and felle uppone hyme, and kyllede hym.
And whenne the Erle of Warwyke sawe his brothere dede, and
the Erle of Oxenforde fledde, he lepte one horse-backe, and
flede to a wode by the felde of Barnett, where was no waye
forthe; and one of Kynge Edwardes menne hade espyede hyme,
and one came uppone hym and kylled hym, and dispolede hyme
nakede.   And so Kynge Edwarde gate that felde.   And ther was
slayne of the Erle of Warwykes party, the Erle hym self, Markes
Montagu, Sere William Tyrelle, knyghte, and many other.   The
Duke of Excetre faugth manly ther that day, and was gretely

despolede and woundede, and lefte nakede for dede in the felde, and so lay ther from vij. of clokke tille iiij. after none ; whiche was take up and brought to a house by a manne of his owne ; and a leche brought to hym, and so afterwarde brought in to sancuarij at Westmynster. And one Kynge Edwardes party was slayne the Lorde Crowmwelle, sonne and heyre to the Erle of Essex, Lord Barnes sonne and heyre, Lorde Say, and dyverse other, to the nombre (of bothe partys) iiij. M^l. menne. And after that the felde was don, Kynge Edwarde commaundyd bothe the Erle of Warwikes body and the Lord Markes body to be putt in a carte, and returned hym with alle his oste ageyne to Londone ; and there commaundede the seide ij. bodyes to be layede in the chyrche of Paulis, one the pavement, that every manne myghte see them ; and so they lay iij. or iiij. days, and afterwarde where buryede. And Kynge Herry, beynge in the forwarde durynge the bataylle, was not hurt ; but he was broughte ageyne to the Toure of Londone, ther to be kept.

And Quene Marget, and Prince Edwarde hire sonne, with other knygtes, squyres, and other menne of the Kyng of Fraunce, hade navy to brynge them to Englond : whiche, whenne thei were schipped in Fraunce, the wynde was so contrary unto them xvij. dayes and nyghtes, that [thei] myght not come from Normandy with unto Englonde, whiche withe a wynd myght have seylede it in xij. oures ; whiche at the xvij. dayes ende one Ester day at the evyne the[i] landed at Weymouthe, and so by lande from Weymouthe the[i] roode to Excetre ; and mette withe hire, at Weymouth, Edmunde Duke of Somersett, the Lorde Jhon his brother, brother to Herry Duke of Somerset slayne at Exham, and Curteney the Erle of Devynschyre, and many othere. And on Ester mounday was brought tithingys to them, that Kynge Edwarde hade wonne the felde at Barnett, and that Kynge Herry was put into the Toure ayene. And anone ryghte thei made oute commaundementes, in the Quenes name and the Prynce, to alle the weste

countre, and gaderet grete peple, and kepte hire wey towarde the
toune of Brystow.   And when the Kynge herd that thei were
landede, and hade gaderede so myche peple, he toke alle his hoste,
and went oute of Londone the wennysday in Ester weke, and
manly-toke his waye towarde them ; and Prynce Edwarde herd
therof; he hastede hym self and alle his oste towarde the towne
of Glouceter, but he enteryd noȝt into the towne, but held forthe
his wey to the towne of Teukesbury, and ther he made a felde
noȝt ferre from the ryver of Saverne ; and Kynge Edwarde and
his oste came uppone hym, the saturday the fourth day of Maij,
the yere aforeseide of oure Lorde a Mˡ. cccclxxj., and the xj yere
of Kynge Edwarde.   And Edmunde Duke of Somersett, and Sere
Hugh Curteneye, went oute of the felde, by the whiche the felde
was broken ; and the moste parte of the peple fledde awaye from
the Prynce, by the whiche the feld was loste in hire party.
And ther was slayne in the felde, Prynce Edward, whiche cryede
for socoure to his brother-in-lawe the Duke of Clarence.   Also
ther was slayne, Curteney the Erle of Devynschyre, the Lorde
Jhon of Somersett, the Lorde Wenloke, Sere Edmunde Hampden,
Sere Robart Whytyngham, Sere William Vaus, Sere Nicholas
Hervy, Sere Jhon Delvis, Sere William Feldynge, Sere Thomas
Fiztharry, Sere Jhon Leukenore, knyghtes ; and these were taken
and behedede afterwarde, where the Kynge hade pardoned them
in the abbey cherche of Teukesbury, by a prest that turnyd oute
at his messe and the sacrament in his handys, whanne Kynge
Edwarde came with his swerde into the chirche, requyrede hyme
by the vertu of the sacrament that he schulde pardone alle tho
whos names here folowe ; the Duke of Somersett, the Lorde of
Seynt Jhones, Sere Humfrey Audeley, Sere Gervis of Clyftone,
Sere William Gremyby, Sere William Cary, Sere Thomas Tresham, Sere William Newbrugh, knyghtes, Herry Tresham, Walter
Curtenay, Jhon Florey, Lowes Myles, Robart Jacksone, James
Gowere, James Delvis, sonne and heire to Sere Jhon Delvis ;

whiche, uppone trust of the Kynges pardone yevene in the same chirche the saturday, abode ther stille, where thei myght have gone and savyd ther lyves; whiche one monday aftere were behedede, noȝtwhitstondynge the Kynges pardone. And afterward these ladyes were takene,—Quene Margaret, Prynce Edwardes wyf, the secunde dowghtere of the Erle of Warwykes, the Countasse of Devynschire, Dame Kateryne Vaus. And these were taken, and noȝt slayne; Sere Jhon Fortescu, Sere Jhon Sentlow, Sire Herry Roos, Thomas Ormonde, Doctour Makerell, Edward Fulforde, Jhon Parkere, Jhon Bassett, Jhon Wallys, Jhon Thromere Throg-mertone, and dyverse other men. And there was takene grete good, and many good horse that were brought frome beyond the see.

And in the same tyme that the batelle of Teukesbury was, Sere Watere Wrotty[s]le and Geffrei Gate, knyȝtes of the Erle of Warwykes, were governers of the towne of Caleys, dide sende Sere George Broke knyghte oute of Caleys, with ccc. of soudyours unto Thomas Bastarde Fakynebrygge, that was one the see with the Erle of Warwykes navy, that he schulde the navy save, and goo into Kent, and to reyse alle Kent, to that entente to take Kynge Herry oute of the toure and distroye Kyng Edwarde, yf he myghte; whiche Bastarde came into Kent, to Caunturbury, and he, withe helpe of other gentylmenne, thei reysed up alle Kent, and came to Londone the v. day of Maij the yere aforeseide. But thenne the Lorde Scales, that Kynge Edwarde hade lefte to kepe the cyte, with the Meyre and Aldermen, wulde noȝt suffre the seid Bastarde to come into the cite; for thei had understondynge that Prince Edwarde was dede, and alle his hoste discomfytede: wherefor the Bastarde loosede his gonnes into the citee, and brent at Algate and at Londone brygge; for the whiche brynnynge, the comons of Londone where sore wrothe, and gretely mevyd ayens them: for and thei had noȝt brent, the comons of the cyte wulde have leett them in, magre of the Lorde Scales hede, the Mayre and alle his brethyr. Wherefor the Bastarde and alle his hoste went overe at Kyngstone Brygge, x. myle westwarde, and hade purposed to have distruyt Kynge Edwarde, or to have dryve hym oute of the londe. And if the Bastarde hade holde forthe his way, Kynge Edwarde be possibilyte coude noȝt be powere haf recisted the Bastarde; for the Bastarde hade moo then xx. mˡ. goode men welle harnessede, and evere as he went the peple felle to hym. The Lorde Scales, and dyverse othere of Kynge Edwardes counselle that were in Londone, sawe that the Bastarde and his oste went westwarde, and that it schuld be a grettere juperdy to Kynge Edwarde thenne was Barnet felde or Teukesbury felde, (in so moche when the felde of Teukesbury was done, his oste was departede from;) wherefor thei promysed to the Bastarde, and to dyverse other that were aboute hym, and in especyalle to one Nicholas Fauntt, Meyre of Caunter-bury, that he schulde entret hym to turne homwarde ageyn. And for as myche as fayre wordes and promyses makes fooles fayne, the Bastarde commaundede alle his oste to turne to Blakhethe ageyn; whiche was distruccion of hyme self and many othere; for anone after, by the Duke of Gloucetre in Yorkeschyre, the seide Bastarde was behedede, noȝtwithstondynge he hade a chartere of pardone; and Nicholas Fauntt was afterward hangede, drawene, and quar-terede in Caunterbury. And whene the Bastarde and alle his oste were come to the Blakheth ageyne, in the next mornynge he withe the soudyours and schypmen of Caleis, to the nombre of vj. c. horsemen, stole awaye frome the oste and roode to Rouchester, and frome thens to Sandwyche, where the Bastard abode the Kynges comynge, and the soudyours saylede overe see to Caleys. And whenne the oste understode that ther Capteyne was stole from them, thei kepte them togedere alle a day and a nyght, and thanne every manne departede to his owne howse. And when Kynge Edward herde thereof, he was gladde, &c.

Here is to knowe that Kynge Edwarde made oute commyssyons to many schyres of Englonde; whiche in a x. dayes ther came to hym, where he was, to the nowmbre of xxx. mˡ., and came

withe the Kynge to Londone, and ther he was worschipfully receyvid. And the same nyghte that Kynge Edwarde came to Londone, Kynge Herry, beynge inwarde in presone in the Toure of
Londone, was putt to dethe, the xxj. day of Maij, on a tywesday
nyght, betwyx xj. and xij. of the cloke, beynge thenne at the Toure
the Duke of Gloucetre, brothere to Kynge Edwarde, and many
other; and one the morwe he was chestyde and brought to Paulys,
and his face was opyne that every manne myghte see hyme; and
in hys lyinge he bledde one the pament ther; and afterward at
the Blake Fryres was broughte, and ther he blede new and fresche;
and from thens he was caryed to Chyrchesey abbey in a bote, and
buryed there in oure Lady chapelle. On the morwe that the
Kynge was come to Londone, for the goode servyse that Londone
hade done to hym, he made knyghtes of the Aldermenne, Sere
Jhon Stokstone, Sire Rauf Verney, Sere Richard Lee, Sere Jhon
Yonge, Sere William Tayliour, Sere George Irlande, Sere Jhon
Stokere, Sere Mathew Philyppe, Sere William Hamptone, Sere
Thomas Stalbroke, Sere Jhon Crosby, Sere Thomas Urswike,
Recordere of Londone. And after that, the Kynge and alle his
oste roode into Kent to Caunterbury, where many of the countre
that where at Blakhethe withe the Bastarde, were arestede and
brought befor hym; and ther was hangyd, drawene, and quarteryd,
one Fauntt of Caunterbury, that was lovynge to the Erle of
Warwyke; whyche entreytede the Bastarde for to departe frome
his oste; and many dyverse menne of the cuntre were hanged
and put to dethe. Aftere that, the Kynge roode unto Sanwyche,
and beside alle the Erle of Warwykes navy there, that the
Bastarde hade reule of, and toke the Bastard withe hyme, and
returned ageyne to Londone. And immediatly after that was the
Lorde Denham and Sere Jhon Fog and dyverse othere made com-
myssioners, that satt uppone alle Kent, Sussex, and Esex, that
were at the Blakhethe, and uppone many othere that were noȝt
there; for some manne payed cc. marke, some a c. pownde, and some

more and some lesse, so that it coste the porest manne vij. ^{s.} whiche was noȝt worthe so myche, but was fayne to selle suche clothinge as thei hade, and borowede the remanent, and laborede for it aftyrwarde; and so the Kynge hade out of Kent myche goode and lytelle luff. Lo, what myschef groys after insurreccion! &c. ɩ

And in [the] same xj. yere of the Kynge, in the begynnynge of of Januarij, there apperyd the moste mervelous blasynge sterre that hade bene seyne. It aroose in the southe este, at ij. of the cloke at mydnyghte, and so contynuede a xij. nyghtes; and it arose ester and ester, tille it aroose fulle este; and rather, and rather; and so whenne it roose playne est, it rose at x. of cloke in the nyght, and kept his cours flamynge westwarde overe Eng-londe; and it hade a white flaume of fyre fervently brennynge, and it flammede endlonges fro the est to the weste, and noȝt upryght, and a grete hole therin, whereof the flawme came oute of. And aftyre a vj. or vij. dayes, it aroose north-est, and so bakkere and bakkere; and so enduryd a xiiij. nyghtes, fulle lytelle chaungynge, goynge from the north-este to the weste, and some tyme it wulde seme aquenchede oute, and sodanly it brent fervently ageyne. And thenne it was at one tyme playne northe, and thenne it compassede rounde aboute the lodesterre, for in the evynynge the blase went ageyns the southe, and in the mornynge playne northe, and thenne afterwarde west, and so more west, flaumyng up ryghte; and so the sterre contynuede iiij. wekys, tylle the xx. day of Feveryere; and whenne it appered yest in the fyrmament, thenne it lasted alle the nyghte, somewhat discendyng withe a grettere smoke one the heyre. And some menne seyde that the blassynges of the seide sterre was of a myle length. And a xij. dayes afore the vanyschynge therof, it appereryd in the evynynge, and was downe anone within two oures, and evyr of a colour pale stedfast; and it kept his course rysynge west in the northe, and so every nyght, it apperide lasse and lasse tylle it was as lytelle as a hesylle styke; and so at the laste it waneschede away the xx. day of Februarij. And some menne saide that this sterre was seene ij. or iij. oures afore the sunne rysynge in Decembre, iiij. days before Crystynmasse, in the south-west; so by that reasoune it compassed rounde abowte alle the erthe, alle way chaungynge his cours, as is afore reherside.

And in the xij. yere of Kynge Edwarde, he lete calle a parleament to be holdene at Westmynstere, the qwhiche beganne the viij. day after Michaelmasse the same yere; in qwiche parleament was a generalle resumpcion of alle lordschippes, tenamentes, and other possesions and feys grawntede be the Kynge, frome the fyrst day of his regne unto the day aforeseid. Also ther was grauntyde, in the same parleamente, that the x. parte of every mannys good, londes, tenamentes, rentys, and feys, thrugheoute alle Englonde, the valowe therof as for a yere; and also a hole quynsyme amonge the comons, to be reysede, of goodes and catelle; and also lj. ᴍˡ. vij. c. ˡⁱ. of money to be raysed, of alle mennys londes, goodes, and other possessions within the reame of Englonde. Also ther was grawntede to the Kynge by the spiritualte, in a con-vocacion two dymes and prestes markes thurghtoute alle Eng-londe: whiche alle was grauntede by the desyre of the Kyng, for he seide he wuld overe see and conquere his right and title in Fraunce, Normandy, Gascoyne, and Guyane.

Also in xiij. yere of Kynge Edwarde, ther was a gret hote somere, bothe for manne and beste; by the whiche ther was gret dethe of menne and women, that in feld in harvist tyme men fylle downe sodanly, and unyversalle feveres, axes, and the blody flyx, in dyverse places of Englonde. And also the hete was so grete, that it brent awey whete and alle other greynis and gresse, in southe partyes of the worlde, in Spayne, Portyngale, Granade, and othere, &c. that a bowsshelle of whete was worthe xx. ˢ; and menne were fayne in that cuntre to yeve away there childeryne for to fynde them. But, blessede be Almyghty God, no suche derthe was noȝt in Englonde, ne in Fraunce.

Also in the same yere Womere watere ranne hugely, withe suche abundaunce of watere, that nevyr manne sawe it renne so moche afore this tyme. Womere is callede the woo watere: for Englyschmen, whenne thei dyd fyrst inhabyde this lond, also sone as thei see this watere renne, thei knewe wele it was a tokene of derthe, or of pestylence, or of grete batayle; wherefor thei callede it *Womere;* (for *we* as in Englysche tonge woo, and *mere* is called watere, whiche signyfieth woo-watere;) for alle that tyme thei sawe it renne, thei knewe welle that woo was comynge to Englonde. And this Wemere is vij. myle frome Sent Albons, at a place callede Markayate; and this Wemere ranne at every felde afore specifyede, and nevere so hugely as it dyd this yere, and ranne stylle to the xiij. day of June next yere folowynge. Also ther has ronne dyverse suche other wateres, that betokenethe lykewyse; one at Lavesham in Kent, and another byside Canturbury called Naylborne, and another at Croydone in Suthsex, and another vij. myle a this syde the castelle of Dodley, in the place called Hungerevale; that whenne it betokenethe batayle it rennys foule and trouble watere; and whenne betokenythe derthe or pestylence, it rennyth as clere as any watere, but this yere it ranne ryght trouble and foule watere, &c. Also ther is a pytte in Kent, in Langley Parke: ayens any batayle he wille be drye, and it rayne nevere so myche; and if ther be no batayle towarde, he wille be fulle of watere, be it nevyre so drye a wethyre; and this yere he is drye, &c. Also this same yere, ther was a voyce cryenge in the heyre, betwyx Laicetere and Bambury, uppon Dunmothe, and in dyverse othere places, herde a long tyme cryinge, "Bowes! Bowes!" whiche was herde of xl. menne; and some menne saw that he that cryed soo was a hedles manne; and many other dyverse tokenes have be schewede in Englonde this yere, for amendynge of mennys lyvynge.

Also this yere, or a lytelle before, George the Archebysshoppe of Yorke, and brother to the Erle of Warwyke, was withe Kynge Edwarde at Wynsoure, and huntede, and hade there ryghte good chere, and supposid he hade stonde in grete favour with the Kynge: for the

Kynge seid to the sayde Archebyschope that he wuld come for to
hunte and disporte withe hyme in his manere at Moore;
whereof he was ryghte glade, and toke his leve and went home
to make purvyaunce therfore; and fett oute of Londone, and
dyverse other places, alle his plate and othere stuffe that he hade
hyde after Barnet felde and Teukysbury feld; and also borowede
more stuff of other menne, and purveyde for the Kynge for two or
iij. dayes for mete and drynke and logynge, and arayed as rychely
and as plesauntly as he coude. And the day afore the Kynge
schulde have comyne to the Archebysshoppe, to the seid manere
of Moore, whiche the saide Archebisshoppe hade purchasshed and
byllede it ryghte comodiusly and plesauntly, the Kynge send a
gentylman to the seide Archebisshoppe, and commaundyd him to
come to Wyndsoure to hyme; and asone as he came he was arested
and apeched of hye treysone, that he schuld helpe the Erle of
Oxenforde; and anone ryght he was put to warde. And forthe-
withe Sere William of Parre, knyghte, and Thomas Vaghan, squyre,
withe othere many dyverse gentilmenne and yomen, were sent to
the seide manere of Moore; and ther by the Kynges comawnde-
ment seysede the seid manere into the Kynges handes, and
alle the good that was therin, whiche was worthe xx. M^l. ^{li}. or
more, and alle other lordschippes and landes that the seid bysshoppe
hade withein Englonde, and alle his stuff and rychesse withein
alle his lordschippes; and sent the same bisschoppe overe the see
to Caleis, and from thens to the castelle of Hammys, and ther he
was kepte presonere many a day; and the Kynge alle that season
toke the prophete of the Archebysshopperyche, &c. And anone
after the Kynge brake the seyd Archebysschoppes mytere, in
the whiche were fulle many ryche stones and preciouse, and
made therof a croune for hyme self. And alle his other juels,
plate, and stuff, the Kynge gaff it to his eldest sonne and heyre
Prynce Edward: for the sayd Archebisshoppe hade be Chaun-
selere of Englond many dayes, and he and his brotheres hade

the reule of the lande, and hade gaderyde grete rychesse many
yeres, whiche in one day was lost; and alle be the hye jugement
of ryghtwisnes (as many manne seide be hym) for his grete cove-
tousenes, and had no pyte of Kynge Harry menne, and was cause of
many mannys undoynge for Kynge Edwardys sake, if he myghte
gete any good by hym. Wherefore *suche goodes as were gaderide
with synne, were loste with sorwe.* And also menne supposid for
cause he was duble to Kynge Herry, and kepte hym in Londone,
where he wulde a be at Westmynstere, he hade a lettere send frome
Kynge Edward to kepe hym oute of sanctuary, and he hade his
charture send hym; where he had be a trewe manne to Kynge
Herry, as the comons of Londone were, Kynge Edward hade not
comene into Londone afore Barnet felde, &c.

Also in the xiij. yere of [the] regne of Kynge Edwarde, Sere Jhon
Veere, Erle of Oxenforde, that withdrewe hym frome Barnet felde,
and rode into Scottlonde, and frome thens into Fraunce asailed,
and ther he was worschipfully received. And in the same yere he
was in the see withe certeyne schippes, and gate grete good and
rychesse, and afterewarde came into westecountre, and, with a
sotule poynte of werre, gate and enteryd Seynt Michaels Mount
in Cornwayle, a stronge place and a mygty, and can noȝt be
geett yf it be wele vytaled withe a fewe menne to kepe hit; for xx^{ti}.
menne may kepe it ageyne alle the world. So the seyde Erle, withe
xx^{ti}. score menne save iij, the last day of Septembre the yere afore
seyd, enteryd fyrst into [the] seyd mount, and he and his menne
came doune into cuntre of Cornwale, and hade riyhte good chere of
the comons, &c. The Kynge and his counselle sawe that therof
myche harme myght growe, &c.; comawndyd Bodrygan, scheff
reulere of Cornwayle, to besege the seid mount. And so he dyd; and
every day the Erle of Oxenfordes menne came doune undere trewis,
spake with Bodrynghan and his menne; and at the laste the seid Erle
lacked vytayle, and the seyde Bodrygan suffryd hyme to be vytailed;
and anone the Kynge was put in knowlache therof; wherefor the

seide Bodrygan was discharged, and Richard Fortescu, squyere for the body, by auctoryte of the Kynge, toke uppone honde to lay scge to the forseide mount, &c. And so gret dyversione roose betwyx Bodrygan and Fortescu, whiche Fortescu was schreve of Cornwayle, &c.; and the seide Fortescu leyed sege, &c. the xx. xiij^{ti}. day of Decembre the yere aforseide; and for the most party every day eche of theme faughte withe othere, and the seide Erles menne kylled dyverse of Fortescu menne; and som tyme whenne thei hade welle y-foughte, thei wulde take a trewis for one day and a night, and some tyme for two or thre dayes, &c. In the whiche trewes eche one of them spake and comaunde with other. The Kynge and his counselle sent unto dyverse that were with the Erle of Oxenforde prevely there pardones, and promysede to them grete yeftes and landes and goodes, by the whiche dyverse of them were turned to the Kynge ayens the Erle; and so in conclusione the Erle hade no3t passynge ane viij. or ix. menne that wolde holde withe hym; the whiche was the undoynge of the Erle. For ther is proverbe and a seyenge, that *a castelle that spekythe, and a womane that wille here, thei wille be gotene bothe :* for menne that bene in a castelle of warr, that wille speke and entrete withe ther enemyes, the conclusione therof [is] the losynge of the castelle; and a womanne that wille here foly spokyne unto hyre, if sche assent no3t at one tyme, sche wille at another. And so this proverbe was prevede trewe by the seide Erle of Oxenforde, whiche was fayne to yelde up the seyde mount, and put hyme in the Kynges grace; if he hade no3t do so, his owne menne wulde have brought hym oute. And so Fortescu enterd into the seyd mount, the xv. day of Februarij. the yere afore sayde, in the whiche was vytayle enogh tylle midsomere aftere. And so was the Erle aforseyd, the Lorde Bemonde, two brotheres of the seide Erles, and Thomas Clyfforde, brought as a presonere to the Kynge; and alle was donne by ther oun ɛfoly, &c.

NOTES.

P. 1, *l.* 1.—The Warkworth Chronicle, in Bernard's Catalogue of the Peterhouse manuscripts, taken from James's Eclogæ, is numbered—230. It may be as well to observe that John Bagford mentions a contemporary Chronicle in English MS. of the events of the commencement of Edward's reign, in MS. Tann. Bodl. 453.

—— *l.* 3.—*At the coronacyone.* King Edward was crowned in Westminster Abbey, on the 29th of June 1461. Warkworth's first passage is both imperfect and incorrect, and would form a very bad specimen of the value of the subsequent portions of his narrative; yet we find it transferred to the Chronicle of Stowe. It must, however, be regarded rather as a memorandum of the various creations to the peerage made during Edward's reign, than as a part of the chronicle. Not even the third peerage mentioned, the Earldom of Northumberland, was conferred at the Coronation, but by patent dated 27 May 1464: and the only two Earldoms bestowed in Edward's first year (and probably at the Coronation) were, the Earldom of Essex, conferred on Henry Viscount Bourchier, Earl of Eu in Normandy, who had married the King's aunt, the Princess Isabel of York; and the Earldom of Kent, conferred on William Neville, Lord Fauconberg, one of King Edward's generals at Towton. The former creaion is mentioned by Warkworth lower down in his list; the latter is omitted altogether.—J. G. N.

—— *l.* 6.—*The Lord Montagu.* " And then Kyng Edward, concidering the greate feate doon by the said Lord Montagu, made hym Erle of Northumberlond; and in July next folowyng th'Erle of Warwyk, with th'ayde of the said Erle of Northumberland, gate agayn the castell of Bamborugh, wheryn was taken Sir Raaf Gray, which said Ser Raaf was after behedid and quartred at York. Also, in this yere, the first day of May, the Kyng wedded Dame Elizabeth Gray, late wif unto the lord Gray of Groby, and doughter to the Lord Ryvers."—*The London Chronicle*, MS. Cotton. Vitell. A. xvi. fol. 126, rᵒ. The MS. of the London Chronicle, from which Sir Harris Nicolas printed his edition, does not contain this passage. It is almost unnecessary to remark the chronological incorrectness of the above, but it serves to show how carelessly these slight Chronicles were compiled. Cf. MS. Add. Mus. Brit. 6113, fol. 192, rᵒ. and MS. Cotton. Otho, B. xiv. fol. 221, rᵒ.

P. 1, *l.* 9.—*Lord Erle of Pembroke.* William Lord Herbert of Chepstow, the first of the long line of Herbert Earls of Pembroke, was so created the 27th May 1468. His decapitation by the Duke of Clarence at Northampton in 1469, is noticed by Warkworth in p. 7.—J. G. N.

—— *l.* 10.—*Erle of Devynschire.* Humphery Stafford, created Baron Stafford of Southwick by patent 24th April 1464, was advanced to the Earldom of Devon 7th May 1469; but beheaded by the commons at Bridgwater before the close of the same year, as related by Warkworth, *ubi supra.*—J. G. N.

—— *l.* 12.—*Erle of Wyltschyre.* John Stafford, created Earl of Wiltshire, 5th Jan. 1470; he died in 1473.—J. G. N.

The Lorde Gray Ryffyne, Erle of Kent. The Earl of Kent, of the family of Neville, died without male issue, a few months after his elevation to that dignity; and it was conferred on the 30th May 1465, on Edmund Lord Grey de Ruthyn, on occasion of the Queen's coronation. He was cousin-german to Sir John Grey, of Groby, the Queen's first husband. On the same occasion the Queen's son Sir Thomas Grey was created Marquess of Dorset; her father Richard Wydevile lord Ryvers was advanced to the dignity of Earl Ryvers; and her brother Anthony married to the heiress of Scales, in whose right he was summoned to Parliament as a Baron.—J. G. N.

Ibid.—*Sere Thomas Blount.* This should be *Walter*, created Lord Montjoy 20th June 1465; he died in 1474.—J. G. N.

P. 1, *l.* 13.—*Sere Jhon Hawarde, Lord Hawarde.* This peerage dates its origin, by writ of summons to Parliament, during the short restoration of Henry VI. in 1470, a circumstance more remarkable as " evidence exists that he did not attach himself to the interest of that Prince, being constitued by Edward, in the same year, commander of his fleet." See Sir Harris Nicolas's memoir of this distinguished person (afterwards the first? Duke of Norfolk) in Cartwright's History of the Rape of Bramber, p. 189.—J. G. N.

—— *l.* 18.—*He ordeyned a parleament.* This was in November.

—— *l.* 19.—*At whiche were atteynted Kynge Henry.* The act for the attainder of Henry is not printed in the authentic edition of the Statutes of the Realm, published by the Commissioners for the Public Records, but occurs on the Rolls of Parliament, vol. v. pp. 476—82. Cf. MS. Ashm. 21, and 862, xxxv; *Cotton's Abridgment,* pp. 670—1; *Fœdera,* xi. 709. " Ubi indutati et atteyntati sunt Henricus, vocatus nuper Rex Anglie, cum Margareta* consore sua, duces et Somerset et Excetre, cum aliis militibus et nobilibus ad numerum quasi centum personarum." MS. Arundel, Coll. Arm. 5, fol. 169, rº. Cf. *W. Wyrcestre Annales,* pp. 490—2.

P. 2, *l.* 3.—*New Fraunschesses.* Cf. MS. Bib. Cantuar. 51.

—— *l.* 6.—*Also Quene Margrett.* This was in the year 1462. Towards the end of the year Edward appears to have made a tour to the West of England, perhaps for the purpose of seeing how the country was disposed towards him:—" Deinde Rex Edwardus, Cantuariam peregre profectus, partes meridionales pertransiit, ubi Willielmum Episcopum Wintonie de manibus querentium animam ejus eripuit, insectatores suos graviter redarguit, et eorum capitaneos carcerali custodi emancipavit. Bristollie apperians, a civibus ejus cum max-

---

* I find, however, in the Pipe Roll of 1 Edw. IV. an entry of £21. 13*s.* for property at Bristol to "Margareta nuper dicta Regina Angliæ," granted to her by Edward; this property, it appears, formerly belonged to Queen Johanna, and " per dominum Regem nunc concess' in partem recompensacionis."

imo gaudio honoratissimè receptus est."—MS. Arundel, Coll. Arm. 5, fol. 169, rº. This Chronicle in the College of Arms was first used, as far as I know, for an historical purpose, in a MS. note in a copy of Carte's History of England in the Bodleian Library, where it is referred to on the important testimony of the death of Henry VI. Mr. Black quotes it in the *Excerpta Historica*, but its value does not appear to be fully appreciated by that author; it is the diary of a contemporary writer on the side of the House of York, and extends to the execution of the Bastard of Fauconberg, and Edward's celebration of the feast of Pentecost which took place immediately afterwards.

The following very curious account of the pageant which received Edward at Bristol is from a MS. in Lambeth Palace, Nº. 306, fol. 132, rº. I am indebted for it to the Rev. S. R. Maitland, F.R.S., Librarian to the Archbishop of Canterbury, who had the extreme kindness, at my request, to send me a transcript.

" *The receyvyng of Kyng Edward the iiijᵗʰ. at Brystowe.*

" First, at the comyng inne atte temple gate, there stode Wylliam Conquerour, with iij. lordis, and these were his wordis :—

> ' Wellcome Edwarde! oure son of high degre ;
> Many yeeris hast thou lakkyd owte of this londe—
> I am thy forefader, Wylliam of Normandye,
> To see thy welefare here through Goddys sond.'

" Over the same gate stondyng a greet Gyant delyveryng the keyes.

" *The Receyvyng atte Temple Crosse next following ;—*

" There was Seynt George on horsbakke, uppon a tent, fyghtyng with a dragon ; and the Kyng and the Quene on hygh in a castell, and his doughter benethe with a lambe ; and atte the sleying of the dragon ther was a greet melody of aungellys."

Sir Bawdan (or Baldwin) Fulford was brought before the King, and beheaded at this place on the ninth of September; his head was placed upon Castle Gate.—Rot. C. 8. Mus. Brit.

P. 2, *l.* 7.—*And other lordes.* Among them was Thomas Lord Roos. *Paston Correspondence*, vol. I. p. 219.

—— *l.* 7-8.—*Certeyne castelles in Northumberlond.* See two contemporary accounts of the sieges of these castles, edited by Mr. Black, in the *Excerpta Historica*, p. 365. Cf. *W. Wyrcestre*, p. 493—449.

—— *l.* 16.—*Sere Peris le Brasylle.* See a curious document printed by Sir Henry Ellis, from Cart. Antiq. Cotton. XVII. 10. in the second series of his collection of Original Letters, vol. I. p. 131.

P. 3, *l.* 7.—*Excepte a castelle in Northe Wales called Harlake.* I cannot resist the temptation of taking the following lines from the poems of Lewis Glyn Cothi, relative to the future siege of Harlech castle—

> " Doves â'i wyr, divasw wedd,
> Dareni daiar Wynedd;
> Jarll, ond ev a'r llu, nid â
> Ar wddv Eryri Wyddva.
> Dau er ei chael dri a chwech,—
> Un dân harddlun yw Harddlech.
> Tynu â gwyr tònau gwin
> Peiriannus, val mab brenin.
> Uchel ewri a *chlariwns*,
> A tharvu gwyr â thwrv *gwns;*
> Saethu 'mhob parth saith mil pen,
> A'u bwa o bob ywen:
> Clod wellwell, cludaw allan
> Goed mawr a fagodau mân;
> O wartha 'r rhai'n, hyd yr hwyr,
> Arvogion a'u rhyvagwyr.
> Trwy'r tair gwart Herbart hirborth
> Ty'nu'r pen capten i'r porth.
> Ennillodd, eu ewyllys,
> Y brenin lech Bronwen Lys.
> *Hywel Davydd ab Jevan ab Rhys.*"

As no translation is added in the published works of Glyn Cothi, it may be as well to give one here;—

> " He tamed, in no trifling manner,
> The lofty heights of Gwyneth ;*
> No earl, save him and his followers, could ever mount
> Upon the neck of Snowdon, the Alpine of Eryri.†
> There would climb up, to gain the ascent,
> Now three,—now six men, all at once ;
> One beautifully formed fiery blaze is Harddlech ! ‡
> Men drawing from men waves of wine,— §
> Loud the shouting—loud the blasts of clarions ;
> Scattering of men, thundering of guns ;
> Arrows flying in every quarter from seven thousand men,
> Using bows made of the yew.
> Bravo ! bravo ! they bring out large trees and faggots ;
> They pile them up, and, behind the pile,
> Armed men are placed to continue there 'til night.
> Then Herbert, through the three wards,
> Brings forth the head captain in the porch.
> Thus King Edward, as it were, with one volition,
> Gained possession of Bronwen's Court."||

This place was possessed in 1468 by Dafydd ap Jeuan ap Einion,— a strong friend of the house of Lancaster, distinguished for his valour and great stature. He was besieged here by William Herbert, Earl of Pembroke, after a march through the heart of our Alps, attended with incredible difficulties ; for in some parts, the soldiers were obliged to climb ; in others, to precipitate themselves down the rocks ; and, at length, invested a place till that time deemed impregnable.

* North Wales.   † The mountains surrounding Snowdon.

‡ This couplet is metaphorical of the rapidity of Herbert's motions.

§ i. e. streams of blood.

|| The castle was anciently called **Twr Bronwen**, after Bronwen, daughter of Llyr (King Lear), and aunt to the great Caractacus. See *The Cambro-Briton*, ii. 71. She is the subject of an old Welsh Romance.

The Earl committed the care of the siege to Sir Richard, a hero equal in size to the British commandant. Sir Richard sent a summons of surrender, but Dafydd stoutly answered that he had kept a castle in France so long, that he made all the old women in Wales talk of him; and that he would keep this so long, that all the old women in France should also talk of him. He at last surrendered, and Herbert had a hard struggle with Edward's barbarous policy to save the noble defender's life.—*Pennant's Tour in Wales*, vol. II. p. 121-2. Margaret of Anjou found refuge in this Castle after the unfortunate battle of Northampton; and it has been conjectured that the song of " Farwel iti Peggy Ban" was composed on the occasion of her quitting it. On the peculiar advantages of the position of this castle, see *The Cambrian Traveller's Guide*, p. 574.

P. 3, l. 15-6.—An hole quinzisme and disme. See *Rot. Parl. V.* 497. This parliament met on the 29th of April, and continued to the following year.

—— *l. 16.—Whereof the peple grocehede sore.* The taxes which Edward appears to have levied were most onerous on the people, and partly served to pay for his extravagant luxury, which he seems to have carried to the extreme.—*Cambrian Register*, I. 78.

—— *l. 17-8.—The Erle of Warwyke was sent into Fraunce.* Gagvin, in his Chronicon Franciæ, informs us that the Earl was received by the King Louis XI. at Rouen with great pomp; had secret conferences with him for twelve days consecutively; and was loaded with presents when he took his departure. It is curious to observe that the author of the fragment printed by Hearne refers to a French writer on this portion of his history.

—— *l. 21.—The Kynge was wedded to Elizabethe Gray.* See a most quaint narrative of this marriage in William Habington's *Historie of Edward the Fourth*, fol. 1640, pp. 33—35. I find it stated in one place (MS. Harl. 2408.) that Edward's mother attempted to hinder the marriage, by causing " another contract to be alleadged made by him with the Lady Elizabeth Lucy, on whom he had begot a child

befor." She seems, indeed, to have been most hostile to this impru-
dent and unpopular connexion :—

> " Married a woman? married indeed!
> Here is a marriage that befits a king!
> It is no marvaile it was done in hast :
> Here is a bridall, and with hell to boote,
> You have made worke."
>
> *Heywood's First Part of Edward IV.* Sig. A. ij.

The author of Hearne's fragment, however, speaks in praise of the
marriage,—" Howbeit that lewde felow that drew thois last brent
cronicles, abusid himsel gretely in his disordrid wriȝting for lakke of
knowlege." (P. 293.)

P. 3, *l.* 23.—*Slayne at Yorke felde.* Sir John Grey was slain at the
second battle of St. Alban's, fought on the 17th Feb. 1460–1.—J. G. N.

—— *l.* 30.—*The Bysshope of Excetre.* George Neville, made Chan-
cellor the 25th July 1460. He was translated to the archbishopric
of York, 17th June 1465.—J. G. N.

—— *l.* 31.—*The Bysshope of Bath.* Robert Stillington. He did not
receive the seal until the 8th June 1468, previously to which Robert
Kirkham had been Keeper.—J. G. N.

P. 4, *l.* 2.—*Kyng Edwarde dide that he myght to feble the Erles powere.*
We have, however, in an act passed subsequently to this period, an
especial clause that the same act " be not prejudiciall or hurtyng unto
Richard Neville, Erle of Warrewyk."—*Rot. Parl.* 4 *Edw. IV.*

—— *l.* 8.—*Gadred a grete peple of the northe contre.* The following
very curious document is from a MS. in the College of Arms (L. 9):—

" *Anno Edwardi quarti quarto et mensis Maij die xxvij. scilicet in die
san[c]te Trinitatis.*

" The Kyng lay in the Palois of York, and kept his astate solemply ; and tho there create he Sir John Nevelle, Lord Mown-
tage, Erle of Northumberland. And than my lorde of Warrewike
toke upon hym the jorney, by the Kynges commandement and
auctoritee, to resiste the Rebellions of the Northe, acompanyed with
hym my sayde Lorde of Northumberland his brother.

" Item, the xxiij^{ti}. day of Juyne, my saide Lorde of Warrewike, with the puissaunce, cam before the castelle of Alwike, and ad it delivered by appointement ; And also the castell of Dunstanboroughe, where that my said Lord kept the feest of Saint Johñ Baptist.

" Item, my said Lorde of Warrewike, and his broder Erle of Northumberland, the xxv. day of Juyn, leyede siege unto the Castelle of Bamburghe, there within being Sir Rauf Grey, with suche power as attendid for to keepe the said castelle ayen the power of the Kinges and my said Lord, as it apperith by the heroudes reporte, by the whiche my Lord sent to charge them to delyvere it under this forme, as ensewithe ; Chester, the Kinges heroude, and Warrewike the heroude, had this commaundement, as foloweth,—to say unto Sir Rauf Gray, and to other that kept his Rebelliouse oppynyon, that they shule delivere that place contynent aftyr that summacion, and every man for the tyme being disposed to receyve the Kynges grace, my said Lord of Warrewike, the Kinges lieutenant, and my Lord of Northumbreland, Wardeyn of themarches, grauntith the Kyng['s] grace and pardon, body, lyvelodes, reservyng ij. persounes, is understoude, Sir Humfrey Neville and Sir Rauf Grey, thoo tweyn to be oute of the Kinges grace, without any redempcion. Than the answere of Sir Rauf Grey followithe unto the said heroudes, he clerely determynyng withinne hymself to liffe or to dye within the said place ; the heroudes, according to my Lordes commandement, charged hym with all inconveniences that by possible myght fall in offence ayenst Allemyghty God, and sheding of bloode ; the heroude saying in this wise, ' My Lordes ensurithe yow, upon their honour, to susteyne siege before yowe these vij. yeres, or elles to wynne yowe.'

" Item, my sayde Lorde Lieutenant, and my Lord Wardeyn, hath yeven us ferther comaundement to say unto yowe, if ye deliver not this Juelle, the whiche the king our most dradde soverain Lord hath so gretly in favour, seing it marcheth so nygh hys awncient enemyes of Scotland, he specially desirethe to have it, hoole, unbroken, with ordennaunce ; if ye suffre any greet gunne laide unto the wal, and be shote and prejudice the wal, it shall cost yowe the Chiftens hede; and so proceding for every gunne shet, to the leest hede of any persoune within the said place. Than the saide Sir Rauf Grey deperted from the saide heroud, ant put hym in devoir to make deffence.

" And than my Lorde lieutenant had ordennede alle the Kinges greet gonnes that where charged at oons to shute unto the said Castelle, Newe-Castel the Kinges greet gonne, and London the second gonne of irne; the whiche betyde the place, that stones of the walles flewe unto the see; Dysyon, a brasin gonne of the Kinges, smote thouroughe Sir Rauf Grey's chamber oftentymes; Edward and Richard Bombartell, and other of the Kinges ordennaunce, so occupied by the ordonnaunce of my said Lord, with men of armes and archirs, wonne the castelle of Bamburg with asawte, mawgrey Sir Rauf Grey, and tooke hym, and brought hym to the Kynge to Doncastre, and there was he execut in this fourme as followith. My lorde Erle of Worcestre, Connestable of Englond, sitting in jugement, told hym jugement, and remambrid hym, saying unto hym; " Sir Rauf Grey, thou hast take the ordir of Knyghthode of the Batthe, and any soe taking that ordir ought to kepe his faithe the whiche he makes; therfor remembre the[e] the lawe! wilt thou shall procede to jugement? thees maters shewith so evidently agayn the, that they nedithe not to examyn the of them, by certein persounes of the Kinges true subgettes, the whiche thou hast wounded, and shewithe here that thou canst not deny this; thou hast drawen the with force of armes unto the Kyng oure most natural soverain Lorde, the whiche tho wotest wele yave unto the suche trust, and in suche wise mynystred his grace unto the, that thou haddist his castels in the Northe partie to kepe; thou hast betraied Sir John Asteley Knyght, and brother of the gartier, the whiche remaignethe in the hand of the Kynges oure soverain Lord enemyes in Fraunce.

" Item, thou hast withstoud and maade fences ageynst the Kynges maiestie, and his lieutenant the worthy Lorde my broder of Warrwike; it apperith by the strookes of the greet gunnes in the Kyng walles of his castell of Bamburghe. For the[se] causes, dispost the to suffre thy penaunce aftyr the lawe. The Kyng had ordenned that thou shuldest have hadd thy sporys striken of by the hard heles, with the hand of the maister cooke, that whiche is here redy to doo, as was promysed at the tyme that he tooke of thy spurres ; he said to yee, as ys accustumed, that ' And thou be not true to thy soverain Lord, I shal smyte of thy sporys with this knyf herd by the helys,' and so shewne hym the maistre cooke redy to doo his office, with apron and his knyff.

" Item, Sir Rauff Grey, the Kyng had ordenned here, thou maist see, the Kynge of armes and heroudes, and thine own propre cote of armes, that whiche they shuld teere of thy body, and so thou shuldist as wel be disgraded of thy worshipp, noblesse, and armes, as of the order of Knyghthode: and also here is an oder cote of thin armes reversed, the which thou shuldest have werne of thy body, going to that dethe warde, for that belongethe aftyr the lawe. Notwithstanding, of the disgrading of knygthode, and of thine armes, et noblesse, the King pardons that for thy noble grauntfader, the whiche suffrid trouble for the Kynges moost noble predecesseurs.*   Than, Sir Rauf Grey, this shal be thy penaunce,—thou shalt goo on thy feet unto the towneseend, and there thou shalt be laide downe and drawen to a scaffold maade for thee, and that thou shalt have thyne hede smite of thi body, to be buriede in the freres ; thi heede where it pleased the Kyng."

P. 4, l. 11—12.—Were takene and afterward behedede. " Quintode-cimo die mensis Maij, apud Exham, decapitati sunt Dux Somersett, Edmundus Fizthu miles, Bradshaw, Wauter Hunt, Blac Jakis. Decimo-septimo die mensis Maii, apud Novum-Castrum, decapitati

---

* Sir Ralph Grey, of Wark, Heton, and Chillingham (lineal ancestor of the Earls of Tankerville, as well as of the present Earl Grey) was the grandson of Sir Thomas Grey, beheaded at Southampton with the Earl of Cambridge, Aug. 5, 1415. See the whole-sheet pedigree of Grey in Raine's North Durham.—J.G.N.

sunt **Dominus de Hungarforde, Dominus Roos, Dominus Thomas Fynderum, Edwardus de la Mare, Nicholaus Massam.** Apud Medetham, xviij° die mensis Maii, decapitati sunt Dominus Philippus Wentworth, Willielmus Penyngton, Warde de Topcliff, Oliverus Wentworth, Willielmus Spilar, Thomas Hunt, *le foteman Regis Henrici.* Apud Eboracum, xxv° die mensis Maii, decapitati sunt Dominus Thomas Husye, Thomas Gosse, Robertus Merfynn, Johannes Butlerus, Rogerus Water, *janitor Regis Henrici,* Thomas Fenwyke, Robertus Cocfeld, Willielmus Bryte, Willielmus Dawsonn, Johannes Chapman. Apud Eboracum, xxviij° die mensis Maii, decapitati sunt Johannes Elderbek, Ricardus Cawerum, Johannes Roselle, Robertus Conqueror."—*MS. Arundel, Coll. Arm.* 5, fol. 170, r°.

P. 4, l. 26.—Chaunged the coyn of Englonde. This whole passage is transcribed by Stowe, nearly word for word, in his Chronicle, pp. 418—19. " Mense Octobris, fecit Rex proclamare Radingiæ, et per totam Angliam, quod unum nobile Regis Henrici valeret viij. s. iiij. d., fecitque novum Cunagium turri Londoniæ, ad summum dampnum magnatum regni." — *W. Wyrcestre Annales,* p. 500. Cf. *Archæologia,* XV. 165; and Sir Henry Ellis's edition of *Grafton's Continuation of Harding's Chronicle,* p. 437.

—— *l. 3.—And also he made angelle noblys of vj. s. viij. d.* i. e. he made the noble of that price, and changed its name to that of angel; *Hearne's Fragment,* p. 294. A very short time previously the noble was of comparatively trifling value.—*MS. Ch. Ant. Eg.* 88.

P. 5, l. 2.—A blacke monke of Abyngtone. In the curious fragment printed by Hearne, at the end of the Chronicle of Sprottus, we are informed that William Cantlow was the name of this rascal. Henry's capture, in the MS. N° 5, in the College of Arms, is placed under the year 1465 :—" Hoc et anno, circiter festum Apostolorum Petri et Pauli, captus est Henricus Sextus, nuper Rex Anglie, du[c]tus et publice per Chepam Londonie, cum aliis secum captis ; ductus usque ad Turrim Londonie, ibique honorifice commendatus custodie mansit." Fol. 170, v°.

P. 5, *l.* 3.—*Bungerley Hyppyngstones.* This was a ford, obtained by stepping-stones, across the river Ribble.—J. G. N.

—— *l.* 4.—*Thomas Talbott, sonne and heyre to Sere Edmund Talbot of Basshalle.* Sir Edmund Talbot, of Bashall, in the parish of Mitton, co. York, died in the 1st Edw. IV. His son, Sir Thomas, was then under age (pedigree in Whitaker's History of Craven, 2d edit. 1812, p. 25) ; but there can be little doubt that, before his traitorous achievement, he had married Alice, daughter of Sir John Tempest, of Brace-well, under whose protection the unfortunate King was then living. Beside the present reward mentioned in the ensuing note, Sir Thomas Talbot appears to have received a grant of a yearly pension of 40*l.*, which was confirmed by Richard III. (pedigree, as above). He survived to the 13th Hen. VII. His father-in-law, Sir John Tempest, was Sheriff of Yorkshire in 18 and 37 Henry VI. (see pedigree of Tempest in Whitaker's Craven, p. 80.)—J. G. N.

—— *l.* 4.—*Thomas Talbott.* In the Issue Rolls of the Exchequer of 5 Edw. IV. are the statements of monies paid to this gentleman and others for taking Henry, late *de facto et non de jure* King of England. It appears that Sir James Haryngton and Sir John Tempest were also concerned in the capture; but the fact of Sir Thomas Talbot being the chief actor is confirmed by the amount of their relative rewards, he receiving 100*l.* and they each 100 marks. Their " costs and charges," amounting to 100 marks, were also paid. John Levesey also received a reward of 20*l.*, and William Rogers of Serne and David Colinley, valets of the King's chamber, together 6*l.* 13*s.* 4*d.* On the 9th of July 1465, Edward, in consideration of " magnam et laboriosam diligentiam suam circa captionem et retinentiam magni proditoris, rebellis, et inimici nostri Henrici nuper vocati Regis Henrici Sexti, per ipsum Jacobum factum," gave to Sir James Haryngton a grant of Thurland Castle and other lands, formerly belonging to Richard Tunstell,* a partizan of Henry.—*Fœdera,* XI. 548.

* The great extent of these possessions may be seen in the Great Roll of the Pipe for 1 Edw. IV. com. Westmorland.

" My ancestor, Sir James Haryngton, did once take prisoner, with his party, this poor prince; for which the House of York did graunt him a parcel of lands in the northern counties, and which he was fool enough to lose again, after the battle of Bosworth, when King Henry the Seventh came to the crown."—*Haryngton's Nugæ Antiquæ, by T. Park,* vol. II. pp. 385–86. Cf. *Rot. Parl.* V. 584, and *Devon's Issue Rolls of the Exchequer,* p. 489.

[Sir James Harrington was of Brierley near Barnsley; a younger brother of Sir John Harrington, of Hornby, who had fallen on the Yorkists' side at the battle of Wakefield in 1460; their father, Sir Thomas, dying also of his wounds the day after the same battle. Sir James had, in 6 Edw. IV. a grant of 340*l.* from the issues of the county of York. Both he and his younger brother, Sir Robert Harrington, were attainted after the battle of Bosworth in 1 Hen. VII. See further respecting him in Hunter's Deanery of Doncaster, vol. ii. p. 403; to which it may be added that it is probably of him that Leland speaks: " There was a younger brother of the Haryngtons that had in gifte Horneby Castelle." (Itin. viii. f. 109 a.), that is, he had it for a time to the prejudice of his nieces, the heirs of his elder brother.—J. G. N.]

P. 5, l. 5.—Jhon Talbott his cosyne of Colebry. That is, of Salesbury, in the parish of Blackburn, co. Lancaster; see Whitaker's Whalley, 3d edit. 1818, p. 432. A yearly fee of twenty marks was granted by King Edward in consideration of the good and faithful service of Johannes Talbot de Salebury, Esq. " in captura magni adversarii sui Henrici," until he received a grant of lands or tenements to the like value; and the same annuity was confirmed to his son Sir John Talbot, of Salebury, by King Richard the Third. See the grant of the confirmation, dated at York 6th June 1484, printed in Baines's History of Lancashire, vol. i. p. 421.—J. G. N.

—— *l.* 6.—*Whiche disseyvide,* i. e. which King Henry, deceived.

—— *l.* 6.—*Wadyngtone Hall.* Waddington is a chapelry within the parish of Mitton, little more than a mile from Bashall. It had belonged to the Tempests of Bracewell from the time of Edward I. Dr. Whitaker says (Hist. of Craven, p. 25), " Waddington Hall, though constructed of strong old masonry, has nearly lost all appearance of antiquity. But one room contains the name of King Henry's chamber." In the History of Whalley, p. 473, will be seen an etching of the ruins. At Bracewell also, (which is now likewise in ruins,) in the older stone portion of the house, " is an apartment called King Henry's Parlour; undoubtedly one of the retreats of Henry VI." (Ibid. p. 82.) At Bolton, in the same neighbourhood, after describing a very ancient hall, and its canopy over the high table, Dr. Whitaker adds, " In this very hall, and probably under the same canopy, that unhappy monarch ate the bread of affliction during a retreat, as it is reported by tradition, of several months. An adjoining well retains the name of King Harry, who is said to have directed it to be dug and walled, in its present shape, for a cold bath." It is at Bolton where there are still preserved three relics of King Henry, a boot, a glove, and a spoon; figures of which are engraved in the Gentleman's Magazine for June 1785, and again in the History of Craven, p. 106. The boot and glove are remarkably small, and show, in Dr. Whitaker's words, that " in an age when the habits of the great, in peace as well as war, required perpetual exertions of bodily strength, this unhappy prince must have been equally contemptible from corporeal and from mental imbecility."—J. G. N.

P. 5, l. 7, 8.—His lege bownde to the styrope. One author, and as far as I have been able to find he is the only authority for it, sa ys, that Henry was immediately cast into chains.—*Matthæi Palmesii Pisani Continuatio Chronici Eusebiani,* ed. Venetiis, 1483, fol. 155, vº. According to some writers, Henry's two religious friends, Drs. Manning and Bedle, were the only companions of his misfortunes.—Cf. *Monstrelet, IV.* 182.

——, *l. 9.—By the Lorde Harberde.* " Et castrum forte in Wallia per dominum Harbarde captum est, et Dominus Ricardus Tunstalle, cum ceteris ibi inventis, captus est, et in Turri Londonie clausus, qui tum in breve gratiam a Rege consecutus est. Duo nobiles ex illic capti decollati sunt."—*MS. Arundel, Coll. Arm.* 5, fol. 171, rº. There is a grant to Lord Herbert for his services in *Rot. Pat.* 3 Edw. IV.

P. 5, l. 16.—*By lawe padowe.* I do not understand the meaning of the word " Padowe," except it be Paduan.

—— *l.* 22.—*And in vij. yere.* An anonymous scribbler says, that in this year there was, throughout England, a hurricane (*vehementissimus ventus*) which lasted for more than thirty-six hours.—*MS. Arundel, Mus. Brit.* 220. fol. 279, v°.

P. 6, *l.* 4.—*Were takene for treasoune and behedede.* See a valuable and curious note by Mr. Stapleton, in his volume of the Plumpton Correspondence, pp. 18, 19. This happened " circiter octavum Epiphanie."—*MS. Arundel, Coll. Arm.* 5, fol. 171, r°.

—— *l.* 19.—*xliij M*[1]. So in MS., but probably a clerical error for xiiij. M[1].

—— *l.* 25.—*A playne byyonde Banbury toune.* Danesmoor is in the parish of Edgecote, near three hills of unequal size, and in their relative position approaching a triangle ; " the spot now called Danesmoor is a small plantation of a few acres, but the name at this period had doubtless a much more extended application."—*Baker's Northamptonshire,* I. 500. This battle is commemorated in " Marwnad Thomas ab Rhosser, arglwydd Herast " of Lewis Glyn Cothi. Three things ought to be remarked, viz. that Herbert, who was beheaded, only made a codicil to his will, and not a new one, as commonly stated ; that the battle took place on the Monday—

" Dyw Llun y bu waed a lladd :"

and that Herbert and his fellow captives were executed on the Wednesday—

" Marchog a las ddyw Merclur,"

as Gutto Glyn remarks in his poetical language. Cf. MS. Cotton. Otho, B. xiv. fol. 221, v°, where an erroneous date is given to the battle,—*in quo cœsi multa milia.* In MS. Tann. Bodl. 2, fol. 104, v°. we find the field called " prelium ad Hegecote, seu Danysmore, prope Banburiam, dictam *Banbery-Feld,* seu *Hegecote-Fyld.*" Hearne's fragment informs us that the land on which the battle was fought belonged to a person named Clarell. In the valuable collection of manuscripts at the seat of W. Ormsby Gore, Esq. are some verses in the Welsh language on this battle; see Sir Thomas Phillipps's Catalogue of these Manuscripts, p. 1.

P. 6. l. 28, 29.—*The names of the gentylmen that were slayne.* See another and more extensive list in *Itinerarium Willelmi de Worcestre,* p. 120.1, although the major part of this catalogue differs from his. Worcester says that at least 168 of the nobility and gentry of Wales fell in this battle, and 1500 men on the English side.

—— *l.* 30, 31.—*Herry Organ, sonne and heyre,* i. e. the son and heir of Henry Organ.

P. 7, l. 5.—*Sere Herry Latymere.* Rather Sir Henry Neville, paternally a cousin-german of the great Earl of Warwick, and whose mother was Lady Elizabeth Beauchamp, half-sister to the heiress Anne, whom the Earl of Warwick married. Leland, in describing the Beauchamp Chapel at Warwick, says : " There lyeth buried (as some saye) in the west end of our Lady Chapell one of the Nevilles L. Latemer, slayne at Edgcote field by Banbury (as some suppose), but there is neither tombe nor scripture seene. This was Sir Hen. Neville, sonne and heire of George Neville, Lord Latemer. But he was never Lord, for he dyed before his father. This Henry Neville was grandfather to the Lord Latemer now livinge." The fact of Sir Henry Neville, and of his brother-in-law John Dudley, also slain in the same battle, having been buried in the Beauchamp Chapel, is proved by the will of his mother Lady Latimer, who on the field of Edgcote lost her only son and the husband of her daughter. Before the close of the same year, (on the 30th Dec.) her husband died insane. Nichols's Beauchamp Monuments, 4to. p. 40.—J. G. N.

—— *l.* 7.—Sir John Conyers of Hornby, com. Ebor. Kt.

—— *l.* 8 —*Olivere Audley, squyere.* For Audley read Dudley. He was a son of John Lord Dudley, K.G. and brother of that John who was grandfather of John Duke of Northumberland. Beauchamp Monuments, p. 39.—J. G. N.

—— *l.* 11-12.—" Hic W. Harberde, gravissimus et oppressor et spoliator ecclesiasticorum et aliorum multorum per annos multos, hunc tandem, justo Dei judicio pro suis sceleribus et nequiciis, recepit mercedem.   Die Sabbati proximo ante assumpcionem beatissime semper Virginis Marie, captus est Dominus de Rywaus, cum domino Johanne filio suo, et, juxta castrum de Kelingworthe, pariter decollati sunt."—MS. Arundel, Coll. Arm. fol. 171 rᵒ.

P. 7, l. 19.—A village bysyde Northampton.   Stowe calls this village Ulney ; that is, Olney, a market-town in Buckinghamshire, but within twelve miles of Northampton.—J. G. N.

―― *l. 31.—A generalle pardone.*   On the 27th of October, Henry Percy of Northumberlond, who had been confined in the Tower, under Lord Dudley, Constable, took the oaths of allegiance and was released.—*Fœdera*, XI. 649.

*P. 8, l. 4.—*I here insert a very curious and valuable document from a MS. Roll in the Ashmolean Museum at Oxford, Nᵒ. 1160, m. 2, dᵒ, et 1, dᵒ.

" *The duc of Clarance, th'archebisshoppe of Yorke, and th'erle of Warwyk.*

" Right trusty and welbelovid, we grete you welle.   And welle ye witte that the Kyng oure soveregne lordys true subgettes of diverse partyes of this his realme of Engelond have delivered to us certeyn billis of Articles, whiche we suppose that ye have in thoos parties, rememberynge in the same the disceyvabille covetous rule and gydynge of certeyne ceducious persones ; that is to say, the Lord Ryvers, the Duchesse of Bedford his wyf, Ser William Herbert, Erle of Penbroke, Humfrey Stafford, Erle of Devenshire, the Lordis Scalis and Audeley, Ser John Wydevile, and his brethern, Ser John Fogge, and other of theyre myschevous rule opinion and assent, wheche have caused oure seid sovereyn Lord and his seid realme to falle in grete poverte of myserie, disturbynge the mynystracion of the lawes, only entendyng to thaire owen promocion and enrichyng.   The seid trewe subgettis with pitevous lamentacion callyng uppon us and other lordes to be meanes to oure seid sovereyne Lord for a remedy and reformacion ; werfore we, thenkyng the peticioun comprised in the seid articles resonabyll and profitable for the honoure and profite of oure seid so-vereyn Lord and the comune welle of alle this his realme, fully purposed with other lordis to shewe the same to his good grace, de-siryng and pray you to dispose and arredie you to accompayneye us thedir, with as many persones defensabyly arrayede as y can make, lettyng you wete that by Goddis grace we entende to be at Caunter-bury uppon Sonday next comyng. Wretyn undre oure signettis and signe manuell the xijth day of Juyll, A^o 1469.

" In three the next articles undrewretin are comprisid and specified the occa-sions and verry causes of the grete inconveniencis and mischeves that fall in this lond in the dayes of Kyng Edward the ij^{de}, Kyng Ric' the ij^{de}, and Kyng Henry the vj^{te}, to the distruccion of them, And to the gret hurt and empoverysshyng of this lond.

" First, where the seid Kynges estraingid the gret lordis of thayre blood from thaire secrete Councelle, And not avised by them; And takyng abowte them other not of thaire blood, and enclynyng only to theire counselle, rule and advise, the wheche persones take not re-spect ne consideracion to the wele of the seid princes, ne to the comonwele of this lond, but only to theire singuler lucour and en-richyng of themself and theire bloode, as welle in theire greet pos-sessions as in goodis; by the wheche the seid princes were so enpo-verysshed that they hadde not sufficient of lyvelode ne of goodis, wherby they myght kepe and mayntene theire honorable estate and ordinarie charges withynne this realme.

" Also the seid seducious persones, not willing to leve the posses-sions that they hadde, caused the seid princes to lay suche imposi-cions and charges as welle by way of untrue appecementes to whom they owed evill wille unto, as by dymes, taxis and prestis noblis and other inordinat charges uppon theire subjettes and commons, to the grete grugge and enpoveryssyng of them, wheche caused alle the people of this lond to grugge.

" And also the seid seducious persones by theyre mayntenaunces, where they have rule, wold not suffre the lawes to be executed, but where they owe favour moved the seid princes to the same; by the wheche there were no lawes atte that tyme deuly ministred, ne putt in execucion, wheche caused gret murdres, roberyes, rapes, oppressions, and extorcions, as well by themself, as by theyre gret mayntenaunces of them to be doon, to the gret grugge of all this lande.

" Hit is so that where the kyng oure sovereigne lorde hathe hadde as gret lyvelode and possessions as evyr had kyng of Engelond ; that is to say, the lyvelode of the Crowne, Principalite of Wales, Duche of Lancastre, Duche of Cornwelle, Duche of York, the Erldome of Chestre, the Erldome of Marche, the Lordeschippe of Irlond, and other, with grete forfaytis, besyde Tunage and Poundage of alle this londe, grauntyd only to the kepynge of the see. The lorde Revers, the Duchesse of Bedford his wyf, and thayre sonnes, Ser William Harbert, Earle of Pembroke, and Humfrey Stafford, Erle of Devonshire, the Lord of Audely, and Ser John Fogge, and other of thayre myschevous assent and oppinion, whiche have advised and causid oure seid sovereigne lord to geve of the seyd lyvelode and possessions to them above theire disertis and degrees, So that he may nat lyf honorably and mayntene his estate and charges ordinarie withinne this lond.

" And also the seid seducious persones next before expressid, not willyng to leve suche large possessions and goodis as they have of oure seid sovereigne lordis gyfte, have, by subtile and discevable ymaginacions, movid and causid oure sovereyne lord to chaunge his most ryche coyne, and mynysshed his most royalle household, to the gret appeycyng of his estate, and the comonwele of this londe.

" Also seid seducious persones, continuyng in theire most deseyvable and covetous disposiscion, have causid oure seid soverayne lord to aske and charge us his trewe comons and subgettis wyth suche gret imposicions and inordinat charges, as by meanes of borowyng withoute payment, takyng goodes of executours of rich men, taxis, dymes, and preestis noblis; takyng gret goodis for his household without payment, impechementes of treasounes to whom they owe any eville will; So that ther can be no man of worshippe or richesse, other spirituelle or temporelle, knyghtis, squiers, marchauntes, or any other honest persone, in surete of his lyf, lyvelode, or goodis, where the seid seducious persones, or any of them, owe any malice or eville wille, to the grete drede and importabylle charges, and the utter empoverysshyng of us his treue Commons and subjettes, And to the gret enrychyng of themself, the premisses amouutynge to ccM^1. markes [this yere] and more.

" Also the seid seducious persones have caused our seid sovereygne lord to spende the goodis of oure holy fadir [the pope], the wheche were yevyn hym for defence of Cristen feyth of many goodely disposyd people of this lond, without repayment of oure seid holy fadir, for the wheche cause this lond stondith in juberdie of Enterdytynge.

" Also the seid seducious persones, be thayre mayntenaunces in the cuntreyes where they dwelt or where they here rule, will not suffre the Kynges lawes to be executyd uppon whom they owyd favere unto, And also movid oure seid sovereyne lord to the same; by the wheche the lawes be not duly mynystered, ne put in execucion; by the wheche gret murdre, robbres, rapes, oppressions, and extorcions, as well be them, as by thayre gret mayntenaunces of theire servauntes, to us daly done and remayne unpunysshed, to the gret hurt and grugge of alle this londe.

" Also the seid seducious persones hath causid oure seid soverayne lord to estrainge the true lordis of his blood from his secrete Councelle, to th'entent that they myghte atteyne and brenge aboughte theyre fals and dysceyvable purpos in premisses aforseid, to the gret enrychynge of themself, And to the gret hurt and poverte of oure seid sovereyne lorde, and to alle us his trewe subjettis and commons of this londe."

*" These undrewretyn are the peticions of us tréue and feythefulle subjettes
and commons of this lond for the gret wele and surete of the Kyng oure
sovereigne lord and his heires, and the commonwele of this lond, evir to be
contynued. Aftir humble praying of trewe lordis, spirituelle and temporelle; to yeve assistence and aid in thys oure true and goodely desyres;
For we take God to record we entende but only for the wele and surete of the
Kyng oure sovereigne lord, And the common-wele of this lond.*

" First, that the seid seducious persones abovenamed, wheche by
theire subtile and malicious meanes have causyd oure said sovereyn
lord to estrainge his goode grace from the Councelle of the nobile and
trewe lordis of his blood, moved hym to breke hys lawes and statutis,
mynysshed his lyvelode and housold, chaunchyng his most richest
coyne, and chargyng this lond with suche gret and inordinat imposicions, as is above expressid ; to the grete appeirement of his most
Royalle estate, and enpoverisshyng of hym and alle his true Commons and subjettis, and only to the enrichynge of themself; may be
punysshed accordyng to theire werkes and untrouethes, So that alle
other hereaftir shall take ensample by thayme.

" Also in eschewyng the occasions and causes of the gret inconveniencis and myschevis that by the same hathe fallen in the Kynges
dayes, above expressid, as well uppon themself, as uppon this lond,
And that in tymes hereaftir myghte falle ; We, the Kyngis
true and feithfulle Commons and subjettes of this lond, mekely
besechen his good grace that hit well lyke hym for the gret wele of
hymself, his heires, and the common-wele of us his true subjettes
and Commons, for evyr to be continued by the advyse and auctorite
of his lordis spirituelle and temporalle, to appoynte, ordeyne, and
stablish for evyr to be hadde suche a sufficiente of lyvelode and pos-
sescions, by the whiche he and alle his heires aftir hym may mayntene and kepe theire most honorable estate, withe alle other ordinarie charges necessarye to be hadde in this lond. So that he nor
noon of his heires, hereafter, of necessite, nede to charge and ley
uppon his true Commons and subjettes suche gret imposicions as
before is expressid ; Unlesse that it were for the gret and urgent

causes concernynge as well the wellthe of us, as of oure seid sovereyne lord; Accordyng to the promyse that he made in his last parliament, openly wyth his owen mouthe unto us.

" Also to be enstablisshid be the seid auctorite, that yf any persone, of what estate or degree that he be, aftir the seid stablisshement so ordeyned, and made, (except the Kynges issue and his brethern), presume or take uppon them to aske or take possessions of any of the lyvelod so appoyntyd, that, by the seid auctorite, he be taken and reputyd as he that wold mynysshe and apeire the royall estate of his sovereyn lord, and the commonwele of this lond. And went pardon so to be punysshed.

" Also that the revenues of Tounage and Poundage may be employed in the kepyng of the see as it was graunted, and too non other use, for the safetie of entrecourse of merchaundizes, to gret enrichyng of this lond, and also for the defence of the enemyes.

" Also that the lawes and the statutis made in the dayes of youre noble progenitours kyng Edward the iij[de]., sethen for the concernyng and kepyng of this lond in good hele and peas, as welle Wales as Engelond, be duly kept, observid, and executyd, for the conservacion of us youre trewe commons and subjettes in peas, and the commonwele of this oure lond."

P. 8, *l.* 5.—*And in the x. yere.* It may be remarked that the regnal years of Edward IV. commence on the fourth of March, " quo die Rex Edwardus iiij[tus]. incepit regnare; "—MS. Magnus Rotulus Pipæ, 1 Edw. IV, com. Cornub. Cf. MS. Bib. Geo. III. Mus. Brit. 52. fol. 33, r°.

—— *l.* 6.—*The Lorde Welles his sonne.* See the *Excerpta Historica,* p. 282, for the confession of Sir Robert Welles, which throws very considerable light on this history. It appears that the Duke of Clarence took a much more active part in the conspiracy than is generally supposed; that the motive which actuated the multitude was chiefly the fear of the King's vengeance; that a servant of Clarence's was in the battle, and afforded Welles considerable assist-tance; that when Lord Welles went to London pursuant to the King's commands, he desired his son, in the event of his hearing that he was in danger, to hasten to his assistance with as many followers as possible; that the real object of the rebellion was to place the crown on Clarence's head; and that both Clarence and Warwick had, for some time, been urging Lord Welles, and his son, to continue firm to their cause.

The following documents are given from the Close Rolls of 10 Edw. IV. (m. 8. dorso.) and are valuable illustrations of the history of this insurrection.

" *De proclamationibus faciendis.*—Rex vicecomiti Warr' et Leicestr' salutem. Præcipimus tibi firmiter injungentes, quod statim, post receptionem præsentium, in singulis locis infra ballivam, tuam tam infra libertates quam extra, ubi magis expediens videris, ex parte nostra publicas proclamationes fieri facias, in hæc verba—

" For as moche as hit hath plesyd God, of his godeness and grace, to send to our soveraigne Lord the victorye of his Rebelles and Traitours of his shire of Lincolne, late assembled in grete nombre, leveyng werre ayenst his Highness, contrary to their ligeaunce and duete; Oure said Soveraigne Lord, therefore, not willing his subgettis, other than such as now attend upon his most Royall Person, to be putte to charge, labour, and businesse, by vertue of his commissions of array, and other writing, late addressed to dyvers shires, citees, and townes, for the resistens of the malicious and traiterous purpose of the said Rebelles, wolle, and in the most straitest wise chargeth, that noon of his subgettes presume, ne take uppon hym, to ryse, ne make any assemble or gadering, by reason of any of the seid commissions or writings, ne be moeving, steryng, writing, or commaundement made, or hereafter to be made, by any persone or persones of what estate, degree, or condition sooever he be of, lesse than hit bee by the Kinges commission, Prive Seal, or writyng under his signet, of new to be made aftir this the xiij. day of Marche. And if any persone or persones presume, or take uppon theym or hym, to doe the contrary hereof, Our Said Soveraigne Lord woll repute and take hym and them soo doyng as his ennemyes and Rebelles, and wool procede to their lawfull Punycion in the most streitest wise, according to his Lawes and Statutes in such case ordeyned.

" Et hoc nullatenus omittas. Teste Rege apud Stamford xiij°. die Martii.

" PER IPSUM REGEM."

(Here follow the names of counties.)

" *De proclamationibus faciendis.*—Rex vicecomiti Eborum salutem. Præcipimus tibi, quod statim post receptionem presentium, in singulis locis infra ballivam tuam, tam infra libertates quam extra, ubi magis expediens videris, ex parte nostra publicas proclamationes fieri facias in hæc verba—

" Howbeit that the King our Soveraine Lord graunted unto Georg Duc of Clarence, and Richard Erle of Warwyk, his pardon generall of all offences committed and doon ayenst him, afore the fest of Christmasse last passed, trusting thereby to have caused theym to have shewed unto him their naturall love, ligeaunce, and duetie, and to have assisted his Highness, as well in subdueing insurrections and rebellions late made ayenst him in the countie of Lincolne, as in all other things concerning the suertie of his persone ; and, in trust that they soo wold have done according to their promises to hym made, his said Highness auctorized theym by his commission undre his grete seal to assemble his subgetts in certain shires, and theym to have brought to his said Highnes, to the entent aforesaid ; yet the said Duc and Erle, unnaturally, unkindly, and untruly intending his destruction and the subversion of his reaume, and the common-wele of the same, and to make the said Duke King of this his said Reaume, ayenst Gods law, mannes law, and all reason and conscience, dissimiled with his seid Highness, and, under colour thereof, falsly and traiterously provoked and stured, as well by their writings as otherwise, Sir Robert Welles, late calling himselfe Great Capitayne of the Commons of the seid shire of Lincolne, to continue the said insurrections and rebellions, and to levee warre ayenst hym, as they, by the same, soe dyd with banners displayed, avauncing theymselfe in plain bataylle, unto the time his said Highnesse, by the help of God, put them to flight; wherein the said Duc and Erle promitted to the said Sir Robert and Commons to have yeven them their assistences to the uttermost of their powers, and soo wolde have done, if God ne had yeven unto hym the said victorie, as the same Sir Robert Welles, Sir Thomas de la Laund, Richard Wareyn, and other have openly confessed and shewed before his seid Highnes, the Lordes of his blood, and the multitude of his subgettis attending upon hym in his host at this tyme; which Sir Robert Welles, and the said other pety capitaynes, affirmed to be true at their dethes, uncompelled, unstirred, or undesired soo to doo; and as by the confession of the said Robert Welles, made under his writing and signe manuell, it apperith. And after that the said Duc and Erle, understanding and seing that this ther seid labours wold not serve to the perfourmyng of their fals and traiterous purpose afore declared, laboured by their writings and messages sent into Yorkeshire into divers persons there, theym straitly charging to doo make open proclamations in their owne names, without making mention of his seid Highnes, that all maner men upon peyn of deth shuld come unto theym, and yeve theym their assistences in resisting of hym; whereupon his seid Highnes sent unto the said Duc and Erle, by Garter King of Armes, summonicion and warnyng of their said accusations undir his prive seal, straitly charging theym to come unto his said Highnes, resonably accompanyed according to their astates and degrees, to answer unto their said accusations; which to doo they presumptuously refused, and withdrew themselfe, and fled with their felaship into Lancashire; soo as his said Highness with his host for lak of vitaill might not follow them, to the intent that they might gadre his subgettes in gretter nombre, and to be able to performe their said fals and traiterous purpose and entent; for the which causes they have deserved to be published as fals traitours and rebelles, and to have the uttermost punition of the law ; yet, nathelesse, our said Soveraigne Lord considering the nighness of blood that they be of unto him, and the tendre love which he hath afore time borne to theym, were therefore loth to lese theym, if they wold submitt theym to his grace, and put hym in suertie of their good demeaning hereafter.

" Wherefore our said Sovereigne Lord woll, and in the most straitest wyse chargeth, the said Duc and Erle, that they, in their persones, come in humble and obeysant wyse, and appier afore his Highnes the xxviij. day of this present month of March, Wednesday next, or afore, wheresoever he than shall be, to answer unto the said accusations; which if they woll soo doo, and come declare theymselfe nat guilty, his Highness woll be thereof right glad, and have hem in his grace and favour; and if they refuse thus to doo, then our said Soveraigne Lord reputeth, taketh, and declareth thaym as his rebelles and traitoures, willing and straitly charging all his subgetts to doo the same, and that noon of his subgetts from that time forth receive theym, ne eyther of theym ayd, favour, or assist with mete, drink, ne money, or otherwise, ne noon other persone which, after the said Duc and Erle have refused to come to our said Soverain Lord as is aforesaid, abydeth with theym, or aydeth theym, or assisteth in any wise ; but that every of the King's subgetts putte hem in effectuell devir to take the said Duc and Erle, and all other soo abyding with theym, or aiding or assisting theym, as is abovesaid, and theym suerly bring to his Highnes uppon peyn of deth ; And he that taketh and bringeth the said Duc or Erle shall have for his reward, to hym and his heires, an C. li. worth of his lond of yerely value, or M¹. li. in redy money, at his election ; and for a knyght xx.li. worth of his lond, or C. marc in money; and for a squyer x. li. worth of his lond, or xl. li. in money; and over that cause our said soveraigne Lord to have hym and theym soo doing in the more tendre favour of his good grace at all tymes hereafter.

" Et hoc sub periculo incumbenti nullatenus omittas.   Teste Rege apud Eborum xxiiijº die Martii.

" PER IPSUM REGEM.

" Consimilia brevia diriguntur vicecomitibus in Com' subscriptis sub data predicta, videlicet,

" Majori et vicecomitibus Civitatis London'." (&c.)

" Rex Vicecomiti Eborum Salutem.   Præcipimus tibi firmiter injungentes, quod, statim post receptionem præsentium, in singulis locis infra ballivam tuam, tam infra libertates quam extra, ubi magis expediens videris, ex parte nostra publicas proclamationes fieri facias, in hæc verba—

" Howbeit that the King our Soveraigne Lord graunted unto Georg Duke of Clarence, and Richard Earl of Warrewyk, his pardon generall of all offences committed and doone ayenst him, afore the fest of Cristemasse last past; trusting thereby to have caused theym to have shewed unto hym theyr naturall love, ligeaunce, and duetee, and to have assisted his Highnesse, as well in subdueing insurrections and rebellyons late made ayenst him in the Counte of Lincolne, as in all other things concerning the suertee of his persone; and in trust that they wold soo have done according to their promisses to hym made, his said Highnesse auctorised theym, by his commission under his great seall, to assemble his subgietts in certain shires, and them to have brought unto his said Highnesse, to th'entent aforesaid; yet the said Duke and Erle unnaturally, unkindely, and untruly entending his destruction, and the subversion of his reaume, and the commonwele of the same, and to make the seid Duke King of this his said Reaume, ayenst God's lawe, mannes lawe, all reason and conscience, dissimiled with his said Highness; and under colour thereof, falsly and traiterously provoked, laboured, and stured, as well by their writings as otherwise, Sir Robert Welles, late calling himselfe Grete Capitayne of the commons of the said Shire of Lincolne, to continue the said insurrections and rebellions, and to levee werre ayenst him, as they by the same soo did, with banners displayed, avauncing theymselfe in pleyn bataille, unto the time his said Highness, by the help of God, put theym to flyght; wherein the said Duke and Erle promytted to the said Sir Robert and Commons to have yeven theym their assistences to the uttermost of their powers, and soo wold have doone, yf God ne had yeven unto hym the said victorye, as the same Sir Robert Welles, Sir Thomas de la Laund, Richard Waryng, and other, have openly confessed and shewed before his said Highness, the Lordes of his blode, and the multitude of his subgietts attending upon him in his host at this time; which Sir Robert Welles, and the other pety Captaynes, affermed to be true at their dethes, uncompelled, unstured, or undesired soo to doe; and as by the confession of the said Sir Robert Wells, made under his writyng and sign manuell, it appereth; and after that the said Duke and Erle, understanding and seing that this ther said labours wold not serve in the performing of their fals and traiterous purpose, afore declared, laboured, by their writings and messages sent into Yorkeshire to dyvers persones there, theym streitly charging to doo make open proclamations in their owne names, without mention makeing of his said Highness, that all manner men, uppon peyn of deth, should come unto theym, and yeve theym their assistence in resisting of him; whereupon his said Highnesse sent unto the said Duke and Erle, by Garter Kyng of Armes, summonition and warnyng of their said accusations undre his privie seal, straitly charging theym to come unto his said Highness resonably accompanyed, according to their astates and degrees, to answere to their said accusations; which to doo they presumptuously refused, and withdrewe themselfe, and fled with their felaship into Lancashire, soo as his said Highness with his host, for lake of vitayl, might not follow theym, to th'entent that they might gather his subgetts in greter noumbre, and to be hable to perfourme their said fals and trayterous purpose and entent; ffor which causes they have deserved to be published as fals traitours

and rebells, and to have the uttermost punytion of the lawe. Yet
nathelesse our said soveraigne Lord considered the nyghnesse of
of blode which they be of unto him, and the tender love which he
hath afore time borne to theym, therefore was loth to have lost theym,
yf they would have submitted theym to his grace, and to have put
hym in suertee of their good beryng hereafter; wherefore he sent his
writts of proclamation unto dyvers open places, straitly charging
theym to have come and appered in their persones afore his Highness in humble and obeysaunt wyse, the xxviijth. day of this present
month of Marche or before, to have aunswered unto the said accusations, shewing by the same that yf they soo would have done, and
could have declared theymselfe not guilty, his Highness would have
be therewith right gladd, and have had theym in his grace and favour,
and that, though they soo cowde not have doon, yet his Highness
would not have forgeten their seid nighness of blode, ne the love
and favour that he aforetime bare to theym, but wold have ministred
to theym ryghtwyssely his lawes with favour and pitee shewyng;
which they did not, but obstinately refused soo to doo, and dayly
aftir withdrew theymself more and more from his Highness; and
after the said proclamations, made as before, it hath be evidently
shewed by open confessions made at his citee of Yorke, afore our
said Soveraigne and his Lordes than there being with hym, by dyvers persones of grete reputation, that the seid Duke and Erle intended the finall destruction of his most royall persone, and the subversion of this his reaume, and the commonwele of the same, which
confessions the said persones have affirmed by their solempne othes,
made upon the receyving of the blessed sacrament, to bee faithfull
and true; wherefore, the præmisses considered, and the grete obsti-
nạcy which they shewed hemself to be of, and yet doo contrarye to
their ligeaunce, faith, and duetee, our said soveraigne Lord, to the
example of all other like offenders, reputeth, taketh, and declareth
the said Duke and Erle as his Rebelles and Traytours, willing and
straitly charging all his subgetts to doo the same; and that noon of

his said subgetts from hensforth receyve theym, ne eyther of theym, ayd, favour, or assist with mete, drynke, or money, or otherwise; nor noo other persone beyng with, or adhering to them, or either of theym, but that every of his said subgetts putt hem in effectuell devoyr to take the said Duke and Erle, and the seid persones soe being with hem, or adhering to theym, or either of theym, and hem surely bring to the King, upon peyn of deth, and forfaiture of all that they may forfait; and he that soo doth shall have for his reward of either of theym C. li. worth of land by yere to him, and to his heires, or a M^l. li. in redy money at his election.

" Et hoc nullatenus omittas. Teste meipso apud Notingham xxxj°. die Martii.

" PER IPSUM REGEM."

(Here follow the names of counties.)

(From Madox's transcripts in the British Museum. MS. Add. 4614.)

P. 8, *l.* 24.—*Wove.* So in MS. for *vowe.*

P. 9, *l.* 32.—*Kynge Henry schuld rejoyse the kyngdome.* " On halmesse evyn, abowt thre after noyne, comyn into the Comowne Howus, the Lordys spiritual and temporal, excepte the Kyng, the Duk of York, and hys sonys; And the Chawnceler reherset the debate had bytwyn owre soveren Lord the Kyng and the Duk of York upon the tytelys of Inglond, Fraunce, and the Lordschep of Erlond, wyche mater was debat, arguet, and disputet by the seyd lordes spiritual and temporal byfore owre soveren Lord and the Duk of York longe and diverse tymys. And at the last, by gret avyce and deliberacion, and by the assent of owre soveryn Lord and the Duk of York, and alle the lordes spiritual and temporal ther assemelyd by vertu of thys present parlement, assentyt, agreyt, and acordyt, that owre sovereyne Lord the Kyng schal pessabylly and quyetly rejoys and possesse the crowne of Inglond and of Fraunce and the Lordchip of Irlond, with al hys preemynences, prerogatyves, and liberteys duryng hys lyf. And that after hys desese the coroun, etc. schal remayne to Rychard

Duk of York, as rythe inheryt to hym, and to hys issue, prayng and desyring ther the comownes of Inglond, be vertu of thys present parlement assemylet, to comyne the seyd mater, and to gyff therto her assent. The wyche comyns, after the mater debatet, comynt, grawntyt, and assentyt to the forseyd premisses. And ferthermore was granted and assentyt, that the seyd Duk of York, the Erl of March, and of Rutlond, schul be sworne that they schuld not compas ne conspyrene the kynges deth ne hys hurt duryng hys lyf. Ferthermore the forseyd Duk schulde be had, take, and reportyt as eyr apparent prince and ryth inheryter to the crowne aboveseyd. Ferthermore for to be had and take tresoun to ymagyne or compas the deth or the hurt of the seyd Duk, wythe othyr prerogatyves as long to the prince and eyr parawnt. And fferthermore the seyd Duk and hys sonys schul have of the Kyng yerly x.M^l. marces, that is to sey, to hemself v.M^l., to the Erl of Marche iijM^l., the Erl of Rutlond ijM^l. marces. And alle these mateyrs agreyd, assentyt, and inactyt by the auctorite of thys present parlement. And ferthermore, the statutes mad in the tyme of Kyng Herry the fowrth, wherby the croune was curtaylet to hys issu male, utterly anullyd and evertyth, wyth alle other statutes and grantys mad by the seyd Kynges days, Kyng Herry the V. and Kyng Herry the vj^{te}, in the infforsyng of the tytel of Kyng Herry the fourth in general."—Rot. Harl. C. 7, Membr. 4, *dorso.*

The following document, from Chart. Antiq. Cotton. XVII. 11, is exceeding curious, and I take the opportunity of inserting it here.

" *Jhesus. Maria. Johannes.*

.... the most nobylle and Crysten prynce, oure most dradde soverayne Lorde Kynge Hary the syxte, verrey true undoutyde Kynge of Englonde and of Fraunce, nowe beynge in the hondys of hys rebellys and gret en[e]my, Edwarde, late the Erl of Marche, usurpur, oppressour, and distroyer of oure seyde Soverayn Lorde, and of the nobylle blode of the reme of Englonde, and of the trewe commenes

of the same, by hys myschevus and inordinate newe founden lawes
and ordenaunces inconveniant, to the uttyrmoste destruccion of the
goode commenes of the seyde reme of Englonde; yf yt so schulde
contenne ffor the reformacion wherof, in especialle for the comen-
welle of alle the seyde reme, the ry3t hyghe and my3ty Prynce
George Duke [of] Clarens, Jasper Erl of Penbroke, Richarde Erl
of Warewyke, and Johnne Erl of Oxenforde, as verrey and trewe
fey3tfulle cosyns, subgettes, and liege men to oure seyde soveraine
Lorde Kynge Harry the syxt, by sufficiante autorite commysyd unto
theme in thys behalfe, be the hole voyse and assent of the moste
nobylle pryncesse Margaret, Quene of Englonde, and the Ry3t Hy3e
and my3ty Prynce Edwarde, atte thys tyme beyng Quene,* into thys
reme to putte theme in ther moste uttermoste devers to dylyver oure
seyd Sopheraine Lord oute of hys grete captivite, and daungere of
hys enmyes, unto hys liberte, and by the grace of Gode to rest hym
in his rialle estate, and crowne of thys hys seyd reme of Englond,
and reforme . . . . . and amende alle the grete myschevus oppressions,
and alle odyr inordinate abusions, nowe raynynge in the seyde reme,
to the perpetualle pese, prosperyte, to the comene welfare of thys
reme. Also ytt ys fully concludyd and grauntyde that alle mail
men within the reme of Englonde, of whatt estat, degre, condicion
that they be of, be fully pardonede of alle maner tresoun or trespace
imagenyd or done, in eny maner of wyse contrary to ther legeyns,
agayne oure soveraine Lorde the Kynge, the Quene, and my Lorde
the prynce, before the day of comynge and entre of the sayde Duke
and Erles in thys sayde reme; so that they putte them in ther uttermost dever, and att thys tyme drawe them to the compeny of the
seyde Duke and Erles, to helpe and to fortefy theme in ther purpose
and jorney; excepte suche persons as be capitalle enmyes to oure
seyde soferaine Lorde, withowte punyschement of the whyche god
pece and prosperite of thys reme cannatte be had; and excepte alle
suche as atte thys tyme make any rescistens ageyns the seyde Duke

---

* This sentence is transposed in the document.

and Erlys, or eny of theme, or of ther compeny. Also the sayde Duke and Erlys, in the name and behalfe of oure seyde soferaine Lorde Kynge Harry the syxt, chargyne and commawndyne that alle maner of men, that be betwen xvj. yeres and lxti., incontinently and immediatly aftyr thys proclamacion made, be redy, in ther best aray defensabell, to attende and awayte upponne the sayde Duke and Erlys, to aschyst theme in ther jorney, to the entente afore rehercyd, upponne payne of dethe and forfiture of alle that they [may forfeyte], withinne the reme of Englond; excepte suche persons as be visette with syknesse, or with suche noune poure that they may not go."

P. 10, *l.* 12.—*Inhabytauntes.*   So in MS. for *inheritaunces.*

P. 11, *l.* 12.—The Harl. MS. 7353, is a most curious roll on vellum, containing pictures on one side representing parts of scripture history, and on the other assumed similar transactions in the life of Edward IV.   We have, I. The King on his throne. II. The King encouraging his soldiers. III. The King with a triple sun shining upon him through three golden crowns, and saying " Domine ! quid vis me facere ?" IV. Pardoning Henry after the battle of Northampton. V. Setting sail for Calais. At the bottom is a genealogical tree, with portraits of all the members of the houses of York and Lancaster, very fantastically arranged.

—— *l.* 12.—*Duke of Burgeyne.*   Charles the Bold, Duke of Burgundy, married Edward's sister on the 18th of June, 1467.   It was to this marriage that Edward owed his preservation abroad, and the final recovery of his kingdom.   An account of the marriage, with the reception of the Princess in Flanders, may be seen in MS. Cotton. Nero, C. ix.   Cf. Cart. Antiq. Mus. Brit. XI. 54.

—— *l.* 22.—*Wrott in alle his lettres.*   Cf. MS. Harl. 7, fol. 64, r°; Sir Harris Nicolas's Chronology of History, p. 304; Cart. Antiq. Mus. Brit. XXII. 42.

P. 12, *l.* 5.—*Was lost in his tyme.*   This was a never-failing source of rebuke against Henry ; so Ocland says—

> " Quippe erat Henricus quintus, dux strenuus olim,
> Mortuus   hinc damni gravior causa atque doloris."

Anglorum prælia. Edit. 1582. Edward, in one of his earlier proclamations, says, " HE that directeth the hertes of all Princes" hath
" putte in oure remembraunce the lamentable state and rayne of this
reaume of Englond, and the losse of th'obeissaunce of the reaume of
Fraunce, and Duchies of Guyenne, and Normandie, and Anjou."
Rot. Claus. 1 Edw. IV. m. 38, dorso.

P. 12, *l.* 26.—*Revertimini,* &c. This is perhaps quoted from memory,
for the reading in the Latin Vulgate is *Convertimini filii revertentes,
dicit Dominus, quia ego vir vester;* which is thus translated,—" Turn,
O backsliding children, saith the Lord, for I am married unto you;"
Jeremiah, iii. 14. It is almost unnecessary to remark that this is
the sermon with which it was usual to preface the opening of a parliament; the present one was most admirably fitted for the occasion.

P. 13, *l.* 6.—*Was behedede.* " His diebus captus est ille trux carni-
fex, et hominum decollator horridus, Comes de Wacester, et in
Turri Londonie incarceratus, et in breve prope dictam turrim decapi-
tatus, et apud Fratres Predicatores, juxta Ludgate, obscure sepultus."
—MS. Arundel, Coll. Arm. 5, fol. 171, v°. This coming from a
partizan of the same side with the Earl, at a period when party
politics necessarily ran so high, is strikingly conclusive of that nobleman's character. Cf. Chron. p. 9, l. 13—21.

—— *l.* 30.—*At Ravenyspore.* See Mr. Jones's Essay on the Rival
Roses, p. xxv.

P. 14, *l.* 11.—*Nevere wulde clayme no title.* He took a solemn oath
to that effect; Cf. MS. Sloan. 3479, and MS. Harl. 2408.

—— *l.* 21.—M¹. M¹. i. e. two thousand.

P. 15, *l.* 18.—*And in dyner tyme Kynge Edwarde was late in.* Edward
was admitted into London on the 11th of April. The Archbishop
suffered himself to be taken at the same time, but was released in two
days afterwards, and obtained full pardon. There is one remarkable
circumstance in this pardon; it remits all crimes before April the
13th, and yet is dated April the 10th, the day probably on which the
Archbishop agreed with Edward to admit him into the city. See

Carte's History of England, book 13, p. 787, *n.*, and *Fœdera,* XI.
709. Warkworth remarks very strongly upon his conduct at p. 26 of
his Chronicle. Cf. MS. Bib. Coll. Trin. Oxon. 62 (10).

P. 16, *l.* 14.—*The sunne with stremys.* The crest of the Kynaston
coat is supposed to have been assumed from this time, and in allu-
sion to this event.

——*l.* 29, 30.—*And ther was slayne.* A very comprehensive list is
given in MS. Arundel, Mus. Brit. 28, fol. 25, v°. The brass matrix
of the seal of the Earl of Warwick, taken from him when he was
slain, is in the British Museum ; an impression may be seen among
the charters, xxxiv. 33.

P. 17, *l.* 6.—*Lord Barnes sonne and heyre.* Sir Humphrey Bourchier.
His gravestone remains in Westminster Abbey, denuded of his figure
in brass plate, but retaining an epitaph of fourteen Latin hexameters,
commemorative of his prowess and the scene of his death. They commence—

> Hic pugil ecce jacens, Bernett fera bella cupiscens,
> Certat ut Eacides, &c. &c.

See engravings in Gough's Sepulchral Monuments, vol. II. pl.
LXXXVI ; Harding's Antiquities in Westminster Abbey, pl. VIII. It
may be remarked that the word in the eighth line read *parvulus* by
Gough, &c. is really *p*ᵢ*mulus,* i. e. *primulus,* used instead of *primus* for
the sake of the metre.—J. G. N.

—— *l.* 7.—*Lord Say.* This nobleman was formerly on the Lancastrian side, but received Edward's pardon on the 5th of May, 1462 ;
Chart. Antiq. Mus. Brit. VIII. 13.

—— *l.* 31-2.—*Kynge Herry was put into the Toure ayene.* See
Devon's Issue Rolls of the Exchequer, p. 491.

P. 18, *l* 1.—*And gaderet grete peple.* Bouchet, in *Les Annales*
d'Acquitaine, says that there were *plus de lx. mil hommes armez.* Edit.
Par. 1558, fol. 121, v°.

—— *l.* 8.—*And ther he made a felde.* The place where the battle
of Tewkesbury was fought is now called Glaston Meadow.—*Rudder's*
History of Gloucestershire, p. 736. I have been further assured that

this field is now called the *Bloody-Field* by the common people living near the spot.

P. 18, *l.* 16.—Cf. *Memoires Olivier de la Marche. Edit. Brux.* 1616, p. 502.

—— *l.* 19.—*And there was slayne in the felde Prynce Edward.*—" Confectus apud Tewkysbery per Edwardum Regem quartum." Rot. Harl. C. 7, Memb. 5.

P. 19, *l.* 3, 4.—*Were behedede.* The prior of St. John's in Smithfield was among them.—MS. Arund. Coll. Arm. 5, fol. 171, v°.

—— *l.* 4.—*No3twithstondynge the Kynges pardon.* Edward's policy was despotic in the extreme; he told De Comines that it was his object to spare the common people, but cut off the gentry. The destruction of these noblemen and gentlemen was an awful example of his barbarity, as well as his deficiency of common honesty.

—— *l.* 28.—*At Algate and at London Brygge.* " Super pontem Londonie, cum dominibus quibusdam adjacentibus, combusserunt, et similiter alias juxta Algate succederunt."—MS. Arundel, Coll. Arm. 5, fol. 171, v°. In MS. Arundel, Mus. 28, fol. 25, v°, this event is stated to have taken place on the 14th of May, — xiiij°. die mensis Maij supra dict' ; the anonymous scribbler of the notes in this MS. informs us that Lord Rivers put the Bastard to flight.

P. 20, *l.* 9.—*Juperdy*, i. e. jeopardy.

—— *l.* 15.—See this proverb illustrated in Sir Walter Scott's novel of the Abbot, iii. 91-2.

—— *l.* 19.—*Was behedede.* This event took place two days before Michaelmas day in the same year, and his head was placed upon London Bridge " lokyng into Kent warde."—*Paston Correspondence,* ii. 82. Cf. MS. Arundel, Mus. Brit. fol. 25, v°.

P. 21, *l.* 1, 2.—*And ther he was worschipfully receyvid.* " Eodem mensis Maii die xxj°. rediit Rex Edwardus ad civitatem Londonie, cum nobili triumpho."—MS. Arundel, Mus. Brit. 28, fol. 25, v°. The same writer says that he brought Queen Margaret with him *in curru precedente exercitum.* In this triumph he was accompanied by the

Dukes of Clarence, Gloucester, Norfolk, Suffolk, and Buckingham ;
also the Earls of Northumberland, Shrewsbury, Rivers, Essex,
Worcester, Pembroke, &c.   See the long list given in the same MS.

    P. 21, *l*. 4.—*Was putt to dethe.* " He dyid put to silence in the Tour
of London, the xxj. day of May, a°. 1471, buryid first at Chertesey
and after at Wyndesore."—Rot. Lansd. Mus. Brit. 6.   In the old
ballad of the " Wandering Jew's Chronicle" this event is thus versi-
fied :—

> " I saw the white and red rose fight,
> And Warwick gret in armour bright,
>   In the Sixth Henries reign ;
> And present was that very hour,
> When Henry was in London Tower,
>   By Crookt-backt Richard slain."

But this subject has been so much before the reader that I refrain
from adding more.   I give, however, a few references, from my mis-
cellaneous notes, which may assist any future inquirer who desires
to investigate more at length into various matters connected with the
popular opinion of Henry VI. after his death, his burial places,
&c. :—*Widmore's History of Westminster Abbey*, pp. 118-120 ; *Ash-
mole's History of the Order of the Garter*, p. 136 ; MS. Cotton. Cleop.
E. III ; *Monast.* I. 277 ; *British Topographer*, II. 112, n ; *Gent. Mag.*
LVI. ; MS. Cole Collect. XLII. 378 ; ib. XIII ; *Hormanni Vulgaria*,
Lond. 1519, fol. 3, r° ; *Barrington on the Statutes*, p. 253 ; *Parker
Antiq. Brit. Eccl.* 229, edit. *Drake*, p. 447 ; *Fuller's Church History*,
IV. 153 ; *Wilkins's Concil.* IV. 635 ; *Spelman*, II. 720 ; *Walpole's
Fugitive Pieces* ; MS. Sloan. 1441.

    —— *l.* 11.—*Caryed to Chyrchesey Abbey in a bote.*   Henry's body
was protected by soldiers from Calais, and, rather singularly, for the
possession of that city had been a hard point of contention between
the rival parties.   The extreme anxiety of Queen Margaret to possess
it, may be seen from a very curious document now preserved in the
Royal Archives of France, and the title of which is given in MS.
Addit. Mus. Brit. 9346, fol. 116, r°.

In the Issue Rolls of the Exchequer, we find money paid to Hugh Brice on the 24th of June for the expenses of Henry's funeral, for conveying his body from the Tower to St. Paul's, and from thence to Chertsey. From these and several other statements of expences in the same rolls, it fully appears that every respect was paid to the corpse; but Mr. Devon has attempted to draw from this an argument for the natural death of the King, not taking into consideration that the very fact of much attention having been paid to his funeral obse-quies would render it more than probable that it was done to conceal the appearance of any hostile feeling : had Henry died a natural death, it appears to me that the haste of Edward's departure into Kent, and the length of time necessarily elapsing before he could have become acquainted with the news, would have almost rendered any definite orders for his funeral next to impossible. Many writers have committed the error of affirming that Henry was buried without honours.—*Camden's Britannia, edit. Gough,* I. 167.

P. 21, *l.* 14.—The names of these aldermen are given by Stowe, Edit. 1755, *Survey of London,* II. 222.

—— *l.* 23.—*One Fauntt of Canterbury.* In the Issue Roll of the Exchequer, 11 Ed. IV. we find the sum of 1*l.* 3*s.* 4*d.* paid to one John Belle, for the value of a horse and harness to conduct this Nicholas Faunte from the Tower of London to the King, then in Kent. Hasted is one of the very few writers who quotes Warkworth's Chronicle, which he does on this point.—*History of Kent,* IV. 433.

In the Introduction I have extracted from Lidgate's poem on the Kings of England; and, for want of a better situation, I here give another version of the stanzas on the reigns of Henry VI. and Edward IV. from a MS. of the commencement of the sixteenth century :—

> " The vj^th Henry his sone was after him fosterde in all vertu,
> By just titull and by inheritaunce,
> By grace afore provyde of Criste Jhesu,
> To were ij crownes bothe in Inglande and in Fraunce.

Above erthly thingis all God was in his remembraunce ;
What vertuus lyfe he led his myraculis now declare !
xxxix. yere he bare dyadym and septure,
In Wyndesore College of the Garter he lyethe in his sepulture.

" After Henry the vj[th], Goddis campyoun and trewe knyght,
Edward the iiij[th] obteynede Septure and Crowne,
From the hy Plantagenate havynge titule and right,
xxij. yere the saide Edwarde flowerede withe wysdome, riches and renowne.
Grete welthe and plente in his dayes all penery put downe,
All Cristyn princes were glade withe hym amyte to make,
Whiche onely with a loke made Fraunce and Scotlande to quake ;
In the College of the Garter where he governoure was and hede,
He chase the place of his sepulture, for his body to be beriede in when he was dede."

MS. Bib. Reg. 18 D. II. fol. 182. v°.

This version is completely remodelled ; the MS. Sloan. 1986 (fol. 199, r°.—213, v°.) contains another different edition of the fifteenth century.

P. 22, *l.* 7.—*The most mervelous blasynge sterre.* See an account of this comet in the Nuremburgh Chronicle, Edit. 1493, fol. 254, r°. " Longum radium in modum flamme ingentis ignis emittens."—MS. Arundel, Mus. Brit. 220, fol. 279, v°. This comet is a return of the one described in a manuscript of the fourteenth century in Sion College Library (xix. 2, fol. 155, v°, b.), and of which there is a drawing on fol. 155, v°, a. Cf. MS. Trin. Cantab. R. xv. 18; Bib. Publ. Cantab. KK. IV. 7.; MS. Cotton. Jul. F. xi.

I give the following fragment relative to this comet from a MS. in the library of Pembroke College, Cambridge :—

" De opinionibus aliquorum de presenti cometa.

" Quidam presumpcionis filius in consulto sermone procacique oracione, volgari verbo tenus ornata, preter phisicas et astrologicas tradiciones, quas tamen similabat, terrenda populo prenunciavit ; sed quoniam sermones sui a tradicionibus antiquorum sapientium similiter et a via veritatis omnino semoti, indignos memoria eos putavi. Dicebat quidem, caudam comete moveri motu simili motui martis in epiciclo, ex quo plura nitebatur concludere. Sed quoniam, ut posterius dicitur, ipsa minus mobilis erat capite comete, imo etiam semper versus occidentem verum [quid]em ex circumvolucione ejus promotum diurno cauda ipsius quandoque respiciebat orientem, sed nunquam movebatur versus orientem. Etiam uno die omnes differencias posicionis mundi respiciebat; mars autem in suo epiciclo nequaquam ita faciebat. Et forsan nullus planetarum epiciclum habet quod magis putandum opinor. Dicebant et alii, cometam a suo astro sicut ferrum a magnete trahi; cui dissonant dicta partis prime de motu cometarum. Et etiam quoniam motus tractus per lineam fit brevissimam. Alio non existenti impedimento continuo mobili ad trahens approximante. Ipso quoque mobili existenti cum trahente, fixum, ad modum ligati, detineretur; quoniam ibi finis est motus tractus. Hæc patent septimo phisicorum libro ad concavum orbis lune delatus fuisset; horum contrarium experiencia lucidissime edocuit, quoniam nulli planetarum conabatur ab omnibus. Discedendo ab ecliptica diversitas, etiam aspectus ejus, ad stellas sibi vicinas, certificavit ipsum magis distare a concavo orbis lune quam a terra, in triplo ferè. Aliqui eciam ni" . . . ατελ.

Much more matter relative to this comet might have been given, but, as these notes have already been extended disproportionately to the length of the text, I reserve them for another occasion.

Cf. MS. Tann. Bodl. 2. fol. 56, r°.

P. 22, l. 10.—Rather=earlier.

P. 23, l. 6-7.—*The viij. day after Michaelmasse.* " About x. of the cloke afore none, the King come into the Parlement chamber in his Parlement robes, and on his hed a cap of mayntenaunce, and sat in his most Royall Majeste, having before hym his Lordes spirituall and temporall, and also the speker of the Parlement, which is called William Alyngton."—MS. Bib. Cotton. Jul. C. vi. fol. 255, r°.

—— *l.* 25.—Axes=Aches.

—— *l.* 33.—*Womere.* So in MS. but should be *wemere.*

P. 24, l. 4.—*A tokene of derthe.* See *Mr. Thoms's Anecdotes and*

Traditions (p. 122), for one instance of this curious superstition; Mr. Thoms refers to Grimm's Mythology for more examples.

P. 24, *l.* 13.—*Lavesham*, i. e. Lewisham.

——— *l.* 15.—*Suthsex*. A mistake in MS. for *Surrey*.

——— *l.* 20.—*A pytte in Kent, in Langley Parke.* This is probably the place where the small stream mentioned in Hasted's History of Kent (II. 140.) took its rise, and joins the river Medway on the south side of it, about half a mile above Maidstone.

——— *l.* 23.—*And this yere he is drye.* This passage shows that these notes of prognosticative prodigies were penned in the same year in which they happened.

P. 25. *l.* 12.—*Hade purchased and byllede.* Moor Park in Hertfordshire, now the seat of the Marquess of Westminster. Clutterbuck (History of Hertfordshire, i. 191) states that the Archbishop had license to inclose 600 acres of pasture and land in Rickmersworth and Watford for a park, and to embattle the site of the manor of Moor in Rickmersworth; and quotes for authority Pat. 9. H. VI. m. 10; but George Neville was then unborn, and on further inquiry we find that the grant was made five years earlier, to Henry (Beaufort) Bishop of Winchester: " Quod Henr' Ep'us Winton' et alii possint kernell' manerium suam de More in Rickmansworth, ac imparcare sexcent, acras terræ, &c. ac liber' warrenn ' ib'm." 2 Pat. 4 Hen. VI. m. 10.—J. G. N.

P. 26, *l.* 16.—*Thens into Fraunce asailed.* i. e. sailed thence into France.

——— *l.* 24.—*xx*ti *score men save iij.* William of Worcester, who is probably correct, says only eighty men (*Itin.* 122.);—" memorandum quod comes de Oxford per quinque annos preteritos die Martis in crastino Sancti Michaelis, tempore quo Fortescue armig. fuit vicecomes Cornubiæ, applicuit ad castrum Mont Mychelle cum LXXX hominibus. Et contra XI millia hominum armatorum ex parte domini Regis Edwardi quarti dictum comitem obsedebant per XXIII septimanas, videlicet usque diem sabbati proxima ante diem martis carniprivii voc. *le clansyng days* pro . . . . . cum domino Rege demittebat fortalicium eundo ad dominum Regem."

P. 27, l. 5.—xx. xiij.—A mistake in MS. for xxiij.

—— *l. 11.—comaunde,* i. e. communed.

It was only at the eleventh hour that I was informed that the first notice I have inserted (Introd. p. viii.) of the death of Henry VI. has been previously printed by Sir Frederick Madden in the *Collectanea Topographica et Genealogica,* i. 278, 280.

I may also observe that Merlin's prophecy of *bellum inter duos dracones, videlicet album et rubeum,* was completely fulfilled in the wars of the Roses.—Cf. MS. Cotton. Vespas. B. x. fol. 23, v°.

INDEX.

CHRONICLE
OF
THE REBELLION IN LINCOLNSHIRE,
1470

Edited by
John Gough Nichols, Esq. F.S.A.

First published for the Camden Society
1847

INTRODUCTION.

THE Rebellion in Lincolnshire was one of the occurrences of that troubled period of the reign of Edward the Fourth, when he was struggling with the machinations of his overgrown subject, Richard Neville, earl of Warwick, through which he was at length compelled to leave his kingdom, and seek personal safety in flight. He had already suffered a period of unkingly restraint, from the time he was seized by the archbishop of York at Honiley, near Warwick,* until his escape from the castle of Middleham; and he had also already been troubled with the insurrection of the Yorkshiremen, who had defeated his army under the earl of Pembroke near Banbury, and beheaded his father-in-law and brother-in-law, earl Rivers and sir John Wydville. For these matters he had granted a pardon, with the mention of which the present narrative commences.

That weak and worthless prince, George duke of Clarence, the king's next brother, had virtually deserted his allegiance on accepting the hand of Warwick's elder daughter and coheir; and it was now the project of the King-maker to depose Edward, and place the duke of Clarence on the throne. This intention was first made apparent by the disclosures which ensued upon the suppression of the Lincolnshire rebellion, as related in the following pages.

* Not Olney, as in the notes to Warkworth's Chronicle, p. 46. See the Gentleman's Magazine for Dec. 1839, vol. XII. p. 616.

The immediate consequence of king Edward's victory near
Stamford was the flight of the duke and earl to France, where they
concluded a treaty* with the queen of Henry VI., and married the
lady Anne Neville, Warwick's younger daughter, to her son
Edward prince of Wales: the duke of Clarence thereupon post-
poning his claim to the crown to that of the house of Lancaster.
On their return to England, fortified by this alliance, the king was
in his turn forced to leave the realm, and take refuge with his
brother of Burgundy; and the temporary restoration of king
Henry the Sixth ensued. King Edward's return, and almost
magical recovery of the crown, forms the subject of the first publication produced by the Camden Society.

The present Chronicle, extending only over the brief space of a
few weeks, will not require further illustration, beyond what a few
notes will supply. Any contribution to so obscure a portion of
English history cannot fail to be welcome; and the present is of
importance, not only because it relates circumstances not elsewhere
recorded, but also because it evidently proceeded from one who
wrote under the immediate influence of the royal authority, and
had consequently the best means of information: appealing, indeed, to documents throughout his narrative. It has been preserved in one of the volumes of the College of Arms (Vincent,
No. 435), and for its communication the Society is indebted
to WILLIAM COURTHOPE, Esq. Rouge Croix Pursuivant.

* On this portion of the history of the period, see " The manner and guiding of the Earl
of Warwick at Angiers," published by Sir Henry Ellis in his Original Letters, Second
Series, vol. I. p. 132.

CHRONICLE

OF

THE REBELLION IN LINCOLNSHIRE,

1470.

A REMEMBRANCE of suche acte3 and dede3 as oure souveraigne
lorde the king hadde doon in his journey begonne at London
the vi. day of Marche in the x. yere of his moost . . . . .
reigne, for the repression and seting down of the rebellyon
and insurreccion of his subgettes in the shire of Linccolne,
commeaved by the subtile and fals conspiracie of his grete
rebelle3 George duc of Clarence, Richarde erle of Warrewike,
and othere, &c.

(Vincent, No. 435, art. IX. in Coll. Arm.)

First, how be it that our saide souveraigne lorde, as a prince
enclined to shew his mercy and pite to his subgettes, raither then
rigure and straitenesse of his lawe3, pardonned of late to his saide
rebelles all tresons and felone3, trespasse3 and offence3 committed
and doon by theym ayeinst his highenese afore the fest of Crist-
enmes last past, (1) trusting that therby he shuld have coraged,
caused, and induced theym from that tyme furthe to have been of
good, kynd, and lovyng demeanyng ayeinst his highenesse ; yit they
unnaturally and unkyndly, withoute cause or occacion yeven to
theym by our saide soveraigne lorde, falsly compassed, conspired,
and ymagened the final destruccion of his most roiall personne,
and of his true subgettes taking parte with him in assisting his
highnesse, in so moche as whan he was commen unto Waltham the

107

vj. day of Marche, on the morue after, the vij. day of Marche, there was brought unto him worde that Robert Welleȝ, calling hym self grete capteyn of the comons of Linccolne shire, (2) had doo made proclamacions in all the churcheȝ of that shire the sonday the iiij. daye of Marche in the kinges name, the duc, erle, and his owne name, everye man to come to Ranby hawe (3) upon the tuesday the vj. day of Marche, upon payne of dethe, to resist the king in comyng down into the saide shire, saying that his comyng thidre was to destroie the comons of the same shire, as apperethe by the copie of the same. And theruppon, the vij. daye of Marche, the king sent to London for the late lorde Welles, (4) sir Thomas Dymmoke, (5) and othere, whiche were come thidre by the kinges prive sealeȝ (6).

Upon the thursday the viij. day of Marche, the king, ryding betwixt Bu[n]ttyngforde and Roiston, toke in the way a childe whiche was sent from John Morling, steward to the lorde Crome-well(7). Wherby appered clerely the gadering of the saide comons, and parte of theire ententeȝ, whiche letres purportith that by the tyme thay came to Stoneford thare shulde be of theym and of Yorkeshyr and other cuntrees that wolde falle to thaym C. M^l. men. And the same lettre was written at Tottersale, (8) the vj. day of Marche, and is redy to be shewed.

The same thursday the king come to Roston, whyther come to hym a servaunt of the duc of Clarence with a letter lattyng hys highnes wyt that, notwithstonding that he had taken hys lyve [a] of hym at London, to have goone westward, yit, for to doo hym service in this his journey, he wolde arredye hym self to com towardes his highenes at suche tyme and place appointed as therle of Warrewike shulde also come, as he hadde promysed the king at London. Wherunto the king then answered, that he was glad, and wrote hym a letre of thanke of hys own hande; whiche message so sent by the duc was fals dissimulacion, as by the warkeȝ aftre it appered. Nevertheles the king, not undrestanding no suche

[a] leave.

doublenesse, but trusting that they ment truly as thay shewed, sent unto the saide duc and erle incontinent his severall comissions (9) for to arreise the people in diverse shires, and to bring theym unto the king to doo hym service ayeinst his rebelles. And soo on the friday the ix. day of Marche the king com to Huntyngdon.

The kyng being at Huntyngdoon did the saide lorde Welleȝ to be examined, and sir Thomas Dymmoke and other severally, in whiche examinacion it was knowleged that in the lorde Welleȝ alle suche counceilleȝ and conspiracions were taken and made betwixt his son, the saide sir Thomas Dynmoke, the commons, and othere; and that he and the saide sir Thomas Dynmoke were prive and knowing of there communicacions, and thay might have lett it and did not, but verray provocars and causers of the same, with othere circumstanceȝ touching it. Wheruppon the king yave hym an inunccion that he shulde send to his sonne, commaunding him to leve hys felaship, and humbly submitte hym, or elles thay for theire seide treasons shulde have dethe, as they had deserved. The king thernne[a] being, com eftsoneȝ tydingeȝ that the saide Robert Welleȝ and commouns were in grete nowmbre, and passed Linccolne towardes Grantham.

Upon the sonday the vj. day of Marche, the king com to Fodrynghay, (10) where he had newe knowlege that his rebelles were passed Grantham towardes hym, but sumwhat thay beganne to chaunge thaire way towards Leycestre; which, as it was aftre clerely confessed, was doon by the stirring and message sent from the duc of Clarence and erle of Warrewike unto the saide late sir Robert Welleȝ and other pety captayneȝ, desiring thaym to have [been] by the monday at Leycestre, where thay promised to have joyned with theym with xx. m̄[l]. men, as it appered aftre in effect and by severall confessions (11) of the saide captayneȝ.

Where it appereth clerely that by all this tyme the saide duc and erle dissimiled falsly with the king, for there,[b] or he went to

---

[a] *So the MS.*   [b] *So the MS. : read the earl.*

London, promysed that he woolde have comen to the king in
resistence of the saide rebelles; uppon trust wherof the king by
his knowlage and assent appoynted his gyste3,[a] and the nombre
of the people that he wolde com withe [to] the king. Also upon the
same trust aftre sent to the saide duc and hym his commissions to
arrise and bring with hym the people of certein shire3 to doo hym
service. Also the saide duc dissimiled right untruly with the
king, for als soon as the lord Welle3 was comen to London to
the king he come also thidre, undre coloure that he wolde have
toke his leve to have goon westward, whedre he had sent his
wyfe. And certeinly he entended principally always to hym
possible to have delaied the kinges comyng forth, sendyng worde
to the saide sir Robert Welle3 that he so wold doo; desiryng
hym not to be ferre, but to com forwardes; the whiche porpose
if he had brought aboute, without eny faile the king, by all
literaly[b] presumpcion, had be distressed and alle his felaship, as
clerely may appere by the warkes aftre.

That the duc thus dissimiled it shewethe; for on the morowe
aftre the king departed owte of London the said duc, the lorde
Welle3, the prioure of Saint Johanne3, (12) and othere divers persons, kept theire counseill secretly at Saynt Johanne3, (13) and
forthwith he departed towards Warrewike, contrary to his saying
afore to the king; and upon the way sent the king a plesaunt
letre as above, whiche letre his highenesse receyved at Roiston,
where he wrote ayein, thanking and trusting verely he wolde so
have doon; and soo diverse other tyme3 thay bothe sent to the
king suche plesaunt mesage3, ever wenyng the king thare writting
and message3 had been feithefulle and true, to the xiiij. day of
Marche, whiche day the king came to Granthame; whiche alle
notwithstonding, falsly and subtylly dissimiled with his highenes; for undre this they sent theire messages daily to the kinges
rebelles, bidding thayme to be of good chere and comforthe, and
hold forthe theire way towardes Leycestre, where they promised to

---

[a] The stages of his march.   [b] *So the MS. qu.* likely.

have joined with theym and utterly to have taken theire parte, wherby theire unnaturelle and fals double treason apperethe.

And if God ne had put in the kinges mynde at Huntyngdon to put the lorde Welleȝ in certeynte of his dethe for his fals conspiracions and concelementes as is afore shewed, onlasse then his sonne wolde have left his felliship, and submutted as above, and theruppon a message sent to the saide sir Robert from his fadre, they had be certeynly joyned with the saide duc and erle ar the king might have had to doo with theym ; but as God of his grace provided for the kinges wele, the same late sir Robert Welles being onwardes on his way towardes Leycestre, undrestonding his fadre life to be in joperdie, by a message brought hym from his fadre, knowing also that the king was that sunday at nyght at Fodringhay, and demyng that he wolde not have passed Stanford the same monday, not entending to make eny submission ne beyng in his felaship, but disposing him to make his parte good ayeinst the king, and traytourly to levie where [a] ayeinst his highnes, arredied hym and his felaship that day to have sett uppon the king in Staunford the monday nyght, and so to have destrest hym and his oost, and so rescued his fadre lyf; and for that entent turned with his hoole oost oute of Leicestre wey and toke his wey towardes Stanford upon that same pourpose.

The king, not undrestonding theeȝ fals dissimilacions, but, of his most noble and rightwise courage, with alle spede pourposing to goo upon his saide rebelles, eerly on the monday afore day drew hym to felde [b] and addressed hym towardes Stanford ; and at his thidre comyng sett furthe his foward towardes his saide rebellion, and bayted hym self and his felaship in the town, whethere com eftsons a message from the saide duc and erle by a prest called sir Richard , and Thomas Woodhille, which brought letres from theym, certefying the king that thay were comyng towardes him in aide ayeinst his rebelles, and that nyght thay were at Coventrie, and on the monday nyght they wolde

[a] war. [b] To the field ; *i. e.* to the march onward.

be at Leycestre; wherof the king delivered theym with letres of thankes of his own hand, and incontinent toke the felde, where he undrestoode the saide sir Robert Welles to be in arme3 with baniers displaied ayeinst hym, disposed to fight; thought it nott according with his honoure ne surtied[a] that he shulde jeoparde his most roialle person upon the same to leve the fadre and the saide sir Thomas Dymmoke of live that suche treason had conspired and wrought, as soo it was thought to alle the lordes, noblemen and othere that tyme being in his oost; wherfore his highnesse in the felde undre his banere displaied comaunded the said lorde Welles and sir Thomas Dymmoke to be executed; and soo furthwith proceding ayeinst his saide rebelles, by the helpe of alle mighty God, acheved the victorie (14) and distressed mo then xxx. m^l. men, usyng therewithe plentyvoufly his mercy in saving of the live3 of his poure and wreched commons (15).

Where it is soo to be remembred that, at suche tyme as the bataile3 were towardes joynyng, the kyng with [his] oost seting uppon [the rebels], and they avaunsyng theymself, theire crye was, *A Clarence! a Clarence! a Warrewike!* that tyme beyng in the feelde divers persons in the duc of Clarence livery, and especially sir Robert Welle3 hymself, and a man of the duke3 own, that aftre was slayne in the chase, and his casket taken, wherinne were founden many mervelous bille3, conteining matter of the grete seduccion, and the verrey subversion of the king and the common wele of alle this lande, with the most abhominable treason that ever were seen or attempted withinne the same, as thay be redy to be shewed; and in the same chase was taken the late sir Thomas Delalande (16). This victorie thus hadde, the king returned to Stanforde late in the nyght, yeving laude and praising to almighty God.

Uppon the tewsday the xiij. day of Marche, the king, yit no thing mystrusting the saide duc and erle, sent from Stanford towarde theym John Down, oon of the swiers for his body, (17) with ij. letres of his own hand, signefyeing unto theym the victorye that

---

[a] *So the MS. q.* suretyhood.

God hadde sent hym, and desired theym to com towarde hym with convenient nowmbre for thaire astates, commaunding theym to departe ᵃ the people of the shire₃ (18) that were arraysed by thayme by virtue of his commyssion, for hym semed full necessarye to sett good direccions in Linccolne shire, for he was thereinne, wherinne the advises were to hym right behovfulle, the king supposing verily that thay had been that monday nyght at Leycestre, as they afore soo had written to his highnes that thay wolde have been. And it is to deme soo they shulde have been, or at the leest upon tewsday, ne had be the kinges victorie on the monday, and that thay had no suche nowmbre of people as thay loked aftre, whiche caused theym to staker and to tary stille at Coventre, where the saide John Down founde theym. It is also to undrestand that ne had be the turnyng backe of the seide late Robert Welles with his oost towards Stanforde, for his fadre₃ reskue, the king couthe not by liklyhode haive hadde at doo with theyme the monday, ne of liklyhode til thay hadd be joyned with the saide duc and erle, as afore written.

Uppon the wednisday and thursday the xiiij. (19) and xv. day of Marche, the king being at Grantham, were taken and brought thidre unto hym alle the captayne₃ in substance, as the saide late sir Robert Welles, Richarde Warine, and othere, severally examyned of there free wille₃ uncompelled, not for fere of dethe ne otherwyse stirred, knowleged and confessed the saide duc and erle to be partiners and chef provocars of all theire treasons. And this plainely, theire porpos was to distroie the king, and to have made the saide duc king, as they, at the tyme that thei shulde take theire dethes, openly byfore the multitude of the kinges oost affermed to be true.

And what tyme the saide John Down had delivered the kinges letres to theim ᵇ at Coventre, thay saide and promysed to hym playnely thay wolde in alle haste com towardes the king, leving theire fotemen, with a Mˡ. or at the most xvᶜ men ; whiche notwithstond-

---

ᵃ *i. e.* disband.   ᵇ Clarence and Warwick.

ing, the said John Down being present, they departed, with alle theire fellaship, towardes Burton-uppon-Trent; and when the saide John Down remembred theym that hym semed they toke not the right way towardes the king, theire aunswere was, that they toke that way for certein fotemen were byfore theym, with whom they wolde speke, and curtesly departed from thens, to thentent thay shulde be the more redy and the better-wele willed to doo hym service here-aftre; and undre colour thereof they went to Burton, and sithen to Darby, for to gadre more people unto theym, to enforce theym self ayeinst the king in all that they couthe or myght soo ever, continually using their accustumed fals dissimilacion.

In this season, the king undrestonding that the commocion in meoving of people in Richemond shire by the stirring of the lorde Scrope and othere, sent by the saide duc and erle there for that cause with many lettres, his highness sent into Northomerland and Westmoreland to arredie certein felaship to a filowed[a] uppon theym if they had com forwarde, and to therle that tyme of Northomerland, nowe markes Mowntague, with his felaship, to have countred theym in theire faces, thay that understanding and havyng tithinges also [of] the kinges victorie, and, as divers gentil-men of that felaship saide, thinkyng by the maner of the saide erle of Warrewike writing sent thidre in his own name oonly, to arreise the people, that theire stirring shulde be ayenst the king, and fering his spedy comyng unto thei3 parties with his oost, left theire gadering, and satt still.

The friday the xvj. day of Marche, the king com to Newerke, and the setyrday, as the king was towardes Horebake, there com to hym from the saide duc and erle Rufford and Herry Wrotesley, and with theym brought pleasaunte writinges, dissimiling eftsone3 that thay wolde com to hym at Ratforde. The king delivered theym the same day, the xvij. of Marche; and on sonday the king sent garter king of arme3 with ij. prive seale3 of summons to theym, that tyme being at Chestrefelde, commaunding theym to com to

---

[a] *i. e.* have followed.

theire aunswere and declaracion upon suche thinges as the forsaide captayns of Linccolneshire had accused theym of, as apperethe by the same seide summons, (20) whereof the tenure filowethe.

"Brothere, we ben enformed by sir Robert Welles, and othere, how ye labowred contrarie to naturalle kyndenes and dutie of ligeaunce divers matiers of grete poise; and also how proclamations have be made in your name and owre cosyn of Warrewike to assemble oure liege people, noo mencion made of us. Furthermore, letres missive sent in like maner for like cause. How be it we wolle foryete that to us perteynethe. And that is to calle you to your declaracion on the same, and to receyve you therunto, if ye wolle com as fittethe a liege man to com to his soveraigne lorde in humble wise. And if ye soo doo, indifference and equite shalbe by us wele remembred, and soo as no resonable man goodly disposed shalle move thinke but that we shalle entrete you according to your nyghenes of oure bloode and oure lawes. Wherfore, our disposicion thus playnly to you declared, we wolle and charge you, upon the feithe and trouthe that ye naturelly owe to bere unto us, and upon payne of your ligeaunce, that ye, departing your felaship, in alle hast aftre the sight herof addresse you to our presence, humbly and mesurably accompayned, and soo as it is convenient for the cause abovesaid, lating you wite if ye soo do not, but contynue that unlefull assemble of our people in perturbacion and contempe of our peas and commandement, we most procede to that we were lothe to doo, to the punyshement of you, to the grevous example of alle othere our subgettes, uppon the which if there filowe eny effucion of Christen bloode of our subgettes of this our realme, we take God, our blissed Lady, saynt George, and all the saintes to our wittenesse that ye be oonly to be charged with the same, and not we. Yeven undre our signet, at Newerke, the xvij. day of Marche, the x. yere of our reign." And a like letre, undre prive seale, was sent to the erle of Warrewike.

The sonday the xviij. day of Marche, the king com to Doncastre, where com to hym from the saide duc and erle a chapleyn

of the saide erleȝ called maister Richarde, bryngyng pleasaunt
letres from theym, signefyeing in the begynyng of his message,
that thay wolde com humbly to the king; but the conclucion was
that, or thay shulde com, thay wolde have suretie for theyme and
theire felaship, with pardonneȝ for theym and alle the lordes and
othere that had take theire partie; wherunto the king aunswered,
that of late, in trust of theire hede[a] demeanyng he had graunted
theym his pardon, and at theire instans and prayour made it
extended to asmoche ferrer day then he had furst graunted it;
and therefore, and the writing and messageȝ to his highnes sent
byfore remembred, he mervailed that thay delaied theire comyng,
and sent eny suche messageȝ for theire excuseȝ, and sithe his
highnes had sent his forsaide summons by the saide garter, his
highnes supposed to have worde from theym the same nyght of
theire comyng, and for that his saide entent shulde more clerely
appere unto theym, he wolde send to theym of newe his prive
sealeȝ of his saide sumons; as soo he dide by the saide maister
Richarde, chargeing hym to deliver theym to the seide duc and
erle.

The monday the xix. day of Marche, before noon, come ayene
from the saide duc and erle unto the king at Doncastre the saide
Rufford, and with hym sir William Pare, (21) with letres creden-
ciales, the credence in effecte conteynyng the saide message
that the saide maister Richarde had brought on sonday afore,
expressing that they wolde not onlesse then they myght have
suretieȝ of theire comyng, abiding, and departing, to have the
kinges pardon in fourme afore rehersed, whiche suretie shulde
have be that the king shuld have be sworne to theym solemply
and theruppon they to be sworne unto hym ayein; wherunto the
king, aftre advise and assent taken with alle his lordes and noblemen being there with hym, openly, thay being present, aunswered,
that he wolde use and entreate theym as a souveragne lord owethe
to use and entreate his subgettes, for his auncient enemyeȝ of

       [a] *So MS.*

France wolde not desire so large a suretie for their comyng to his rialle presens; and he doubt it not but it was wele in theire remembraunce how he of late had graunted theym his pardonne, and sithe that what insurreccions and rebellions were in his shire of Linccolne comitted ayenst hym and the common wele of his lande, and as his highnesse hathe knowlage by the confessions of sir Robert Welles called grete capteigne of Linccolneshire, Waryn capteyn of the fotemen, and other, they were styrers and provokers and causers of the same; and if he shulde be to liberalle of his pardonne, considering the hanyous accusacions, and thay not harde what they couth say for their declaracions, it shulde be to perlioux and to evel example to alle other his subgettes in like case, and to gret an unsurtie to his personne and comon wele of his realme; whiche meaved his highne3 to telle theym his aunswere3, and if they couthe have a declared theym self, and shewed the saide accusacions van and untrue, he wolde have be therewith as gladde as theym self, and so have taken theym in his grace and favour. And thoughe thay couthe not so have doon, yit his highnesse wolde not have forgoten the nyghnesse of blode which they were of to hym, ne the olde love and affeccion whyche of long tym he had borne to theym, but wolde have mynistred to theym rightwisseness with favour and pite. And where sedicious langage3 have be shewen, as it is saide, by theire meanes in the northe partie3 and elle3 where to stir his subgettes ayeinst hym, in that he wolde not abide by his saide pardon late graunted, if thay or eny other knyght withinne his saide realme would soo say, he wolde in his own personn, as j knyght, make it goode uppon hym that he saide falsly and untruly; and furthermore, he bad the saide sir William and Rufford say to the saide duc and erle, that if thay wolde com to his presence, according to his saide summons, he wolde therewith be plesed; and if thay ne wold, but refused so to do, he wolde repute, take, and declare theym, as reason wolde, aftre as theire demerites, obstinacy, and unnaturelle demeanyng required, and charged the saide sir William

Parre and Rufford, that sith they were gentilmen borne of his
realme, if they self [a] theym of such contumacy, they then shulde
leve theym and com to hym, according to theire duty and ligeance,
and to yeve hym [b] assistence ayenst theym, and that thay shulde
give [c] like charge to all other knyghtes, swiers, and other subgettes
being there with the saide duc and erle to do the same, upon the
payne of ligeance; wheruppon the saide sir William Par and
Rufford, fering that they shuld not be suffred to opyn the kinges
commandment, humbly besought the kinges gode grace that it
might please the same to send an officer of armes with theym to
doo it, as he soo did, sendyng with theym Marche, oon of his kinges
of arme3.

The monday nyght, whan his message was commen to the saide
duc and erle at Chestrefelde, they, taking noo regarde therunto,
but presumptuosly refusing by the same obstinacy, withdrew
theymself and their felliship into Loncastre shire, trusting there to
have encresing their strenghe3 and by the comforthe that thay
shulde have had there, and oute of Yorkshire to [have] assembled
so gret a puyssaunce that thay might have be able to have fought
with the kinges highnes in plein felde.

The tewsday, in the mornyng, the king, uncerteined how they
wolde demean theym upon the saide summons and message,
addressed hymself to the felde, and there put his hoole oast in [d]
noble ordre of bataille, awowching his baner towardes Chestrefelde,
undrestonding noon othere but that thay [should] be there, and then
their aforeryders were com to Rotherham to take theire lod[ging],
therefore the night filowing he came to Rotherham, where he
loged [that ny]ght, and there had certeyn tidinges of their departing,
and that knawlege had [for as mo]che as it was thought by his
highnes, his lordes, and other noble[men there bei]ng with hym, that
he might not conveniently p[roceed] with soo [great an] host, for
that the saide duc and erle, with their felaship [had consum]ed the
[vitaile] afore hym, and the contrey afore hym self wa . . not

[a] *So apparently the MS. q.* found ?   [b] *MS.* them.   [c] *MS.* if.   [d] *MS.* and.

able to susteyn so gret an oost as the kinges highnesse had with him withowt a newe refresshing; the king for that cause, and for that he shulde lie betwene them and the strengest of the north parte, wheruppon thay hoped and wolde have beene fayne joyned with, addressed hym with his saide oost towardes his citie of Yorke, fully determyned there to have refresshed and vitailed his saide oast, and so vitailed to have entered into Lanccastreshire that wey, and there, if they wold have biden, to have recountred theire malice; and that night he loged at his castelle of Powmfrett; and from thens the next day, thursday the xxij. day of Marche, he cam to his saide citie of Yorke. And at Yorke the king taried friday, (23) saturday, sonday, and monday the xxvj. day of Marche, esta[blishing] suche ruleȝ and direccions as were and might be for the surtie of alle the northe partieȝ and for sufficient provicion of vitaile for his oost for thaccomplishing of his pourpose into Lanccastreshire. And there com to the king the lorde Scrope (24), sir John Conyers (25), yong Hilyard of Holdrenes (26), and other, which had laboured, specially provoced, and stirred the people in thieȝ partieȝ to have [made] commocion ayeinst the king, wherinne they frely submitted them to the kinges grace and mercy, and humbly bysought hym of his pardone and grace; and also of ther fre willeȝ, unconstreyned and undesired, they clerely confessed that so to make commocions they were specially laboured and desired by the saide duc and erle, th[r]oughe theire writing and messages, by their own servauntes delivered and opened, and at they shulde [have] assembled as many as they couthe have made in thieȝ partieȝ, and have drawen to Rotherham, and there to have countred the king, and to have doon asmuche as in them had been to have distressed hym and his ost; which alle they affermed to be true by theire otheȝ, solemply made upon the blissed sacrament, and by they[m] receyved upon the same. And the said late sir Robert Welleȝ, Waryn, and other, confessed pleinly at theire detheȝ taking afore the multitude of the kinges oost at Donccastre, that they were specially laboured, provoked, and stirred, by writing and messaige; sent to theym from the saide duc and erle, and by their servauntes delyvered, that they shuld have comen to Leycestre, and there have joyned with theym, and not to have countred the king, but to have suffred hym to have passed northwardes to thentent that [a] soo the saide duc and erle, and they, with theire powers soe joyned, myght have been betwen the king and the southe parties, and enclosed hym betwixt theym and the power of the northe, to the likly uttur and finalle distruccion of his rialle person, and the subversion of alle the land, and the common wele of the same.

[a] *In MS.* that he.

NOTES.

(1.) *The king's pardon.* "This yere, soone after Alhalowe tyde, proclamacyons were made thorough the cytie of London, that the kynge had pardoned the Northyrn men of theyr riot, and as well for the deth of the lorde Ryvers, as all displeasures by theym before that tyme done." Fabyan's London Chronicle.

(2.) *Sir Robert Welles.* Very few particulars are on record respecting this captain of the rebels, whom it is impossible not to regard as having been, in some measure, the victim of filial duty. He was the only son of his parents, who are noticed in Note 4. He had married Elizabeth, daughter of John Bourchier lord Berners ; she made her will on the 10th October following her husband's death, and therein bequeathed her body to be buried in the church of the Friars at Doncaster, where that of her husband lay interred. As they had no children, the inheritance devolved on his sister Joane, the wife of Richard Hastings esquire, brother to William lord Hastings, lord chamberlain ; which Richard was afterwards summoned to Parliament as lord Welles.

(3.) *Ranby Hawe.* The principal estates of the family of Welles were the manors of Hellowe, Aby, Welle, and Alford, in the county of Lincoln, in the first of which they also possessed the advowson of the free chapel of Wellys. (Act 19 Hen. VII.) By consulting the map of Lincolnshire, the town of Alford will be found near the eastern coast, and the other places mentioned in its immediate vicinity. Ranby, where sir Robert Welles mustered his forces, is about fifteen miles east of Alford, and towards the city of Lincoln ; to which city he afterwards marched, and thence to Grantham, as noticed in more than one passage of the present narrative. The commencement of the rebellion is thus described in Warkworth's Chronicle: "In the moneth of March, the lorde Willowby, the lorde Welles his sonne, Thomas de la Lond knyght, and sere Thomas Dymmoke knyght the kynges champyon, droff out of Lyncolnschyre sere Thomas à Burghe, a knyght of the kynges howse, and pullede downe his place, and toke alle the comons of the shyre, to the nowmbre of xxx.ᴍl., and cryed, *Kynge Henry!* and refused kynge Edwarde." Sir Thomas Burgh was obnoxious to the partizans of Warwick, because, in conjunction with sir William Stanley, he had recently assisted king Edward in escaping from durance at Middleham Castle. He resided in the ancient manor-house of Gainsborough, which he partly rebuilt ; but it does not appear probable that the rebels went so far north.

(4.) *Richard lord Welles* had married Joane daughter and heir of Robert lord Willoughby of Eresby, who died in 1452, by his first wife Elizabeth Montacute, daughter of John earl of Salisbury. (Collectanea Topogr. et Geneal. vii. 155.) Thus it will be found that the earl of Warwick and sir Robert Welles (the Lincolnshire "captain") were second-cousins, John earl of Salisbury having been the great-grand-father of both. There had also been another connection between the families of Neville and Willoughby ; for sir Thomas Neville, one of the earl of Warwick's younger brothers (he was slain at the battle of Wakefield in 1460), had married Maud dowager lady Willoughby, the second wife of Robert, and cousin and co-heir of Ralph lord Cromwell, lord treasurer. She survived to the 30th Aug. 1497. In consequence of his marriage, sir Richard Welles was summoned to parliament during his father's lifetime, by writ directed "Ricardo Welles de Willoughby militi," from the 26th May, 1455. His father, Lionel lord Welles, K.G. was slain at the battle of Towton in 1461, fighting on the Lan-castrian side, and was consequently attainted ; but the son was restored in blood in 1468 (Nicolas's Synopsis of the Peerage), and then became entitled to the barony of Welles, which was of older date than that of Willoughby. By an act passed in the parliament of 1475 Richard Welles late of Hellowe in the countie of Lincolne knyght, Robert Welles of the same place knyght, and Thomas Delalaunde late of Horblyng in the same shire knyght, were declared attainted of high treason, for the present rebellion. (Rot. Parl. vol. vi. p. 144.) The attainder of the two Welles, father and son, was reversed in the first parliament of Henry VII. (Ibid. 286.) It may here be noticed that the author of Hearne's Fragment was under a misapprehension when he wrote, "And anon there-upon the lord Welles *(that had married Margaret duchess of Somerset)* began a new commotion in Lincolnshire ;" for that had been a second marriage made by his father, Lionel. It was to John, the son of that marriage, that Henry the Seventh gave the lady Cecily Plantagenet, his queen's sister, together with the dignity of a viscount and the order of the garter, he being the king's uncle, viz. half-brother, *ex parte maternâ*, of Margaret countess of Richmond.

(5.) *Sir Thomas Dymmoke*, of Scrivelsby, son of sir Philip who officiated as champion at the coronation of king Henry VI., had married Margaret, daughter of Lionel lord Welles by his first wife Joane daughter and heir of sir Robert Waterton : and was thus implicated with his brother-in-law and nephew. He was not, however, included in their subsequent attainder.

(6.) *The king's privy seals.* Polydore Vergil (Camden Society's edition, p. 127) represents that lord Welles and sir Thomas Dymmoke had taken sanctuary at Westminster ; that "king Edward gave his faith and promise for their safeties, and called them out of sanctuary." Afterwards, when the king beheaded them, the same historian remarks that it was "contrary to faith and promise given, and to the worst example that might be."— After perusing the present narrative, it may be fairly questioned whether this statement, which is that adopted by most subsequent writers, is not exaggerated in some of the attendant circumstances.

(7.) *Lord Cromwell.* This was Humphrey Bourchier, third son of Henry earl of Essex, by Isabel daughter of Richard of Coningsburgh earl of Cambridge, king Edward's grandfather. Having married Joane Stanhope, neice and co-heir of Ralph lord Cromwell, of Tattershall, he was summoned to parliament by that title in 1461. It is not to be supposed that he had any concern in the rebellion. He died the next year at Barnet field, fighting on the side of the king, his cousin.

(8.) *Tattershall*, lord Cromwell's castle, was in the immediate vicinity of the insurrection. The remaining tower, built by the lord treasurer Cromwell temp. Hen. VI. is a remarkably fine specimen of brick architecture, views of which will be found in Britton's Architectural Antiquities, and elsewhere ; and its chimney-pieces, curiously carved with heraldic insignia and lord treasurer's purses, are represented in Gough's Sepulchral Monuments, and in Weir's Horncastle.

(9.) *Commissions.* These commissions had been prepared the day before, being dated "Apud Waltham Abbatis septimo die Martii." They were addressed, 1. to George duke of Clarence, Richard earl of Warwick and Salisbury, sir Walter Sculle, Richard Crofte senior, Thomas Throgmerton, Thomas Everton, and Thomas Lygon, for the county of Worcester ; and 2. to George duke of Clarence, Richard earl of Warwick and Salisbury, sir Thomas Ferrers, sir Simon Mountford, sir William Catesby, sir Richard Verney, sir John Greyville, Thomas Burdyt, Thomas Hygford, John Hygford, Henry Botyller, Thomas Muster, and John West, for the county of Warwick ; and are printed from the Patent Rolls in Rymer, xi. 652.

(10.) *Fotheringay.* This, as is well known, was a royal castle, and at this time was one of the customary residences of Cecily duchess of York, the king's mother. The bodies of Richard duke of York and his second son Edmund earl of Rutland had been brought hither from Pontefract, and re-interred with great pomp on the 22nd July, 1466, the king and duke of Gloucester being present.

(11.) *Confessions.* The confession of sir Robert Welles was published in the Excerpta Historica, 1831 ; but its close relation to the present narrative will justify its repetition here :—

CONFESSION OF SIR ROBERT WELLES.

(MS. Harl. 283, f. 2.)

" Aboute Candelmasse last, a chapelein of my lordes of Clarence, called maister John Barnby, and with him sir John Clare, prestes, came to my lord my fadir and me to Hellow, with letres of credence yeven to the sayd maister Johan, which he opned in this wyse : that my lorde of Warwike was at London with the kinge, wherupon for thaire bothe sureties he praied us in bothe thaire names to be redy with alle the felaship we couth or might make and assemble of the comons, what tyme so ever my sayd lord of Clarence shuld send us word. Nathelesse he willed us to tary, and nott stur, to suche time as my lord of Warwike were come agayne from London, for doubte of his destruccion. And anone after my lorde of Clarence sent me a patent of the stewerdship of Cawlesby in Lincolnshire by the saide sir John Clare.

"The cause of oure grete risinge at this time was grounded upon this noise raisid amonges the people, that the kinge was coming downe (and with him sir Thomas Borogh*), with grete power, into Lincolnshire, where the kinges jugges shulde sitte, and hang and draw grete noumbre of the comons. Wherfore, with as many as we might make be alle meanes possible, we came to Lincolne upon the Tuseday ; and upon the Wenesday a servaunt of my said lord of Clarence, called Walter   , yoman of his chawmbre, by his commaundment, told us the same, and that the gentilmen of the contre shuld passe upon us in such wyse that nedely gret multitud must dye of the comons ; therupon desiring us to arise and procede in oure purpose, as we loved ourselfes. And for that my lord my fadir was att London, and peraventure shuld there be endaungered, which he ne wold, for that cause him self wold go to London to help excuse my sayd lord my fadir, and to delaye the kinges coming forth.

"The said Walter   , servaunt of my lorde of Clarence, went with me to the feld, and toke grete parte of guiding of our hoost, nott departing from the same to the end. And afore that, as sone as I came to Lincolne, I sent sir John Clare to my lord of Warwike, to have understanding from him how he wold have us guidid forthwardes ; but, for us semed he taried long, we sent hastily after him oon John Wright, of Lincolne, for the same cause ; and thereupon I departed with oure hoost towardes Grantham ; and in the way, aboute Temple Brewere, sir John Clare mett with me, saing of my lord of Warwikes behalfe, that he grett us welle, and bad us be of gode comforth, for he and my said lord of Clarence wold araise alle the peple they couth in alle hast, and come towardes us, and utterly take suche parte as we shuld take, saing over, that he saw my sayd lord of Warwike lay his hand on a boke that he wold so do. And so the said sir John Clare often times declared aforn the peple.

"The Sunday after came John Wright to Grantham, and broght me a ring from my said lord of Warwike, and desired me to go forward, bidding me and us alle be of gode comfort, for he was in araising alle that he might make, and wold be at Leycestre on Monday night with xx. ml. men, and joyne with us. Wherefore he willed me to suffre the felaship that came with the king fro by south to passe northwardes, and yeve him the way, to th'entent he and we might be betwix them and the south.

"Also, when my lord my fadir went to London, he charged me that if I understode him att eny tyme to be in jupartye, I shuld with alle that I might make come to socoure him.

"Also, my lord of Clarence servaunt Walter   , that cam to us to Lincolne, stured and meved often times our hoost, and in many places of the same, that att such tyme as the matir shuld come nerre the point of batelle they shuld calle upon my lord of Clarence to be king, and to distroye the kinge that so was aboute to distroye them and alle the realme : so ferforthly that, at such tyme as the king was beforne us in the feld he

---

* These words are erased with a pen.

toke a spere in his hand, and said he wold therwith as frely renne agains the king as agains his and his maister's mortalle enemy.

" Also, I have welle understand by many mesagges, as welle fro my lord of Clarence as of Warwike, that they entended to make grete risinges, as forforthly as ever I couth understand, to th'entent to make the duc of Clarence king : and so it was oft and largely noised in our hoost.

" Also, I say that ne had beene the said duc and erles provokinges, we at this tyme wold ne durst have maid eny commocion or sturing, but upon there comfortes we did that we did.

" Also, I say that I and my fadir had often times lettres of credence from my said lordes of Clarence and Warwike, of thankinges for our devoires, and praied us to continue our gode hertes and willes to the above sayd purpose. One that broght fro my lord of Clarence was called William Uwerke ; oone that broght lettres from my lord of Warwike was called Philip Strangways ; * of the other I remember nott the names. The credence in substance rested onely in this, yevyng of thankes, praing to continue, and to sture and meve the peple to do the same ; which lettres be to be broght forth."

(12.) *Prior of saint Johannes.* Sir John Longstrother, bailiff of the Eagle and seneschal of the reverend the high master of Rhodes, was elected prior of the hospital of saint John of Jerusalem in England, in the year 1469, and swore fealty to king Edward on the 18th November that year, and again to king Henry on the 20th Oct. 1470; see the documents recording both ceremonies in Rymer, vol. xi. pp. 650, 664, derived from the Close Rolls : and repeated at p. 670 from the Patent Rolls. Being a zealous Lancastrian, he was on the same day as last mentioned appointed treasurer of the exchequer (ibid. 665). On the 16th Feb. following king Henry sent him to conduct the queen and prince from France to England, and granted him " of oure tresoure cc. marc to have of oure yefte by way of rewarde, for his costs and expences in that behalve " (ibid. 693); and on the 24th of the same month, in conjunction with John Delves esquire, he was appointed warden of the mint (ibid. 698.)

He returned out of France with queen Margaret in April 1471, being " at that time called treasurer of England " (Fleetwood's MS.); and he was one of those who were beheaded after the battle of Tewkesbury.

(13.) *At Saint Johannes.* That is, at the preceptory of the order at Clerkenwell near London.

(14.) *The victorie.* The battle was fought " at Empyngham, in a felde called Horne-

---

* A younger son of sir James Strangways, by Elizabeth, daughter and coheir of Philip lord Darcy and Meynell. His sister Margaret had for her second husband Richard Hastings lord Welles and Willoughby. See the Collectanea Topogr. et Genealogica, ii. 162.

felde." (Act of Attainder of Richard Welles, &c. 14 Edw. IV.) " The place where it was fought, about five miles north-west of Stamford, near the road to York, retains the name of *Bloody Oaks* to this day. We are told that some of the Lancastrians who fled from the battle threw off their coats, that they might not be incumbered by them in their flight ; and that the field called *Losecote-field,* between Stamford and Little Casterton, which, by erroneous tradition, has been fixed upon as the field of battle, received its name from that circumstance. Perhaps that was the place where some of them were severely pressed by their pursuers." Blore's History of Rutland, fol. 1811, p. 142.

(15.) *His poor and wretched commons.* Edward's vindictive conduct towards all the nobility who opposed him is conspicuous throughout the history of his reign. Philip de Comines alludes to his practice in battle to call out to spare the common soldiers, and kill only the gentlemen ; but states that at the battle of Barnet he did so no more, having conceived a mortal hatred against the commons of England, for the favour they had manifested towards the Earl of Warwick.

(16.) *Sir Thomas Delalande,* of Horbling in Lincolnshire, was a brother-in-law of lord Welles, as well as sir Thomas Dymmoke, having married his sister Katharine. In Nicolas's Testamenta Vetusta is the following brief extract of a will. " John De la Laund knight, being very aged, this 4th day of Feb. 1465 make my will. My body to be buried in the convent of the Augustine friars London. Thomas my son. Proved April 4th, 1471." This, therefore, seems to have been the father's will, proved in consequence of the son's death.

Sir Thomas is, however, termed a Gascon both by Olivier de la Marche and by William of Wyrcestre, in their notices of the tournaments performed in London on the visit of the bastard of Burgundy (see the Excerpta Historica, 1831, pp. 213, 214). The bastard came accompanied by sire Jehan de Chassa and sir Philippe Bouton. The bastard himself was encountered by the lord Scales ; sire Jehan de Chassa by Loys de Bretailles, a Gascon esquire, servant to lord Scales ; and " on the morrow (says Olivier de la Marche) messire Philippe Bouton, (who was chief esquire to the comte de Charoloys,) did arms against an esquire of the king. This esquire was a Gascon, and was named Thomas de la Lande ; and this Thomas was a fine companion, and a good man." The words of Wyrcestre are, " Et alio die sequenti (it was the 15th June 1467) congressi sunt in campo ibidem equites cum acutis lanceis Thomas de la Launde Gascon' contra . . . . Boton' Burgund' idemque Thomas de la Launde magis audacter et honorabiliter [*not* horribiliter, *as in the Excerpta Historica*] se habuit."

(17.) *John Down, one of the esquires of the king's body.* This was probably John Dwnn, of Kydweli, co. Carmarthen, who married Elizabeth, sister to William lord Hastings, the lord chamberlain; and whose portrait and that of his lady, both of them wearing king Edward's livery collar of roses and suns, is one of the most curious pictures in the duke of Devonshire's collection at Chiswick (and described in the Gentleman's Magazine, Nov. 1840, vol. XIV. p. 489). His brother Harry Dwnn had fallen at the battle of Banbury; and there was another of the name there killed, who is styled " John Done of Kydwelli " in Warkworth's Chronicle: but from William of Worcestre's list of the slain, in which that person is described as " Henr. Don de Kedwelly: filius Ewin Don," combined with the present passage, it may probably be concluded that John Dwnn of Kidwelly, whose father's name was Griffith, did not fall in that battle. He is stated to have been buried at Windsor, or at Westminster. (Gent. Mag. ubi supra.)

(18.) *The king's proclamation* to this effect, dated at Stamford the 13th of March, has been printed, from the Close Rolls, in the notes appended to Warkworth's Chronicle, p. 52.

(19.) *Coventry.* This city, lying in the immediate vicinity of the castles of Warwick and Kenilworth, was a place entirely under the control of the earl of Warwick. Here it was that earl Rivers and his son sir John Widville had lost their lives ; and in the same neighbourhood the king himself had been seized and rendered a prisoner (as noticed in the Introduction). In order to ascertain whether the archives of Coventry contained any record of the commotions of the year 1470, I applied to Mr. William Reader, who when a resident there devoted much time to their investigation, and he has favoured me with the following document, which is a royal mandate, issued before the king's departure from Westminster, commanding the citizens to send their contingent to meet the king, and it is remarkable that the day on which they were appointed to meet him at Grantham, was the same on which the battle was fought near Stamford. Of course they had not reached him : in all probability, their march was altogether stayed through the influence of the earl of Warwick.

" This lettre was brought to the Meyr [of Coventry], the xix. day of Feverer, late in the evenyng, aº. ixº.

" By the Kynge.

" Trusty and welbyloved, we grete yow well, and for somuche as we be acertayned that our rebelles and owtward enemies intende in haste tyme to aryve in thys our royaume, and that certain our subgietts, ther adherents, contrary to ther duté and legiance, in divers parties of our lande arredy and assemble hemselfe for the reteyning of our sayd ennemies and rebelles, so that yffe their malice be not in briffe tyme mightily withstondon it myght growe to the grett juparté of us and the destruccion of al our trew subgietts, we therfor with alle diligence fully dispose us by Goddes grace to go in our own person to resiste ther sayde malicyows purpose, in the whiche it apperteinith of very ryght and dueté to every our subgietts to yeve on to us ther assistens with bodies and godes ; wherfore we desire and pray yow, and natheles in the straitest wyse charge yow, that ye do sende unto us persones hable and of power wel and defensibly arayd to labour in our servise in suche competent nowmbre as ye may goodly beere, sufficiantly wagyd for, and that they be with us at our town of Grantham, the xij. day of Marche next coming, to wayte apon us in our sayd jornee ; and, over that, that ye charge everi person beinge within your liberté or franches having eny office of our yefte, or of our derist wyfe the quene, for terme of hys lyfe, wheroff the wagis extende to iij^d. by the day or above, that he com unto us in his per-sone, if he be of power to laboure, or finde a souffisant man for hym at the sayd day and plase waged as aforne, and that everi persone having moo offices than oon of our grant, or of our sayd wyfe as above, with lyke fees or wages, that for everi such office he finde us a souffisant man as hit ys aforesayd, putting yow in suche devoir for the premisses that we may perceyve that ye tender the wele and suerté off us and our sayde royaume, as ye wol ansuer unto us at your perilles. Yeven onder owr signet, at our Paleys off Westminster, the ix. day of Feverer."

In pursuance of this letter twenty men were raised, and they were made to take the following oath :—

(The MS. is torn here) that were sende towards the kyng to Grantam. I shall be trewe [to the king my sovereign] lege lord, and truly abyde with hym at better and werse, and truly performe hyr. al manner [servyce, and] not depart from hym on to the ynde of owr reteygn, and tyll we may com to the kynges hyghnes we shall duly attende and wayte apon Wyllyam Shyppey, the meyrs serjant. I shan quarell with no persone onresonabely a monge owr selffe, but be well rulyd. So helpe me [God and] holydame.

In April following 40 men were raised in Coventry at 12*d.* a day, for a month, to go with king Edward into the South, and 100*l.* was collected from the ten wards to pay them.

(20.) *On Wednesday the 14th of March* the king was at Stamford, as appears by two documents in Rymer, one appointing ambassadors to Castille, the other constituting John earl of Worcester constable of England.

(21.) *The king's summons to the duke of Clarence.* This letter of summons has been printed by sir Henry Ellis in his Second Series of Original Letters, vol. i. p. 138, from a copy by Stowe in the MS. Harl. 543 ; but, as it there immediately follows a letter which Clarence and Warwick sent out of France, the editor was misled to attribute its date to the period of their return from that country.

(22.) *Sir William Parr* was a knight of the garter and comptroller of the royal household at the death of Edward IV. He had married the king's cousin-german, Eli-zabeth daughter and coheir of Henry lord Fitzhugh, by Alice daughter of Ralph earl of Westmerland and sister to Cecily duchess of York. His eldest son, sir Thomas, was the father of queen Katharine Parr. See further of him in Davies's York Records, 1843, p. 40.

(23.) *On Friday 23d March*, the king wrote from York " to Edmund Dudley esquyer, deputie lieftenaunt to our cousyn John erle of Worcestre, lieftenaunt of our lord of Ireland, and to our chauncellor and counceill there," announcing that he had dis-charged the duke of Clarence from the office of lieutenant of Ireland, and appointed the earl of Worcester thereto ; and, suspecting that the duke and the earl of Warwick might repair to the said land, requiring them to be arrested, and offering to him that took either of them a reward of 100*l.* of land in yearly value, to him and to his heirs, or 1000*l.* in ready money, at his election. Rymer, xi. 654.

On Saturday the 24th the king issued at York the proclamation against the duke of Clarence and earl of Warwick, printed in the notes to Warkworth's Chronicle, p. 53 ; which was followed by another dated at Nottingham, the 31st March, printed ibid. p. 56 ; and also in the Appendix to the Rolls of Parliament, vol. vi. p. 233.

On the 26th, the king, having discovered that the duke and earl were fled towards Devonshire, directed commissions of array to that and several other of the western counties ; printed in Rymer, xi. 655.

On the last day of March Edward had come as far southwards as Nottingham, and thence wrote to the mayor, &c. of Salisbury, announcing that he purposed to pursue the rebels into the West, and charging them to provide a contingent for his service, and provisions to entertain an army of 40,000 men ; this is printed in Hatcher's History of Salisbury, (Hoare's Modern Wiltshire,) fol. 1843, p. 174.

(24.) One of the "Paston Letters" (vol. II. Reign of Edward IV. Letter XXXII.) which was written from York on the 27th of March, confirms the present narrative in many particulars. It is as follows.

" To my cosyn, John Paston.

" The king camme to Grantham and there taried thoresday all day, and there was headed sir Thomas Dalalaunde, and one John Neille, a greate capteyn ; and upon the Monday nexte after that at Dancastre, and there was headed sir Robert Wellys and anothre greate capteyn,* and than the king hadde warde that the duke of Clarence and the erle of Warwick was att [Ch]esterfeld,† xx. mile from Dancastre. And uppon the tewesday, at ix. of the bell, the king toke the feld, and mustered his people, and itt was seid that were never seyn in Inglond so many goodly men and so well arreiyed in a fild ; and my lord ‡ was whorsshupfully accompanyed, no lord there so well ; wherfor the king gaffe my lord a greate thanke ; and than the duke of Clarence and the erle of Warwike harde that the king was comyng to them-warde, incontynent they departed, and wente to Manchestre in Lancasshire, hopyng to have hadde helpe and socour of the lord Stanley; § but in conclusion there they hadde litill favor, as it was enformed the king ; and so men

---

* Dr. Miller, in his History of Doncaster, 4to. p. 46, has here appended a note stating that " this great captayn was sir Ralph Grey of York, who was taken the year 1463 by the Yorkists in the battle of Bamburgh ;" but that was a distinct occurrence, which had passed seven years before, and is very incorrectly stated by Dr. Miller. Sir Ralph Grey, of Wark (not York) was captain of the castle of Bamborough for king Henry ; it was taken by assault soon after the battle of Hexham in June 1464, and sir Ralph was thereupon brought to king Edward, who happened to be then at Doncaster, and forthwith beheaded. See a particular narration of these events, from a MS. in the College of Arms, in the notes to Warkworth's Chronicle, p. 36.

† This place is printed Esterfield, in Sir John Fenn's modernised version ; and was conjectured to be Austerfield by the Editor of the 12mo. edition, in 1841.

‡ " I believe it means John Mowbray, duke of Norfolk."—FENN.

§ Thomas lord Stanley was lord steward of the king's household (Fœdera, xi. 845). He

sayn they wente Westward, and som men demen to London. And whan the king harde they wer departed and gone, he went to York, and came theder the thoresday next aftre, and there camme into hym alle the gentilmen of the shire ; and uppon our Lady day made Percy erle of Northumberland,† and he that was erle affore markeys Muntakew,‡ and the king is purposed to come Southwarde. God send hym god spede. Writen the xxvij. day of March.   (Signed, in place of a name, thus—) "for trowyth."

It may here be remarked that letter xxxvi. of vol. IV. of the Paston Letters evidently belongs to this year, 1470, and not to 1462, to which it was assigned by the editor. It was written at Stamford the 13th day of March, " by youre sone and servant, John Paston the older," to John Paston, at the Inner Temple, the writer being then in attendance on the king, and charged to have his horse and harness in constant readiness. Sir John Fenn imagined it was written from a place named Stamford either in Northumberland or Yorkshire.

(24.) *Lord Scrope*. It appears doubtful whether this was John lord Scrope of Bolton, K.G. or Thomas lord Scrope of Upsal and Masham, who were both living at this period. No other notice of either of them opposing the authority of king Edward has been found.

(25.) *Sir John Conyers*, of Hornby Castle, co. York (afterwards a K.G. in the reign of Richard III.) had commanded the army of Northern men which defeated the king's friends at Edgecote, near Banbury, and his eldest son, James, was killed in that battle (see Warkworth's Chronicle, p. 7). His wife was a cousin of the earl of Warwick, namely, Alice, daughter and coheir of William Neville lord Fauconberg, and earl of Kent.

(26.) *Young Hilliard of Holdreness*. This was the popular leader of the Northern insurrection, who was best known by the name of " Robin of Riddesdale." His father, sir William Hilliard, or Hildyard, had fallen on the Lancastrian side at the battle of Towton, and the son had probably been reared under a forfeiture of his estates, which were at Winestead, near Pocklington. From whence he derived his popular name has not been ascertained. Sir Robert Hildyard was afterwards knighted at the coronation of Richard III. and was the ancestor of sir Robert Hildyard, a colonel in the army of Charles the First, whose loyalty was at the Restoration rewarded with a baronetcy, which continued in the family to the year 1814.

---

was brother-in-law to the earl of Warwick, having married lady Alianor Neville. He was afterwards the husband of Margaret countess of Richmond, mother of king Henry VII. and was created earl of Derby.

† " Herry Percy" had been released from the Tower of London, and had sworn fealty to king Edward at Westminster, on the 27th Oct. 1469. See the Memorandum upon the Close Rolls recording the ceremony printed in Rymer, xi. 649.

‡ It was at York that sir John Neville had first received the earldom of Northumberland, six years before, in May 1464. See Notes to Warkworth's Chronicle, p. 36.

HISTORIE

OF THE ARRIVALL OF EDWARD IV IN ENGLAND
AND THE FINALL RECOUERYE OF HIS KINGDOMES
FROM HENRY VI. A.D. M.CCCC. LXXI.

Edited by
John Bruce, Esq. F.S.A.

First published for the Camden Society
1838

INTRODUCTION.

THE principal original historical authorities for the period to which the following narrative relates are, I. The Second Continuation of the History of Croyland * ; II. Fabyan's Chronicle † ; III. An English Chronicle from which there are large extracts in Leland's Collectanea ‡ ; IV. The *Anglica Historia* of Polydore Vergil § ; and V. The *Memoires* of Philip de Comines ‖ : to these is now added, in the following narrative, a sixth authority, of greater value than any of them.

The Continuator of the History of Croyland is one of the best of our English Historians of the class to which he belongs. His name is unknown, but it appears in his work that he was a Doctor of Canon Law, was one of Edward the Fourth's Councillors, and was employed by that monarch upon a foreign mission.

* Published in Gale's Rerum Anglicarum Script. Vet. I. 549.
† I have used Sir Henry Ellis's edition, 4to. Lond. 1811.
‡ Vol. II. of the edition of 1774, p. 499.
§ I have used the Edition of Basil, fol. 1557.
‖ My references are to the edition printed at Brussels in 1706, 4 vols. 8vo.

Thus connected with the house of York, but not writing until after the battle of Bosworth,* he holds the balance pretty evenly between the rival parties. He does not dwell much upon minute facts; but the general current of events is clearly, and, in all probability, accurately, detailed by him.

Fabyan's narrative is such an one as might be expected from a citizen and an alderman of the reign of Henry VII.; full, and no doubt correct, upon all points connected with the popular feeling and with transactions which took place in the City of London, but brief and inaccurate respecting events which passed elsewhere. Fabyan's bias was towards the Lancastrian party.

Of *the Chronicler from whom Leland extracted* we know absolutely nothing. The extracts contain many anecdotes and minute particulars, and the spirit and feeling of a contemporary are evident throughout, but I have not observed anything which has enabled me to identify the author. He writes with a very palpable inclination towards the party of " the innocent Henry."

From what sources *Polydore Vergil* derived his account of these events is unknown; but he has given an excellent narrative, superior in style, more abundant in facts, and more copious in description than any of those before mentioned. It of course strongly favours the house of Lancaster; and may indeed be considered as the account which that party was desirous should be believed.

* Gale, I. 575.

I have added *Philip de Comines* to the catalogue of authorities, principally with a view to his account of Edward the Fourth's proceedings on the Continent preparatory to his return into England, and his narrative of the battle of Tewkesbury; which last he seems to have received from some of those who fled from thence to the Continent *. His relation of the intermediate events is extremely inaccurate.

Upon these authorities, which in many points are most singularly contradictory, all our subsequent Chroniclers, with one exception, which will be noticed hereafter, have based their statements. Rastell abridges Fabyan ; Hall translates Polydore Vergil and Philip de Comines; Stowe transcribes the Chronicle quoted by Leland; and the rest follow some one author and some another.

The present narrative has higher claims to authority than any of those I have noticed. It was written upon the spot; immediately after the events to which it relates ; by some person possessed of full means of knowledge ; and it will be seen that it was adopted by Edward IV. as an accurate relation of his achievements. All the other narratives either emanated from partisans of " the adverse faction," or were written after the subsequent triumph of the House of Lancaster, when it would not have been prudent—perhaps not safe—to publish any thing which tended to relieve the Yorkists from the weight of popular odium which attached to the real or supposed crimes of their leaders. We have

---

* Comines, I. 209, " *comment m'ont dit ceux qui y estoient.*"

here an authorised relation put forth by the Yorkists themselves, and giving their own account of the events upon which many of the heavy charges brought against their "house" have been founded.

The author says of himself, that he was a servant of Edward the Fourth, and that he " presently saw in effect a great parte of his exploytes, and the resydewe knew by true relation of them that were present at every tyme; " (p. 1.) and these assertions are corroborated, not merely by the narrative itself, which possesses all the characteristics of a relation of an eye-witness, but in a singular manner also by a communication made to the Society of Antiquaries in the year 1820, and published in the Archæologia, vol. xxi. p. 11. It appears from that communication, and from a MS. relating to the same subject, in the possession of Thomas Amyot, Esq. with the use of which I have been kindly favoured, that on the 29th May 1471, three days only after the termination of the following narrative, Edward IV., being then at Canterbury, addressed a letter in French to the Nobles and Burgomasters of Bruges, thanking them for the courteous hospitality he had received from them during his exile, apprising them of the great success which had attended his expedition, and referring them to the bearer of the letter for further particulars of his victories. Those " farther particulars " were contained in a very brief French abridgment of the following narrative ; and in the Public Library at Ghent there is a quarto MS. volume in vellum, which contains a contemporary transcript of the abridgment, and of the King's letter, all written with great care, and ornamented with four illuminations, representing the battles of Barnet and Tewkesbury, the execution of the Duke of Somerset, and the attack of the Bastard Fauconberge upon London. It is probable that the Ghent MS. is a copy of the communication received from Edward IV. which was transmitted by the Citizens of Bruges to their brethren of Ghent, who were equally interested in the subject matter with themselves.

The identity of the Ghent MS. as an abridgment of the present narrative is unquestionable. Brief, meagre, and spiritless as it is, it yet contains quite enough to render the connexion indisputable. In both, the succession of events, even down to the most minute that are stated, is precisely the same; in both, whenever several persons or several facts are mentioned in one sentence, they stand in the same order; even in the re-translation from the French back into English, which alone is published in the Archæologia, the same epithets are frequently applied to the same events; and, with the exception of some obvious mistakes in the publication in the Archæologia,* the same names, dates, and numbers—as, for instance, the numbers of killed in the several battles, and the numbers of the troops engaged, as to

* For example, in p. 20, for the Earl of Exeter, read the Earl of Essex. In p. 21, the death of Henry VI. is said to have occurred on the 24th of the said month of *June;* May is the only month which can be alluded to, and the

which there is the greatest discrepancy in all the other accounts, are exactly the same.

The identity of the two narratives, the one as the original, and the other as an abridgment of it, lifeless, uninteresting, and almost useless for historical purposes, but still an abridgment of the more important work now published, being established, we become secure both as to the age and authority of the present work; and if we inquire further whether its contents be of sufficient importance to justify its publication, the result will be most satisfactory.

The events to which it relates have few parallels in history. A fugitive and an exile, Edward IV. at the commencement of the year 1471, seemed to have lost all present chance of restoration. The imbecility of the actual monarch was amply compensated by the vigour of the Earl of Warwick, the principal regent, a nobleman whose importance both parties in the state had by turns seen ample reason to appreciate, and whose present measures gave sufficient indication of the energy with which he was prepared to defend the throne he had raised. The inhabitants of the eastern coast, from the Thames to the borders of Scotland, were raised and arrayed to oppose any hostile landing; the Duke of Clarence, one of Edward's brothers, was

day in our MS. is the 23d. Upon that point, it would be satisfactory if the Ghent MS. were again consulted. In p. 22, the battle of Tewkesbury is dated on the 14th of May, instead of the 4th.

bound to the restored dynasty by being associated, according to some of the authorities, with the Earl of Warwick in the regency, by a marriage with Warwick's elder daughter, and by a parliamentary entailment of the crown upon him, in exclusion of his elder brother, in case of failure of the descendants of Henry VI.; and the new order of things was further strengthened, and the three great families of Lancaster, York, and Neville bound together, as it were, with a triple cord, by the union of the Prince of Wales with Warwick's younger daughter, the sister of the Duchess of Clarence. Nor was there wanting that only sure foundation for the throne—the affection of the great majority of the people. The simplicity and meek piety of Henry; the generous hospitality of Warwick; the hard fortunes of the youthful Prince of Wales; the licentiousness of Edward the Fourth's life; his undignified marriage; and the unpopularity of his friend Worcester, "the butcher of England;"* all these circumstances, operating upon various classes of the community, produced a wide-spread feeling in favour of the cause of Henry VI.

The aspect of affairs upon the Continent seemed equally encouraging to the House of Lancaster. The Duke of Burgundy, the only prince to whom Edward could look for support, was little likely to enter warmly into his cause; for, although married to his sister, he was connected by relationship with

* Fabyan, 659.

139

Henry VI. and was involved in a war with France, which would become doubly perilous if, upon any opposition to the Lancastrian party, the influence of England were thrown into the scale against him.

Whilst every thing seemed thus secure and prosperous, Queen Margaret and the Prince of Wales prepared to pass into Eng land. Warwick went to the sea coast to receive them; and, if they had landed at that time, their progress to the capital would have resembled a triumph. Detained on the coast of Normandy from February until April by the unusual boisterousness of the weather, they at length, with some difficulty, secured a landing at Weymouth; and what were the tidings with which they were greeted? That, amidst the tempests by which they had been detained, Edward and a small band of followers had landed in the north amongst a people up in arms to oppose him, but whom he had deceived by false representations of the purpose of his coming; that he had obtained possession of the metropolis and of the person of the King; that Clarence—" false, fleeting, perjured Clarence "—had deserted the cause of Lancaster; that a great battle had been fought; and that Warwick, the centre of all their hopes, had been defeated and killed. " When," says Hall, paraphrasing the words of Polydore Vergil, " when she harde all these miserable chaunces and misfortunes, so sudainly, one in another's necke, to have taken effect, she, like a woman all dismaied for feare, fell to the ground, her harte was perced with sorowe, her speache was in a manner passed, all her spirits were tormented with malencholy." *

The remainder of the story may be soon told. The friends of the House of Lancaster gathered around the Queen and Prince ; a considerable force was raised ; a strong position was taken near Tewkesbury ; and on the fourth of May 1471 the two armies met. The results were fatal to the House of Lancaster. The Prince of Wales was killed ; after the battle, sixteen of his principal adherents were selected from amongst the prisoners and beheaded ; and Edward returned to London, bearing Margaret with him as a captive.

One death more brought the tragedy to a close. Edward IV. entered London on the 21st of May, and on the 23rd, according to the following narrative, Henry VI. died in the Tower " of pure displeasure and melancoly."

The interest which attaches to the persons and situations of the chief actors in these events; the controversies to which the events themselves have given rise; the picture they present of the state of moral degradation to which the English people were reduced by the long civil war,—to which alone Edward's rapid recovery of the throne and the success of the deceptions and crimes by which it was accompanied are to be attributed,— are quite sufficient to justify the addition to our historical authorities of a writer whose means of information were more

* Hall, p. 297.

ample, and whose narrative is anterior in date to any that we possess.

The deaths of the Prince of Wales and Henry VI. are popularly considered to constitute deep blots upon the escutcheon of the House of York; and although the acuteness of some modern writers has a little shaken the general faith in the justice of the share in those deaths attributed to the Duke of Gloucester, it has not at all affected the almost universal belief that those Princes were murdered—and murdered through the instrumentality of the heads of the House of York. In the following pages we have a representation of the facts relating to both those deaths set forth by the Yorkists themselves, within a few days after their occurrence, and before the public mind had been filled with the rumours which were soon afloat. This is not the place in which to enter upon any disquisition as to the manner in which the Yorkist narrative affects their cause; at any event, we shall all agree that they ought to be heard. In the notes, I have brought together the statements of the various contemporary authorities relating to the deaths of the Prince and Henry VI.; and the juxta-position will not only be useful to those who are desirous to approximate towards the truth, but, by displaying the contradictions between the existing authorities, will be found to prove the importance of obtaining further information.

The fate of the following narrative has been singular. Adopted as we have seen by Edward IV., and an abridgment of it translated and sent abroad at the time it was written, it either remained unknown to the English writers of the period, or was considered to be too entirely Yorkist in its tone and spirit to be used during the subsequent ascendancy of the House of Lancaster. After the lapse of a century, a MS. of it is ascertained to have been extant in the library of Fleetwood, the well-known Recorder of London in the time of Queen Elizabeth; and from that MS. Fleetwood, without acknowledging his authority, compiled a narrative of Edward's restoration, which was inserted in Holinshed's Chronicle,* and is referred to its author by the name " W. Fleetwood" in the margin. In passing under Fleetwood's hand, the orthography was modernised, many passages were omitted, many softened, and in some of the most important places the narrative of Hall, translated from Polydore Vergil, was adopted as "more pleasing to Lancastrian ear." After it had been thus diluted by Fleetwood, it received an infusion of Lancastrian spirit from Abraham Fleming, the editor of that part of Holinshed, who interpolated a number of passages from Stowe, derived from the Chronicler with whom we are made acquainted by the extracts in Leland's Collectanea. In these various ways the red rose was blanched, the colour of the narrative was changed in all its more important passages, and the servant of Edward IV. was transformed into a Lancastrian Chronicler.

* Vol. III. p. 303, Edit. 1808.

It was through the partial representation in Holinshed alone, that the facts contained in this narrative were at all known, until Mr. Sharon Turner, whose endeavours to discover MS. historical authorities cannot be too highly praised, drew attention to the narrative itself, by using and commending it in his History of England during the Middle Ages.* To that work I am indebted for my first knowledge of it; and I am not aware that it has ever been noticed by any other writer.

What became of Fleetwood's MSS. is not, I believe, known; but Stowe, who had access to them, made a copy of the original of the following paper, and that copy, written in the small clear hand of the Chronicler, found its way into the Harleian Library through Sir Symonds D'Ewes. It now forms the third article, in a small quarto volume of Stowe's Transcripts, numbered 543, amongst the Harleian MSS. It commences on folio 31, and is thus described in a title page written by another hand; " The Historie of the arrivall of King E. 4. in England, and the finall recouerie of his Kingdomes from H. 6. in A°. Dᶦ. 1471. Written by an Anonymus whoe was liuing at the same time and a seruant to the saied King E. 4. Transcribed by John Stowe the Chronicler with his owne hand." The work now published is a copy of Stowe's MS.

I cannot conclude without an expression of my thanks to the

* Vol. III. p. 281. Edition 1830, 8vo.

Council of the Camden Society for the readiness with which they adopted my suggestion for the publication of this Document, and also for the kind assistance I have received from them whilst it has been passing through the press.

8th *May* 1838.   JOHN BRUCE.

THE

HISTORIE

OF THE

ARRIVALL OF KING EDWARD IV.

A.D. 1471.

Here aftar folowethe the mannar how the moaste noble and right victorious
prince Edwarde, by the grace of God, Kinge of England and of
Fraunce, and Lord of Irland, in the yere of grace 1471, in the monethe
of Marche, departed out of Zeland; toke the sea; aryved in England;
and, by his force and valliannes, of newe redewced and reconqueryd the
sayde realme, upon and agaynst th'Erle of Warwicke, his traytor and
rebell, calling himselfe Lievetenaunte of England, by pretensed aucto-
ritie of the usurpowre Henry, and his complices; and, also, upon and
agains Edward, callynge hymselfe prince of Wales, sonne to the sayde
Henry than wrongfully occupienge the Royme and Crowne of England;
and, upon many othar greate and myghty Lords, noble men, and othar,
beinge mightily accompaigned. Compiled and put in this forme suinge,
by a servaunt of the Kyngs, that presently saw in effect a great parte of
his exploytes, and the resydewe knewe by true relation of them that
were present at every tyme.

IN the yere of grace 1471, aftar the comptinge of the churche of England, the ij. day of Marche, endynge the x. yere of the reigne of our sove-
raign Lord Kynge Edwarde the IV. by the grace of God Kynge of England and of Fraunce, and Lord of Irland, the sayde moaste noble kynge
accompanied with ij thowsand Englyshe men, well chosen, entendynge to
passe the sea, and to reentar and recovar his realme of England, at that
tyme usurpyd and occupied by Henry, callyd Henry the VI., by the tray-

147

torous meanes of his greate rebell Richard, Erle of Warwicke, and his
complices, entred into his shipe, afore the haven of Flisshinge, in Zeland,
the sayde ij. day of Marche ; and, forasmoche as aftar he was in the shippe,
and the felowshipe also, with all that to them appertayned, the wynd fell
not good for hym, he therefore wold not retorne agayne to the land, but
abode in his shipe, and all his felowshipe in lyke wyse, by the space of ix
dayes, abydynge good wynde and wether ; whiche had the xj. daye of
Marche, he made saile, and so did all the shipps that awayted upon hym,
takyng theyr cowrse streyght over [towards] the coste of Norfolke, and
came before Crowmere, the Tusedaye, agayne even, the xij. day of Marche ;
whithar the Kynge sent on land Ser Robart Chambarlayne, Syr Gilbert
Debenham, Knyghts, and othar, trustinge by them to have some knowledge how the land inward was disposed towards hym, and, specially, the
countries there nere adioyninge, as in party so they browght hym knowledge from suche as for that caws wer sent into thos parties, from his trew
servaunts and partakars within the land, whiche tolde them, for certayne,
that thos parties wer right sore beset by th'Erle of Warwyke, and his adherents, and, in especiall, by th'Erle of Oxenforde, in such wyse that, of lykly-
hood, it might not be for his wele to lande in that contrye ; and a great
cawse was, for the Duke of Norfolke was had owt of the contrye, and all
the gentlemen to whom th'Erle of Warwyke bare any suspicion ware, afore
that, sent for by letars of privie seale, and put in warde about London, or
els found suerty ; natheles, the sayd ij Knyghts, and they that came on
land with them, had right good chere, and turned agayne to the sea.
Whos report herd, the Kynge garte make course towards the north partyes.   The same night followinge, upon the morne, Wenesday, and
Thursday the xiiij. daye of Marche, fell great stormes, wynds and tempests
upon the sea, so that the sayde xiiij. day, in great torment, he came to
Humbrehede, where the othar shipps were dissevered from hym, and every
from other, so that, of necessitye, they were dryven to land, every fere
from other.   The Kynge, with his shippe aloone, wherein was the Lord
Hastings, his Chambarlayne, and other to the nombar of v c well chosen
men, landed within Humber, on Holdernes syde, at a place callyd Ravener-
sporne, even in the same place where somtime the Usurpowr Henry of
Derby, aftar called Kynge Henry the IV. landed, aftar his exile, contrary
and to the dissobeysance of his sovereigne lord, Kynge Richard the II.

whome, aftar that, he wrongfully distressed, and put from his reigne and regalie, and usurped it falsely to hymselfe and to his isswe, from whome was linially descended Kynge Henry, at this tyme usinge and usurpinge the corone, as sonne to his eldest sonne, somtyme callyd Kynge Henry the V. The Kyng's brothar Richard, Duke of Glowcestar, and, in his company, iijᶜmen, landyd at an othar place iiij myle from thens. The Earle Rivers, and the felowshipe beinge in his companye, to the nombar of ijᶜ, landyd at a place called Powle, xiiij myle from there the Kynge landyd, and the reminaunt of the felowshipe wher they myght best get land. That night the Kynge was lodgyd at a power village, ij myle from his landynge, with a few with hym; but that nyght, and in the morninge, the resydewe that were comen in his shipe, the rage of the tempest somewhate appeasyd, landyd and alwaye drewe towards the Kynge. And on the morne, the xv. day of Marche, from every landynge place the felowshipe came hoole toward hym. As to the folks of the countrye there came but right few to hym, or almost none, for, by the scuringe of suche persons as for that cawse were, by his said rebells, sent afore into thos partes for to move them to be agains his highnes, the people were sore endwsed to be contrary to hym, and not to receyve, ne accepe hym, as for theyr Kynge; natwithstondynge, for the love and favour that before they had borne to the prince of fulnoble memorye, his father, Duke of Yorke, the people bare hym right great favowr to be also Duke of Yorke, and to have that of right apartayned unto hym, by the right of the sayde noble prince his fathar. And, upon this opinion, the people of the countrie, whiche in greate nombar, and in dyvars placis, were gatheryd, and in harnes, redye to resiste hym in chalenginge of the Royme and the crowne, were disposyd to content them selfe, and in noo wyse to annoy hym, ne his felowshipe, they affirmynge that to such entent were [they] comen, and none othar. Whereupon, the hoole felowshipe of the Kyngs comen and assembled togethar, he toke advise what was best to doo, and concludyd brifely, that, albe it his enemies and chefe rebells were in the sowthe partes, at London and ther about, and that the next way towards them had be by Lyncolneshire, yet, in asmooche as, yf they shulde have taken that waye, they must have gon eft sones to the watar agayne, and passyd ovar Humbar, whiche they abhoryd for to doo; and also, for that, yf they so dyd it would have be thowght that they had withdrawe them for feare, which note of sklaundar they wer right lothe to suffar; for thes, and othar goode considerations, they determined in themselves not to goo agayne to the watar, but to holde the right waye to his City of Yorke. The Kynge determined also, that, for as longe as he shuld be in passynge thrughe and by the contrye, and to the tyme that he myght, by th'assistaunce of his trew servaunts, subiects and lovars, whiche he trustyd veryly in his progres shuld come unto hym, be of suche myght and puissaunce as that were lykly to make a sufficient party, he, and all thos of his felowshipe, shuld noyse, and say openly, where so evar they came, that his entent and purpos was only to claime to be Duke of Yorke, and to have and enioy th'enheritaunce that he was borne unto, by the right of the full noble prince his fathar, and none othar. Thrwghe whiche noysynge the people of the contrye that were gatheryd and assembled in dyvars placis, to the number of vi or vij thowsand men, by the ledinge and gwydynge of a priste the vycar of   , in one place, and a gentleman of the same contrye, callyd, Martyn of the See, to th'entent to have resisted and lettyd hym his passage, by the stiringe of his rebells, theyr complices, and adherents, toke occasyon to owe and beare hym favowre in that qwarell, not discoveringe, ne remembringe, that his sayd fathar, bisydes that he was rightfully Duke of Yorke, he was also verrey trew and rightwise enheritoure to the roylme and corone of England &c. and so he was declared by [the] iij astates of the land, at a parliament holden at Westmynster, unto this day never repelled, ne revoked. And, under this manar, he kepinge furthe his purpos with all his felowshipe, toke the right way to a gode towne called Beverley, being in his high way towards Yorke. He sent to an othar gode towne, walled, but vj myle thens, called Kyngstown upon Hull, desyringe th'enhabitants to have openyd it unto hym, but they refused so to doo, by the meanes and stirings of his rebells, whiche aforne had sent thethar, and to all the contrye, strict commande-ments willing, and also charginge, them, at all their powers, to withstonde the Kinge, in caase he there aryved. And, therefore, levinge that towne, he kept his way forthe streight to Yorke. And nere this way were also assembled great compaignies in divars places, muche people of the con-trie, as it was reported, but they cam not in syght, but all they suffred hym to pas forthe by the contrye; eythar, for that he and all his felowshipe pretendyd by any manar langage none othar qwarell but for the right that was his fathars, the Duke of Yorke; or ells, for that, thowghe they were in nombar mo than he, yet they durst not take upon them to make hym any manifest warre, knowynge well the great curage and hardines that he was of, with the parfete asswrance of the felowshipe that was with hym; or ells, paradventure, for that certayne of theyr capitaines and gadrers were some whate enduced to be the more benivolent for money that the Kynge gave them; wherfore the Kynge, keping furthe his way, cam beforn Yorke, Monday the xviij. day of the same monithe.   Trewthe it is that aforne the Kynge came at the citie, by iij myles, came unto him one callyd Thomas Coniers, Recordar of the citie, whiche had not bene afore that named trwe to the Kyngs partie.   He tolde hym that it was not good for hym to come to the citie, for eyther he shuld not be suffred to enter, or els, in caas he enteryd, he was lost, and undone, and all his.   The Kynge, seeing so fer-forthly he was in his iorney that in no wyse he might goo backe with that he had begone, and that no good myght folowe but only of hardies, decreed in hymselfe constantly to purswe that he had begon, and rathar to abyde what God and good fortune woulde gyve hym, thowghe it were to hym uncertayne, rathar than by laches, or defaulte of curage, to susteyne reprooche, that of lyklihode therby shulde have ensued; And so, therfore, notwithstondynge the discoraginge words of the Recordar, which had be afore suspecte to hym and his partie, he kept boldely forthe his iorney, streyght towards the citie.   And, within a while, came to hym, owt of the citie, Robart Clifford and Richard Burghe, whiche gave hym and his felowshipe bettar comforte, affirmyng, that in the qwarell aforesayde of his father the Duke of Yorke, he shuld be receyvyd and sufferyd to passe; whereby, better somewhate encoragyd, he kepte his waye; natheles efte sonnes cam the sayde Coniers, and put hym in lyke discomforte as afore. And so, sometyme comfortyd and sometyme discomfortyd, he came to the gates afore the citie, where his felashipe made a stoppe, and himself and xvj or xvij persons, in the ledinge of the sayde Clifford and Richard Burgh, passed even in at the gates, and came to the worshipfull folks whiche were assembled a little within the gates, and shewed them th'entent and purpos of his comming, in suche forme, and with such maner langage, that the people contentyd them therwithe, and so receyvyd hym, and all his felawshipe, that night, when he and all his feloshipe abode and were refreshed well to they had dyned on the morne, and than departed out of the cite to Tadcastar, a towne of th'Erls of Northumbarland, x mile sowth-

wards. And, on the morow after that, he toke his waye towards Wake-
fielde and Sendall, a grete lordshipe appartayninge to the Duke of Yorke,
leving the Castell of Pomfrete on his lefte hand, wher abode, and was, the
Marqwes Montagwe, that in no wyse trowbled hym, ne none of his fellowshipe, but sufferyd hym to passe in peasceable wyse, were it with good
will, or noo, men may iuge at theyr pleaswre; I deme ye; but, trouth it is,
that he ne had nat, ne cowthe not have gatheryd, ne made, a felashipe of
nombar sufficient to have openly resistyd hym in hys qwarell, ne in Kyng
Henries qwarell; and one great caws was, for great partie of the people in
thos partis lovyd the Kyngs person well, and cowthe nat be encoragyd
directly to doo agayne hym in that qwarell of the Duke of Yorke, which in
almannar langage of all his fellawshipe was covertly pretendyd, and none
othar. An othar grete cawse was, for grete partye of [the] noble men and
comons in thos parties were towards th'Erle of Northumbarland, and would
not stire with any lorde or noble man other than with the sayde Earle, or
at leaste by his commandement. And, for soo muche as he sat still, in
suche wise that yf the Marques wolde have done his besines to have assembled them in any manier qwarell, neithar for his love, whiche they bare
hym non, ne for any commandement of higher auctoritie, they ne wolde in
no cawse, ne qwarell, have assisted hym. Wherein it may right well
appere, that the said Erle, in this behalfe, dyd the Kynge right gode and
notable service, and, as it is deemed in the conceipts of many men, he
cowthe nat hav done hym any beter service, ne not thowghe he had openly
declared hym selfe extremly parte-takar with the Kynge in his rightwys
qwarell, and, for that entent, have gatheryd and assemblyd all the people
that he might have made; for, how be it he loved the Kynge trewly and
parfectly, as the Kynge thereof had certayne knowledge, and wolde, as of
himselfe and all his power, have served hym trwely, yet was it demyd, and
lykly it was to be trewe, that many gentlemen, and othar, whiche would
have be araysed by him, woulde not so fully and extremly have determyned them selfe in the Kyng's right and qwarell as th'Erle wolde have
done hymselfe; havynge in theyr freshe remembraunce, how that the Kynge,
at the first entrie-winning of his right to the Royme and Crowne of England, had and won a great battaile in those same parties, where theyr
Maistar, th'Erlls fathar, was slayne, many of theyr fathars, theyr sonns,
theyr britherne, and kynsemen, and othar many of theyr neighbowrs;

wherefore, and nat without cawse, it was thowght that they cowthe nat have borne verrey good will, and done theyr best service, to the Kynge, at this tyme, and in this quarell.   And so it may be resonably judged that this was a notable good service, and politiquely done, by th'Erle.   For his sittynge still caused the citie of Yorke to do as they dyd, and no werse, and every man in all thos northe partes to sit still also, and suffre the Kynge to passe as he dyd, nat with standynge many were right evill disposed of them selfe agaynes the Kynge, and, in especiall, in his qwarell.   Wherefore the Kynge may say as Julius Cesar sayde, he that is nat agaynst me is with me.   And othar right greate cause why the Marqwes made nat a felawshippe agaynst hym for to have trowbled hym [was], for thowghe all the Kynges [felowshipe] at that season were nat many in nombar, yet they were so habiled, and so well piked men, and, in theyr werke they hadd on hand, so willed, that it had bene right hard to right-a-great felashipe, moche greatar than they, or gretar than that the Marquis, or his frends, at that tyme, cowthe have made, or assembled, to have put the Kynge and his sayde felawshipe to any distresse.   And othar cawse [was,] where as he cam thrwghe the cuntre there, the people toke an opinion, that yf the people of the contries wherethrwghe he had passed aforne, had owght him any mannar of malice, or evill will, they would some what have shewed it whan he was amongs them, but, inasmoche as no man had so don aforne, it was a declaration and evidence to all thos by whome he passyd after, that in all the othar contries wer none but his goode lovars ; and greate foly it had bene to the lattar cuntries to have attempted that the former cuntries would not, thinkynge verilie that, in suche case, they, as his lovars, would rathar have ayded hym thann he shulde have bene distressed; wherefore he passed with moche bettar will.

Abowte Wakefylde, and in thos parties, came some folks unto hym, but not so many as he supposed wolde have comen ; nevarthelesse his nombar was encreasyed.   And so from thens he passyd forthe to Doncastar, and so forthe to Notyngham.   And to that towne came unto hym two good Knyghts, Syr William Parre, and Ser James Harington, with two good bands of men, well arrayed, and habled for warr, the nombar of vi ^{c} men.

The Kynge, beinge at Notyngham, and or he came there, sent the scorers alabowte the contries adioynynge, to aspie and serche yf any gaderyngs were in any place agaynst hym; some of whome came to

Newerke, and undarstode well that there was, within the towne, the Duke of Excestar, th'Erle of Oxforde, the Lord Bardolf, and othar, with great felowshipe, which th'Erle and they had gatheryd in Essex, in Northfolke, Sowthfolke, Cambridgeshire, Huntyngdonshire, and Lyncolneshire, to the nombar of iiij ᴹ men. The sayde Duke and Erll, havynge knowledge that the sayde forrydars of the Kyngs had bene aforne the towne in the evenynge, thinkynge verily that the Kynge, and his hole hoste, were ap- prochinge nere, and would have come upon them, determyned shortly within themselfe that [they] might not abyde his comynge. Wherefore, erly, abowte two of the cloke in the mornynge, they flede out of the towne, and ther they lost parte of the people that they had gatheryd and browght with them thethar. Trewthe it was, that, whan the Kynges aforne-ridars had thus espyed theyr beinge, they acertaynyd the Kynge therof, at No- tyngham, which, incontinent, assembled all his felowshipe, and toke the streyght waye to-them-wards, within three myle of the towne. And, there, came to hym certayne tydings that they were fledd owt of Newerke, gonn, and disperpled; wherefore he returnyd agayne to Notyngham, determyned to kepe the next and right way towards his sayd great Rebell, th'Erle of Warwike, the which he knew well was departyd out of London, and comen into Warwikeshire, where he besterd hym, and in the countries nere adioynynge, t'assemble all that he myght, to th'entent to have made a myghty filde agaynst the Kynge, and to have distressyd hym. Wherefore, from Notyngham, the Kynge toke the streyght way towards hym, by Lei- cestre; but, as sonne as he hard of the Kyngs comyng onwards, and approchinge nere, eythar for that hym thowght not to be of swfficient powere to gyve hym batayle in that playne filde, or els, for that he lacked hardines and cowrage soo to doo, albe it he had assembled greatar nom- bar than the Kynge had at that tyme; for by the pretensed auctoritie of Henry, than callyd Kynge, he was constitute Lievetenaunt of England, and, whereas he cowthe nat arrayse the people with good will, he streyghtly charged them to come forthe upon payne of deathe; he withdrew hym- selfe, and all his fellowshipe, into a strong wallyd towne there nere by hym, callyd Coventrye.

At Leycestar came to the Kynge ryght-a-fayre felawshipe of folks, to the nombar of iij ᴹ men, well habyled for the wers, suche as were veryly to be trustyd, as thos that wowlde uttarly inparte with hym at beste and worste in his qwarell, withe all theyr force and myght to do hym theyr trew service. And, in substaunce, they were suche as were towards the Lorde Hastings, the Kyngs Chambarlayne, and, for that entent above sayd, came to hym, stiryd by his messages sent unto them, and by his servaunts, frinds, and lovars, suche as were in the contrie.

And so, bettar accompanyed than he had bene at any tyme aforne, he departyd from Leycestar, and cam before the towne of Coventrie, the xxix. day of Marche. And when he undarstode the sayde Earle within the towne [was] closyd, and with hym great people, to the nombar of vj or vij ᴹ men, the Kynge desyred hym to come owte, with all his people, into the filde, to determyne his qwarell in playne fielde, which the same Earle refused to do at that tyme, and so he dyd iij dayes aftar-ensuinge continually. The Kynge, seinge this, drwe hym and all his hooste streght to Warwike, viij small myles from thens, where he was receyvyd as Kynge, and so made his proclamations from that tyme forthe wards; where he toke his lodgyngs, wenynge thereby to have gyven the sayde Earle gretar cowrage to have yssyed owte of the towne of Coventrye, and to have taken the fielde, but he ne would so doo. Nathelesse dayly came certayne personns on the sayde Erlls behalve to the Kinge, and made greate moynes, and desired him to treat withe hym, for some gode and expedient appoyntment. And, how be it the Kynge, by the advise of his Counseylors, graunted the sayd Erle his lyfe, and all his people beinge there at that tyme, and dyvers othar fayre offers made hym, consythar his great and haynows offenses; which semyd resonable, and that for the wele of peax and tranquilitie of the Realme of England, and for ther-by to avoyde th'effusyon of Christen bloode, yet he ne woulde accepte the sayde offars, ne accorde thereunto, but yf he myght have had suche apoyntment unresonable as myght nat in eny wyse stande with the Kyngs honowr and swretye.

Here is to be remembride how that, at suche season aforne, as whan the Kynge was in Holand, the Duke of Clarence, the Kyngs second brothar, consyderinge the great inconveniences whereunto as well his brother the Kynge, he, and his brother the Duke of Glocestar, were fallen unto, thrwghe and by the devisyon that was betwixt them, whereunto, by the subtyle compassynge of th'Erle of Warwike, and his complices, they were browght, and enduced; as, first to be remembred, the disheritinge of them all from the Royme and Crowne of England, and that therto apperteynyd; and, besyds that, the mortall warre and detestable, lykely to falle betwixt them; and, ovar this, that yt was evident that to what party so evar God woulde graunte the victorye, that, notwithstandynge, the wynner shuld nat be in eny bettar suerty therefore of his owne estate and parson, but abyde in as greate, or greatar, dangar than they wer in at that tyme. And, in especiall, he considred well, that hymselfe was had in great suspicion, despite, disdeigne, and hatered, with all the lordes, noblemen, and othar, that were adherents and full partakers with Henry, the Usurpar, Margaret his wyfe, and his sonne Edward, called Prince; he sawe also, that they dayly laboryd amongs them, brekynge theyr appoyntments made with hym, and, of lyklihed, aftar that, shuld continually more and more fervently entend, conspire, and procure the distruction of hym, and of all his blode, wherethrwghe it apperyd also, that the Roylme and Regalie shuld remaygne to suche as thereunto myght nat in eny wyse have eny rightwyse title. And, for that it was unnaturall, and agaynes God, to suffar any suche werre to continew and endure betwixt them, yf it myght otharwyse be, and, for othar many and great considerations, that by right wyse men and virtuex were layed afore hym, in many behalfs, he was agreed to entend to some good apointment for this pacification. By right covert wayes and meanes were goode mediators, and mediatricis, the highe and myghty princis my Lady, theyr mothar; my lady of Exceter, my lady of Southfolke, theyre systars; my Lord Cardinall of Cantorbery; my Lord of Bathe; my Lord of Essex; and, moste specially, my Lady of Bourgoigne; and othar, by mediacions of certayne priests, and othar well disposyd parsouns. Abowte the Kyngs beinge in Holland, and in other partes beyond the sea, great and diligent labowre, with all effect, was continually made by the high and mighty princesse, the Duches of Bowrgine, which at no season ceasyd to send hir sarvaunts, and messengars, to the Kynge, wher he was, and to my sayd Lorde of Clarence, into England; and so dyd his verrey good devowre in that behalfe my Lord of Hastings, the Kyng's Chambarlayne, so that a parfecte accord was appoyntyd, accordyd, concludyd, and assured, betwixt them; wherein the sayde Duke of Clarence full honorably and trwly acquited hym; for, as sune as he was acertaygned of the Kyngs arivall in the north parties, he assembled anon suche as would do for hym, and, assone as he godly myght, drew towards the Kynge, hym to ayde and assyste agaynste all his enemyes, accompanied with mo than iiij ᴹ.

The Kynge, that tyme beinge at Warwyke, and undarstondynge his neere approchinge, upon an aftarnone isswyd out of Warwike, with all his felowshipe, by the space of three myles, into a fayre fylde towards Banbery, where he saw the Duke, his brothar, in faire array, come towards hym, with a greate felashipe. And, whan they were togedars, within lesse than an halfe myle, the Kynge set his people in aray, the bannars [displayed] and lefte them standynge still, takynge with hym his brothar of Glocestar, the Lord Rivers, Lord Hastings, and fewe othar, and went towarde his brothar of Clarence. And, in lyke wyse, the Duke, for his partye takynge with hym a fewe noble men, and levinge his hoost in good order, departyd from them towards the Kynge. And so they mett betwixt both hostes, where was right kynde and lovynge langwage betwixt them twoo, with parfite accord knyt togethars for evar here aftar, with as hartyly lovynge chere and countenaunce, as might be betwix two bretherne of so grete nobley and astate. And than, in lyke wyse, spake togethar the two Dukes of Clarence and Glocestar, and, aftar, the othar noble men beinge there with them, whereof all the people there that lovyd them, and awght them theyr trew service, were right glade and ioyows, and thanked God highly of that ioyows metynge, unitie, and accorde, hopynge that, therby, shuld growe unto them prosperows fortune, in all that they shuld aftar that have a doo. And than the trompetts and minstrels blew uppe, and, with that, the Kynge browght his brothar Clarence, and suche as were there with hym, to his felowshipe, whom the sayd Duke welcomyd into the land in his best manner, and they thanked God, and hym, and honoryd hym as it apparteygned.

Aftar this, the Kynge, yet levinge his hooste standynge still, with the sayd few persons went with his brothar of Clarence to his hoste, whome he hertily welcomyd, and promised hym largely of his grace and good love, and, from thens, they all came hoole togethars to the Kyngs hooste, when ethar party welcomyd and jocundly receyvyd othar, with perfect frindlynes; and, so, with greate gladnes, bothe hostes, with theyr princes, togethars went to Warwyke, with the Kynge, and ther lodged, and in the countrie nere adioyninge.

Sone aftar this the Duke of Clarence, beinge right desyrows to have procuryd a goode accorde betwyxt the Kynge and th'Erle of Warwyke; not only for th'Erle, but also for to reconsyle therby unto the Kyngs good grace many lordes and noble men of his land, of whom many had largly taken parte with th'Erle; and this for the weale of peax and tranquilitie in the land, and in advoydynge of cruell and mortall were, that, of the contrary, was lykly, in shortyme, to enswe; he made, therefore, his mocions, as well to the Kynge as to th'Erle, by messagis sendynge to and fro, bothe for the well above sayde, as to acquite hym trwly and kyndly in the love he bare unto hym, and his blood, wheréunto he was allied by the marriage of his dowghtar. The Kynge, at th'ynstaunce of his sayd brothar, the Duke, was content to shew hym largly his grace, with dyvars good condicions, and profitable for th'Erle yf that he woulde have acceptyd them. But th'Erle, whether he in maner dispaired of any good pardurable continu-aunce of good accord betwixt the Kynge and hym, for tyme to come, con-syderinge so great attemptes by hym comytted agaynst the Kynge; or els, for that willinge to enterteigne the greate promises, pacts, and othes, to the contrary, made solempnily, and also priuately sworne, to the Frenche Kynge, Qwene Margarete, and hir sonne Edward, in the qwarell of them, and of his owne sechinge, wherefrom he ne couthe departe, without grete desklaundar; or els, for that he had afore thowght, and therefore purveyed, that, in caase he myght nat get to have the ovar-hand of the Kynge, his meanes were founden of sure and certayne escape by the sea to Calais, whiche was enswryd to hym selfe in every caas that myght hape hym, so that it myght fortwne hym for to come thethar; or els, for that certayne parsons beinge with hym in companye, as th'Erle of Oxenforde, and othar, beinge desposed in extrem malice agaynst the Kynge, wolde not suffre hym t'accepte any mannar of appoyntment, were it resonable or unresonable, but causyd hym to refuse almannar of appointements; whiche as many men deme was the verray cawse of none acceptinge of the Kyngs [grace]; wherefore all suche treaty brake and toke none effecte.

In this meane season of the Kyngs beinge at Warwyke, cam to the Erle of Warwyke, to Coventrye, the Duke of Excestar, the Marques Mountagwe, th'Erle of Oxenforde, with many othar in great nombar, by whos than commynge dayly grew and encreasyd the felowshipe of that partye. The Kynge, withe his brithern, this consyderinge, and that in no wyse he cowthe provoke hym to come owt of the towne, ne thinkynge it behoffoll to assayll, ne to tary for the asseginge therof; as well for avoydaunce of greate slaghtars that shuld therby enswe, and for that it was thowght more expedient to them to draw towards London, and there, with helpe of God, and th'assystaunce of his trwe lords, lovars, and servaunts, whiche were there, in thos partes, in great nombar; knowynge also, that his principall advarsarye, Henry, with many his partakers, were at London, ther usurpynge and usynge the authoritie royall, which barred and letted the Kyng of many aydes and assystaunces, that he shuld and mowght hav had, in divars parties, yf he myght ones shew hymselffe of powere to breke their auctoritie; wherefore, by th'advyse of his sayd brithern, and othar of his cownsell, he toke his purpos to London wards, and so departyd fro Warwicke; yet, efte sones, shewinge hym, and his hoste, before Coventrie, and desyringe the sayd Erle, and his felashipe, to come owte, and for to determyne his qwarell by battayle, whiche he and they utterly refused, wherefore the Kynge and his brethern kept forthe theyr purpos sowthewardes. And this was the v. day of Aprell the Friday.

On the Satarday, the Kynge, with all his hooste, cam to a towne called Daventre, where the Kynge, with greate devocion, hard all divine service upon the morne, Palme-Sonday, in the parishe churche, wher God, and Seint Anne, shewyd a fayre miracle; a goode pronostique of good aventure that aftar shuld befall unto the Kynge by the hand of God, and mediation of that holy matron Seynt Anne. For, so it was, that, afore that tyme, the Kynge, beinge out of his realme, in great trowble, thowght, and hevines, for the infortwne and adversitie that was fallen hym, full often, and, specially upon the sea, he prayed to God, owr Lady, and Seint George, and, amonges othar saynts, he specially prayed Seint Anne to helpe hym, where that he promysed, that, at the next tyme that it shuld hape hym to se any ymage of Seint Anne, he shuld therto make his prayers, and gyve his offeringe, in the honor and worshipe of that blessyd Saynte. So it fell, that, the same Palme Sonday, the Kynge went in procession, and all the people aftar, in goode devotion, as the service of that daye askethe, and, whan the processyon was comen into the churche, and, by ordar of the service, were comen to that place where the vale shulbe drawne up afore the Roode, that all the people shall honor the Roode, with the anthem, *Ave*, three tymes begon, in a pillar of the churche, directly aforne the place where Kynge knelyd, and devowtly honoryd the Roode, was a lytle ymage of Seint Anne, made of alleblastar, standynge fixed to the piller, closed and clasped togethars with four bordes, small, payntyd, and gowynge rownd abowt the image, in manar of a compas, lyke as it is to see comonly, and all abowt, where as suche ymages be wont to be made for to be solde and set up in churches, chapells, crosses, and oratories, in many placis. And this ymage was thus shett, closed, and clasped, accordynge to the rulles that, in all the churchis of England, be observyd, all ymages to be hid from Ashe Wednesday to Estarday in the mornynge. And so the sayd ymage had bene from Ashwensday to that tyme. And even sodaynly, at that season of the service, the bords compassynge the ymage about gave a great crak, and a little openyd, whiche the Kynge well perceyveyd and all the people about hym. And anon, aftar, the bords drewe and closed togethars agayne, withowt any mans hand, or touchinge, and, as thowghe it had bene a thinge done with a violence, with a gretar might it openyd all abrod, and so the ymage stode, open and discovert, in syght of all the people there beynge. The Kynge, this seinge, thanked and honoryd God, and Seint Anne, takynge it for a good signe, and token of good and prosperous aventure that God wold send hym in that he had to do, and, remembringe his promyse, he honoryd God, and Seint Anne, in that same place, and gave his offrings. All thos, also, that were present and sawe this worshippyd and thanked God and Seint Anne, there, and many offeryd; takyng of this signe, shewed by the power of God, good hope of theyr good spede for to come.

The Kynge from that towne went to a good towne callyd Northampton, wher he was well receyved, and, from thens toke the next way towardes London, levynge alway behynd hym in his jowrney a good bande of speres and archars, his behynd-rydars, to countar, yf it had neded, suche of th'Erls partye as, peradventure, he shuld have sent t ha ve trowbled hym on the bakhalfe, yf he so had done.

Here it is to be remembred, that, in this season of the Kyngs comynge towards and beinge at Warwyke, and of the comynge to hym of his brothar the Duke of Clarence, Edmond callynge hymselfe Duke of Somarset, John of Somarset his brother, callyd Marqwes Dorset, Thomas Courtney, callynge hym self th'Erle of Devonshire, beinge at London, had knowledge owt of Fraunce, that Qwene Margaret, and hir sonne, callyd Prince of Wales, the Countes of Warwyke, the Prior of Seint Johns, the

Lord Wenloke, with othar many, theyr adherents and parte-takers, with all that evar they myght make, were ready at the sea-syde commynge, purposynge to arive in the West Contrie; wherefore they departyd owt of London, and went into the west parties, and ther bestyrd them right greatly to make an assemblye of asmoche people for to receyve them at theyr comynge, them to accompany, fortyfy, and assyst, agaynst the Kynge, and all his partakars, in the qwarels of Henry, callyd Kynge, and occupinge the regalie for that tym.   And trew it was that she, hir sonne, the Countes of Warwike, the Lords, and othar of theyr fellowshipe, entryd theyr ships for that entent the xxiiij. of Marche, and so continuyd theyr abode in theyr ships, or they myght land in England, to the xiij. day of Aprell, for defawlt of good wynd, and for grete tempests upon the sea, that time, as who saythe, continuynge by the space of xx dayes.   But leve we this, and retorne agayne to the Kyngs progrese in his jowrney towards London, tellynge how that he came upon the Twesday, the ix. day of Aprill, from whens he sent comfortable messagis to the Qwene to Westminstar, and to his trew Lords, servaunts, and lovars, beynge at London; wherupon, by the moste covert meanes that they cowthe, [they] avised and practysed how that he myght be receyved and welcomyd at his sayde city of London.   Th'Erle of Warwike, knowenge this his iowrneynge, and approchinge to London, sent his lettars to them of the citie, willinge and chargynge them to resyste him, and let the receyvynge of hym and of his.   He wrote also to his brothar, th'Archbysshope of Yorke, desyrynge hym to put hym in the uttarmoste devowr he cowthe, to provoke the citie agayns hym, and kepe hym owt, for two or three dayes; promisynge that he wolde not fayle to come with great puisance on the bakhalfe, trustinge utterly to dystrese and distroye hym and his, as to the same he had, by his othar writyngs, encharged the maior, and the aldermen, and the comons of the citie.

Hereupon, the ix. day of Aprell, th'Archbyshope callyd unto hym togethars, at Seint Powles, within the sayde Citie of London, suche lords, gentlemen, and othar, as were of that partye, [with] as many men in harneys of theyr servaunts and othar as they cowthe make, which, in all, passed nat in nombar vj or vij ᴹ men, and, thereupon, cawsed Henry, callyd Kynge, to take an horse and ryde from Powles thrwghe Chepe, and so made a circute abowte to Walbroke, as the generall processyon of London hathe bene accustomyd, and so returned agayne to Powles, to the Bysshops Palays,

161

where the sayd Henry at that tyme was lodged, supposynge, that, whan he had shewyd hym in this arraye, they shuld have provokyd the citizens, and th'enhabitants of the citie, to have stonde and comen to them, and fortified that partye; but, trewthe it is, that the rewlars of the citie were at the counsell, and hadd set men at all the gates and wardes, and they, seynge by this manner of doinge, that the power of the sayde Henry, and his ad-herents, was so litle and feble as there and then was shewyd, they cowld thereby take no corage to draw to them, ne to fortefye theyr partye, and, for that they fearyd, but rathar the contrary, for so moche as they sawe well that, yf they wolde so have done, ther myght was so lytle that it was nat for them to have ones attemptyd to have resystid the Kynge in his com-ynge, whiche approched nere unto the citie, and was that nyght at Seint Albons. They also of the citie in great nombar, and, namly, of the moaste worshipfull, were fully disposed to favowr the Kynge, and to have the citie opne unto hym at his comynge.   They of the citie also consideryd, that he was notably well accompanied with many good, hable, and well-willed men, whiche, for no power, nor no resistence that myght be made, would spare to attempt, and suporte, the takynge the citie, by all wayes possible; whereof they ne shuld have failled, consideringe that the Kynge at that tyme had many greate and myghty frinds, lovars, and servitors, within the sayd citie, whiche would not have fayled by dyvers enterprises have made the citie open unto hym; as this myght nat be unknowne unto right many of the sayde citie; and, also, as might appere by that was don aftar in that behalfe and to that entent.   Thus, what for love that many bare to the Kynge, and what for drade that many men had, how that, in caas the citie shuld have bene wonne upon them by foarce, the citiesens shuld therefore have susteygned harmes and damagis irreparable, and for many othar great consyderations, the maior, aldarmen, and othar worshipfull of the citie, de-termined clerly amongs them selfe to kepe the citie for the Kynge, and to opne it to hym, at his comynge; as so they sent to hym that therein they would be gwydyd to his pleaswre. Th'Archebyshope of Yorke, undarstond-ynge the Kyngs commyng, and approchinge nere to the citie, sent, se-cretly unto hym desyringe to be admittyd to his grace, and to be undar good appoyntement, promittynge therefore to do unto hym great pleaswre for his well and swertye; whereunto the Kynge, for good cawses and con-

siderations, agreed so to take hym to his grace. Th'Archbyshope, therof
assuryd, was ryght well pleasyd, and therefore wele and trwlye acquite
hym, in observynge the promyse that he had made to the Kynge in that
behalfe.

The same nyght followynge the towre of London was taken for the
Kyngs beholfe; whereby he had a playne entrie into the citie thowghe
all they had not bene determyned to have receyvyd hym in, as they were.
And on the morow, the Thursday, the xj. day of Aprell, the Kynge came,
and had playne overture of the sayd citie, and rode streight to Powles
churche, and from thens went into the Byshops paleis, where th'Archbyshope of Yorke presentyd hym selfe to the Kyngs good grace, and, in his
hand, the usurpowr, Kynge Henry; and there was the Kynge seasyd of
hym and dyvars rebels. From Powles the Kynge went to Westmynstar,
there honoryd, made his devout prayers, and gave thankyngs to God,
Saint Petre, and Saint Edward, and than went to the Qwene, and comfortyd hir; that had a longe tyme abyden and soiourned at Westmynstar,
asswringe hir parson only by the great fraunchis of that holy place, in
right great trowble, sorow, and hevines, whiche she sustayned with all manar pacience that belonged to eny creature, and as constantly as hathe bene
sene at any tyme any of so highe estate to endure; in the whiche season
natheles she had browght into this worlde, to the Kyngs greatyste joy, a
fayre sonn, a prince, where with she presentyd hym at his comynge, to his
herts synguler comforte and gladnes, and to all them that hym trewly loved
and wolde serve. From thens, that nyght, the Kynge retornyd to London, and the Qwene with hym, and lodged at the lodgynge of my lady
his mothar; where they harde devyne service that nyght, and upon the
morne, Good Fryeday; where also, on the morn, the Kynge tooke advise
of the great lords of his blood, and othar of his counsell, for the adventures
that were lykely for to come.

Th'Erle of Warrewike, callynge hymselfe lievetenaunt of England, and so
constitute by the pretensed auctoritie of Kynge Henry, beynge at Coventrie, and undrestandinge well that the Kynge wolde moche doo to be received in at London, and wist nat, in certeyne, ye or no, isshued owt of
Coventrie with a great puissaunce, the lords, and all that he might make
with hym, and, by Northampton, tooke theire way aftar the Kynge, sup-
posinge verrely to have had right great advantage upon hym by one of the

two waies; eithar, that the citie shuld have kepte the Kynge owte, whiche failed; or els, in caas he were received in, he shulde there [have] kepte and observyd the solempnitie of Estar, and, yf he so dyd, he thowght sodaynly to come upon hym, take hym, and distroy hym, and his people [to have] disceaveyed, but the Kyng, well advertised of this yvell and malicious purpos, dyd grate diligence to recountre hym, or he might come nere to the citie, as ferre from it as he goodly myght; and, therfore, with a great armye, he departyd out of the citie of London towards hym, upon the Saturdaye, Ester's even, the xiij. day of Aprell. And so he toke in his companye to the felde, Kynge Henrye; and soo, that aftar none, he roode to Barnete, x myles owte of London, where his aforne-riders had founden the afore-riders of th'Erles of Warwikes hooste, and bet them, and chaced them out of the towne, more some what than an halfe myle; when, undre an hedge-syde, were redy assembled a great people, in array, of th'Erls of Warwike. The Kynge, comynge aftar to the sayde towne, and undarstanding all this, wolde [ne] suffre one man to abyde in the same towne, but had them all to the field with hym, and drewe towards his enemies, without the towne. And, for it was right derke, and he myght not well se where his enemyes were enbataylled afore hym, he lodged hym, and all his hoste, afore them, moche nere[r] then he had supposed, but he toke nat his ground so even in the front afore them as he wold have don yf he might bettar have sene them, butt somewhate a-syden-hande, where he disposed all his people, in good arraye, all that nyght; and so they kept them still, withowt any mannar langwage, or noyse, but as lytle as they well myght. Bothe parties had goons, and ordinaunce, but th'Erle of Warwike had many moo then the Kynge, and therefore, on the nyght, weninge gretly to have anoyed the Kinge, and his hooste, with shot of gonnes, th'Erls fielde shotte gunes almoste all the nyght. But, thanked be God! it so fortuned that they alway ovarshote the Kyngs hoste, and hurtyd them nothinge, and the cawse was the Kyngs hoste lay muche nerrar them than they demyd. And, with that also, the Kyng, and his hoste, kept passinge greate silence alnyght, and made, as who saythe, no noyse, whereby they might nat know the very place where they lay. And, for that they shulde not know it, the Kynge suffred no gonns to be shote on his syd, all that nyght, or els right fewe, whiche was to hym great advauntage, for, therby, they myght have estemed the ground that he lay in, and have leveled theire gunns nere.

On the morow, betymes, The Kynge, undarstandinge that the day approched nere, betwyxt four and five of the cloke, natwithstandynge there was a greate myste and letted the syght of eithar othar, yet he commytted his cawse and qwarell to Allmyghty God, avancyd bannars, dyd blowe up trumpets, and set upon them, firste with shotte, and, than and sone, they joyned and came to hand-strokes, wherein his enemies manly and coragious-ly receyved them, as well in shotte as in hand-stroks whan they ioyned; whiche ioynynge of theyr bothe batteyls was nat directly frount to frount, as they so shulde have ioyned ne had be the myste, whiche suffred neythar party to se othar, but for a litle space, and that of lyklyhod cawsed the bataile to be the more crewell and mortall; for, so it was, that the one ende of theyr batayle ovarrechyd th'end of the Kyngs battayle, and so, at that end, they were myche myghtyar than was the Kyngs bataile at the same [end] that ioyned with them, whiche was the west ende, and, there-fore, upon that party of the Kyngs battayle, they had a gretar distres upon the Kyngs party, wherefore many flede towards Barnet, and so forthe to London, or evar they lafte; and they fell in the chace of them, and dyd moche harme. But the other parties, and the residewe of neithar bataile, might se that distrese, ne the fleinge, ne the chace, by cawse of [the] great myste that was, whiche wolde nat suffre no man to se but a litle from hym; and so the Kyngs battayle, which saw none of all that, was therby in nothing discoragyd, for, save only a fewe that were nere unto them, no man wiste thereof; also the othar party by the same distres, flyght, or chace, were therefore nevar the gretlyar coragyd. And, in lyke-wise, at the est end, the Kyngs batayle, whan they cam to ioyninge, ovar-rechyd theyr batayle, and so distresyd them theyr gretly, and soo drwe nere towards the Kynge, who was abowt the myddest of the battayle, and sus-teygned all the myght and weight thereof. Netheles upon the same litle distresse at the west end anon ranne to Westmynstar, and to London, and so forthe furthar to othar contries, that the Kynge was distressed, and his fielde loste, but, the lawde be to Almyghty God! it was otharwyse; for the Kynge, trusting verely in God's helpe, owr blessyd ladyes, and Seynt George, toke to hym great hardies and corage for to supprese the falcehode of all them that so falcely and so traytorowsly had conspired agaynst hym, where-thrwghe, with the faythefull, welbelovyd, and myghty assystaunce of his felawshipe, that in great nombar deseveryd nat from his parson, and were as well asswred unto hym as to them was possyble, he mannly, vigorowsly, and valliantly assayled them, in the mydst and strongest of theyr battaile, where he, with great violence, bett and bare down afore hym all that stode in hys way, and, than, turned to the range, first on that one hand, and than on that othar hand, in lengthe, and so bet and bare them downe, so that nothing myght stande in the syght of hym and the welle asswred felowshipe that attendyd trewly upon hym; so that, blessed be God! he wan the filde there, and the perfite victory remayned unto hym, and to his rebells the discomfiture of xxx ᴹ men, as they nombrid them selves.

In this battayle was slayne the Erle of Warwyke, somewhat fleinge, which was taken and reputed as chefe of the felde, in that he was callyd amongs them lyvetenaunt of England, so constitute by the pretensed aucthoritye of Kynge Henry. Ther was also slayne the Marques Montagwe, in playne battayle, and many othar knyghts, squiers, noble men, and othar. The Duke of Excestar was smytten downe, and sore woundyd, and lafte for dead; but he was not well knowne, and so lafte by a lytle out of the fielde, and so, aftar, he escaped. The Erle of Oxenford fled, and toke into the contrie, and, in his flyenge, fell in company with certayne northen men, that also fled from the same filde, and so went he, in theyr company, northwards, and, aftar that, into Scotland.

This battayle duryd, fightynge and skirmishinge, some tyme in one place and some tyme in an othar, ryght dowbtefully, becawse of the myste, by the space of thre howrs, or it was fully achivyd; and the victory is gyven to hym by God, by the mediacion of the moaste blessyd virgen and modre, owr lady Seint Mary; the glorious martire Seint George, and all the saynts of heven, mayntaynynge his qwarell to be trew and rightwys, with many-fold good and contynuall prayers, whiche many devout persons, religiows and othar, ceasyd not to yelde unto God for his good spede, and, in especiall, that same day and season, whan it pleasyd God t'accepte the prayers of people being confessyd and in clene lyfe, whiche was the Estare mornynge, the tyme of the servyce-doynge of the resurection, comonly, by all the churches of England. And, albe hit the vyctorye remayned to the Kynge, yet was it not without grete danger and hurt, for ther were slayne in the filde the Lorde Cromwell, the Lord Say, the Lord Mountjoies sonne and heyre, and many othar good Knyghts, and squiers, gode yemen, and many othar meniall servaunts of the Kyngs. And it is to wete, that it cowthe not be judged that the Kyngs hoste passyd in nombar ix ᴹ men; but, suche a great and gracious Lorde is Almyghty God, that it plesythe hym gyvythe the victory as well to fewe as to many, wherefore, to hym be the lawde and the thanks. And so the Kynge gave him speciall lovinge, and all that were with hym. This thus done, the Kynge, the same day, aftar that he had a little refresshed hym and his hoste, at Bar-nette, he gathered his felowshipe togethars, and, with them, returned to his Citie of London, where into he was welcomyd and receyvyd with moche ioy and gladnesse. And so rode he forthe streyght unto Powles at London, and there was receyvyd with my Lorde Cardinall of England, and many othar bysshops, prelates, lords spirituall, and temporall, and othar, in grete nombar, whiche all humbly thanked and lovyd God of his grace, that it plesyd hym that day to gyve to theyr prynce, and soveraygne lord, so prosperous a iowrney, wherby he had supprised them that, of so great malice, had procured and laboryd at theyr powers his uttar destruc-tion, contrary to God, and to theyr faythes and liegeances.

On the morow aftar, the Kynge commandyd that the bodyes of the deade lords, th'Erle of Warwicke, and hys brothar the Marques, shuld be browght to Powles in London, and, in the churche there, openly shewyd to all the people; to th'entent that, aftar that, the people shuld not be abused by feyned seditiows tales, which many of them that were wonnt to be towards th'Erle of Warwyke had bene accustomyd to make, and, par-adventure, so would have made aftar that, ne had the deade bodyes there be shewyd, opne, and naked, and well knowne; for, dowbtles ells the ru-more shuld have bene sowne abowte, in all contries, that they bothe, or els, at the leaste, th'Erle of Warwyke, was yet on lyve, upon cursed entent therby to have cawsyd newe murmors, insurrections, and rebellyons, amongst indisposed people; suche, namely, as many dayes had bene lad to great inconveniences, and mischevs-doynge, moyenaunt the false, faynyd fables, and disclandars, that, by his subtiltie and malicious moyvyng, were wont to be seditiously sowne and blowne abowt all the land, by suche persons as cowthe use, and longe had usyd, that cursed custome; whereof, as it is comonly sayde, right many were towards hym, and, for that entent, returnyd and waged with hym.

Here aftar folowithe how that Qwene Margaret, with hir sonne Edward,
called Prince of Wales, aftar theyr arryvall in the west contrye,
assembled greate people and cam to Tewkesberye, where the Kynge
delyveryd theym battayle, distressed theym and theyr felawshipe, [and]
the sayd Edward, the Duke of Somarset, and othar, were slayne.

Aftar all thes things thus fallen, the Twseday in Estar weke, the xvj.
day of Aprile, came certayn tydyngs to the Kynge how that Qwene Margaret, hir sonne Edward, callyd Prince of Wales, the Countese of Warwyke, the Priowr of Seint Johns, that tyme called Tresorar of England, the Lord Wenloke, and many othere knyghts, squiers, and othar of
theyr party, whiche longe had bene owt of the land with them, with suche
also as, with the sayde Priowr of Seint Johns, had gon into Fraunce to fet
them into England, were arryved, and landed in the west-contrye, upon
Estar day, at Waymowthe, aftar longe abydynge passage, and beyng on
the sea, and landinge agayne for defawlte of good wynde and wethar. For,
trewthe it is, that the Qwene, and Edward hir sonne, with all theyr felowshipe, entendinge to passe out of Normandy into England, toke first the
sea, at Humflew, in the monithe of Marche, the xxiiij. day of the same,
and, from that tyme forthe wards, they cowlde nat have any stable wethar
to passe with; for and it were one day good, anon it chaunged upon
them, and was agaynst them, and fayne they were therefor to goo to land
agayne. And so, at divars tymes, they toke the sea, and forsoke it agayne,
tyll it was the xiij. day of Aprill, Estars Even. That day they passyd.
The Countysse of Warwyke had a shippe of avaunctage, and, therefore,
landyd afore the othar, at Portsmowthe, and, from thens, she went to
Sowthampton, entendynge to have gon towards the Qwene, whiche was
landyd at Wemowthe. But, beinge there, she had certayne knowledge
that the Kynge had wonne the fielde upon her howsband, at Barnet, and
there slayne hym, wherefore she would no farthar goo towards the Qwene,
but, secretly, gat ovar Hampton-watar into the new forreste, where she
tooke hir to the fraunches of an abbey called Beawlew, whiche, as it is
sayde, is ample, and as large as the franchesse of Westmynstar, or of
Seint Martins at London.

The Qwene, Margarete, and hir sonne went from there she landyd to an abbey nere by, callyd Seern, and all the lords, and the remenaunt of the fellowshipe with them. Thethar came unto them Edmond, callyd Duke of Somerset, Thomas Courteney, callyd th'Erle of Devonshire, with othar, and welcomyd them into England; comfortyd them, and put them in good hope that, albe it they had lost one felde, whereof the Qwene had knowledge the same day, Monday, the xv. day of Aprell, and was therefore right hevy and sory, yet it was to thinke that they shuld have ryght good spede, and that, for that los, theyr partye was nevar the febler, but rathar strongar, and that they dowted nothinge but that they shuld assemble so great puisaunce of people in dyvars partis of England, trewly asswred unto theyr partye, that it shuld not mowe lye in the Kyngs powere to resyste them; and in that contrye they would begyne. And so, forthewith, they sent alabout in Somarsetshere, Dorsetshire, and parte of Wiltshere, for to arredy and arays the people by a certayne day, suche, algats, as the sayde lords, and theyr partakers, afore that had greatly laboryd to that entent, preparinge the contry by all meanes to them posseble. And, for that they would gather and arrays up the powere of Devonshire and Cornewaile, they drew from thens more west ward to the citie of Excestar, movinge Edward, callyd Prince, and his mothar, the Qwene, to doo the same; trustynge that theyr presence-shewynge in the contrye shuld cawse moche more, and the sonnar, the people to com to theyr helpe and assistaunce.

At Excestar, they sent for Syr John Arundell, Syr Hughe Courteney, and many othar on whom they had any trust, and, in substaunce, they araysed the hoole myghte of Cornwall and Devonshire, and so, with great people, they departyd out of Excestre, and toke the ryght waye to Glastonberye, and, from thens, to the city of Bathe, withar they came the day of Aprell; and, as they went, they gatheryd the hable men of all thos partes. The cuntrie had bene so longe laboryd afore by th'Erle of Warwike, and such as he for that caws sent thethar to move them to take Kynge Henry's partie, and, now of late, they were also sore laboryd for the same entent, and thereunto the more lyghtly enducyd, by Edmond, callyd Duke of Somarset, and Thomas Courtney, callyd th'Erle of Devonshire, for that they reputyd them old enheritors of that contrie.

The Kynge beynge at London, and havynge knowledge of all this theyr demeanyng from tyme to tyme, anon purveyed for the relevynge of his sycke and hurt men, that had bene with hym at Barnet fielde, which were ryght many in nombar, what left at London, and what in the contrye, and sent to all partes to get hym freshe men, and, incontinent, prepared all things that was thowght behovefull for a new field; whiche he saw was imminent and comyng on. So purveyed he artilary, and ordinaunce, gonns, and othar, for the filde gret plentye. And Fryday, the xix. day of Aprille, he departyd out of London, and went to Wyndsore, ther to thanke and honor God, and Seint George, where he kept also the feaste of Seint George, tarienge somwhat the longar there for that he had commaundyd all the people, and thos that wold serve hym in this iourney, to draw unto hym thithar, and from thens, suche waye as shulde happen hym take towards his enemyes. And, for so moche as they at that season were in an angle of the land, and nedes they must take one of the two wayes, that is to say, eythar to come streight to Salisbery, and so, that way, towards London; or ells, alonge by the sea-coaste into Hampshire, Sussex, and Kent, and so to London, to make in the way theyr people the mo in nombar; or els, they, nat thynkyng themselves to be of puisaunce lykly to have a doo with the Kynge, and, therefore, paradventure, wowlde drawe north-wards into Lancasshyre and Cheshere, trustynge also to have in theyr waye th'assystaunce of Walchemen, by the meane of Jasper called Erle of Penbroke, whiche, for that cawse, had bene afore sent into the contrie of Wales, to arays them, and make them redy to assyst that partye at theyr comynge; for whiche consyderations, the Kynge cawsed great diligence to be done by meane of espies, and by them he had knowledge, from tyme to tyme, of theyr purposes in that behalfe. Yf they would have taken est-wards theyr way, his entent was to encountar them as sonne as he myght, and the farthar from London that shuld be to hym posseble, for th'entent that they shuld assemble no myght owt of eny contrye but where they then were, but, for so moche as he undarstode well they toke the othar waye, towards northwest, he hastyd hym, with his host, all that he myght, upon the purpos that he had taken to stope them theyr waye and passage into thos parties whereunto their desyre was to goo, and to make them the more myghty, whiche passagis of lykelyhode eythar must be at Glow-cestar, or els at Tewkesbery, or farthar of at Worcestar. And, algates, the Kynge lay so that, would they or no, he nedes shuld nowe recountar them, or stope them, and put them bake. They in lyke wyse, thynkynge by theyr wysdomes that suche was, or of convenience muste be, the purpos of the Kyngs party, therefore put them gretly in devowre to abwse the Kyngs party in that behalfe, for whiche cawse and purpos they sent theyr aforerydars streight from Excestar to Shaftesbery, and aftarwards to Salisbery, and toke them the streight way to Tawnton, and to Glastonberye, to Wells, and there abouts, hovinge in the contrye; from whens, an othar tyme, they sent theyr forrydars to a towne called Yevell, and to a towne callyd Bruton, to make men to undarstond that they would have drawne towards Redynge, and by Barkeshire, and Oxfordshire, have drawne towards London, or ells fallen upon the Kynge at some great advantage. Suche mannar sendynge natheles servyd them of two thyngs; one was, to call and arays the people to make towards them for theyr helpe owt of all thos parties; an othar was, to have abusyd the Kynge in his approchyng towards them but, thanked be God, he was nat hereof unadvertysed, but, by goode and sad advyse, purveyed for every way, as may appere in tellyng furthe his progres from Wyndsowr towards them; from whence he departyd the Wedensday, the morne aftar Saynt Georgis day, the xxiiij. day of Aprell, so kepinge his iorney that he cam to Abyndon the Satarday next, the xxvij. day; where he was the Sonday; and, on the Monday, at Cicestre; where he had certayne tydyngs that they wowld, on Twesday next, [be] at Bathe, as so they were; and that on the morne next, the Wedensday, they wowld com on streight towards the Kyngs battayle. For whiche cawse, and for that he would se and set his people in array, he drove all the people owt of the towne, and lodgyd hym, and his hoste, that nyght in the fielde, iij myle out of the towne. And, on the morow, he, having no certayne tydyngs of theyr comynge forward, went to Malmesbury, sekynge upon them. And there had he knowledge that they, undarstandynge his approchinge and marchinge neare to them, had lefte theyr purpos of gevynge battayle, and turned asyde-hand, and went to Bristowe, a good and stronge wallyd towne, where they were greatly refreshed and relevyd, by such as were the Kyngs rebells in that towne, of money, men, and artilarye; wherethrwghe they toke new corage, the Thursday aftar to take the filde, and gyve the Kynge battayll, for whiche intent they had sent forrydars to a towne ix myle from Bristow, callyd Sudbury, and, a myle towards the Kynge, they apoyntyd a grownd for theyr fielde at a place callyd Sudbury hill. The Kynge, heringe this, the same Thursday, first day of May, with all his hooste in array and fayre ordinaunce came towards the place by them apoyntyd for theyr fielde. Th'enemyes alsoo avauncyd them forthe, the same day, owt of Bristow, makynge semblaunce as thowghe they would have comen streyght to the place appoyntyd, but, havynge knoledge of the Kyngs approochinge, they lefte that way, albe it theyr herbengars were come afore them as ferre as Sudberye towne; where they distressed certayne of the Kyngs partye, five or six, suche as neglygently pressed so ferre forwards, dredynge no dangar, but only entendyng to have purveyed ther theyr masters lodgyngs; and so they changyd theyr sayd purpos, and toke theyr way streyght to Berkley, travelyng all that nyght, and, from thens, towards the towne of Gloucestar. The Kynge, the same Thursday, sonne aftar none, came nere to the same grownd, called Sudbury hill, and, nat havynge eny certaynty of his enemys, sent his scowrers alabowte in the cuntrye, trustynge by them to have wist where they had bene. Aboute that place was a great and a fayre large playne, called a would, and dowbtfull it was for to pas ferther, to he myght here somewhate of them, supposynge that they were right nere, as so they myght well have bene, yf they had kepte forthe the way they toke owt of Bristow. And, when he cowthe nat here any certayntye of them, he avauncyd forwards his hoole battayle, and lodgyd his vaward beyonde the hill, in a valley towards the towne of Sudberye, and lodged hymselfe, with the remenaunt of his hooste, at the selfe hill called Sudbery hill. Early in the mornynge, sonne aftar three of the cloke, the Kynge had certayne tydyngs that they had taken theyre way by Barkley toward Gloucestar, as so they toke indede. Whereupon he toke advise of his counsell of that he had to doo for the stopynge of theyr wayes, at two passagys afore namyd, by Glocestar, or els by Tewkesberye, and, first, he purvayed for Glouces-tar, and sent thethar certayne servaunts of his owne to Richard Bewchamp, sonne and heyr to the Lord Bewchampe, to whom afore he had comyttyd the rule and govarnaunce of the towne and castell of Gloucestar, commaundynge hym to kepe the towne and castle for the Kynge, and that he, with suche helpe as he myght have, shuld defend the same agaynst them, in caas they woulde in any wise assayle them; as it was suppos they so would doo that same aforenone; lettynge them wete that he would have good espye upon them yf they so did. And, yf he myght know that they so dyde, he promised to come theyr rescows, and comforte. With this the Kyngs message they were well receyved at Gloucestar, and the towne and castell put in sure and save kepinge of the sayd Richard, and the sayde Kynges servaunts. Whiche message was sent and done in right good season, for certayne it is the Kyngs enemyes were put in sure hope, and determyned to have enteryd the towne, and ethar have kept it agaynst the Kynge, or, at the leaste, to have passed thrwghe the towne into othar contries, where they thowght [to] have bene myghtely assysted, as well with Welchemen, which they demed shuld have fallen to them in thos parties, in the company of Jasper, called Earle of Penbroke, as also for to have goten into theyr companye, by that way-takynge, greate nombar of men of Lancashire, and Chesshere, upon whom they muche trustyd. For whiche cawses they had greatly travayled theyr people all that nyght and mornynge, upon the Fryday, to the about ten of the cloke they were comen afore Gloucestar; where there entent was uttarly denyed them by Richard Bewchampe, and othar of the Kyngs servaunts, that, for that cawse, the Kynge had sent thethar. Natwithstandynge, many of the inhabytaunts of that towne were greatly disposed towards them, as they had certayne knowledge. Of this demenynge they toke right great displeasure, and made great manasys, and pretendyd as thowghe they wowlde have assaultyd the towne, and wonne it upon them, but, as well thos that kepte the towne as the sayde enemyes that so pretendyd, knewe well, that the Kynge with a myghty puisawnce was nere to them, and, yf eny affraye had there be made, he myght sone have bene upon them, and taken upon them ryght grete advantage; wherefore they in the towne nothynge dowbtyd, and they withoute durste not for feare begynne any suche werke; and, therefore, they shortly toke theyr conclusyon for to go the next way to Tewkesbery, whithar they came the same day, about four aftar none. By whiche tyme they hadd so travaylled theyr hoaste that nyght and daye that they were ryght wery for travaylynge; for by that tyme they had travaylyd xxxvj longe myles, in a fowle contrye, all in lanes and stonny wayes, betwyxt woodes, without any good refresshynge. And, for as mooche as the greatar parte of theyr hooste were fotemen, the othar partye of the hoste, whan they were comen to Tewkesbery, cowthe, ne myght, have laboryd any furthar, but yf they wolde wilfully have forsaken and lefte theyr fotemen behynd them, and therto themselves that were horsemen were ryght werye of that iorwney, as so were theyr horses. So,

whethar it were of theyr election and good will, or no, but that they were
veryly compelled to byde by two cawses; one was, for werines of theyr
people, which they supposed nat theyr people woulde have eny longer
endured; an other, for they knew well that the Kynge ever approchyd
towards them, nere and nere, evar redy, in good aray and ordinaunce, to
have pursuyd and fallen uppon them, yf they wolde any ferther have gon,
and, paradventure, to theyr moste dyssavantage. They therefore determyned t'abyde there th'aventure that God would send them in the qwarell
they had taken in hand. And, for that entent, the same nyght they pight
them in a fielde, in a close even at the townes ende; the towne, and the
abbey, at theyr backs; afore them, and upon every hand of them, fowle
lanes, and depe dikes, and many hedges, with hylls, and valleys, a ryght
evill place to approche, as cowlde well have bene devysed.

The Kynge, the same mornynge, the Fryday, erly, avanced his banners,
and devyded his hole hoost in three battayles, and sent afore hym his forrydars, and scorars, on every syde hym, and so, in fayre arraye and ordinaunce, he toke his way thrwghe the champain contrye, callyd Cottes-
wolde, travaylynge all his people, whereof were moo than iij ^{M} fotemen,
that Fryday, which was right-an-hot day, xxx myle and more; whiche his
people might nat finde, in all the way, horse-mete, ne mans-meate, ne so
moche as drynke for theyr horses, save in one litle broke, where was full
letle relefe, it was so sone trowbled with the cariages that had passed it.
And all that day was evarmore the Kyngs hoste within v or vj myles of
his enemyes; he in playne contry and they amongst woods; havynge
allway good espialls upon them. So, continuynge that iourney to he came,
with all his hooste, to a village callyd Chiltenham, but five myles from
Tewkesberye, where the Kynge had certayn knolege that, but litle afore
his comynge thethar, his enemyes were comen to Tewkesbury, and there
were takynge a field, wherein they purposed to abyde, and delyver him
battayle. Whereupon the Kynge made no longar taryenge, but a litle
confortyd hymselfe, and his people, with suche meate and drynke as he
had done to be caried with hym, for vitalyge of his hooste; and, incontinent, set forthe towards his enemyes, and toke the fielde, and lodgyd
hym selfe, and all his hooste, within three myle of them.

Upon the morow followynge, Saterday, the iiij. day of May, [the Kynge]
apparailed hymselfe, and all his hoost set in good array; ordeined three

wards; displayed his bannars; dyd blowe up the trompets; commytted his caws and qwarell to Almyghty God, to owr most blessyd lady his mothar, Vyrgyn Mary, the glorious martyr Seint George, and all the saynts; and avaunced, directly upon his enemyes; approchinge to theyr filde, whiche was strongly in a marvaylows strong grownd pyght, full difficult to be assayled. Netheles the Kyngs ordinance was so conveniently layde afore them, and his vawarde so sore oppressyd them, with shott of arrows, that they gave them right-a-sharpe shwre. Also they dyd agayne-ward to them, bothe with shot of arrows and gonnes, whereof netheles they ne had not so great plenty as had the Kynge. In the front of theyr field were so evell lanes, and depe dykes, so many hedges, trees, and busshes, that it was right hard to approche them nere, and come to hands; but Edmond, called Duke of Somarset, having that day the vawarde, whithar it were for that he and his fellowshipe were sore annoyed in the place where they were, as well with gonnes-shott, as with shot of arrows, whiche they ne wowld nor durst abyde, or els, of great harte and corage, knyghtly and manly avaunsyd hymselfe, with his fellowshipe, somewhat asyde-hand the Kyngs vawarde, and, by certayne pathes and wayes therefore afore purveyed, and to the Kyngs party unknowne, he departyd out of the field, passyd a lane, and came into a fayre place, or cloos, even afore the Kynge where he was enbatteled, and, from the hill that was in that one of the closes, he set right fiercely upon th'end of the Kyngs battayle. The Kynge, full manly, set forthe even upon them, enteryd and wann the dyke, and hedge, upon them, into the cloose, and, with great vyolence, put them upe towards the hyll, and, so also, the Kyng's vaward, being in the rule of the Duke of Gloucestar.

Here it is to be remembred, how that, whan the Kynge was comyn afore theyr fielde, or he set upon them, he consydered that, upon the right hand of theyr field, there was a parke, and therein moche wood, and he, thinkynge to purvey a remedye in caace his sayd enemyes had layed any bushement in that wood, of horsemen, he chose, out of his fellashyppe, ij ^{c} speres, and set them in a plomp, togethars, nere a qwartar of a myle from the fielde, gyvenge them charge to have good eye upon that cornar of the woode, if caas that eny nede were, and to put them in devowre, and, yf they saw none suche, as they thowght most behovfull for tyme and space, to employ themselfe in the best wyse as they cowlde; which pro-

visyon cam as well to poynt at this tyme of the battayle as cowthe well
have been devysed, for the sayd spers of the Kyngs party, seinge no lyk-
lynes of eny busshement in the sayd woode-corner, seinge also goode
oportunitie t'employ them selfe well, cam and brake on, all at ones, upon
the Duke of Somerset, and his vawarde, asyde-hand, unadvysed, whereof
they, seinge the Kynge gave them ynoughe to doo afore them, were gretly
dismaied and abasshed, and so toke them to flyght into the parke, and
into the medowe that was nere, and into lanes, and dykes, where they best
hopyd to escape the dangar; of whom, netheles, many were distressed,
taken, and slayne; and, even at this point of theyr flyght, the Kynge
coragiously set upon that othar felde, were was chefe Edward, called
Prince, and, in short while, put hym to discomfiture and flyght; and so fell
in the chase of them that many of them were slayne, and, namely, at a
mylene, in the medowe fast by the towne, were many drownyd; many rann
towards the towne; many to the churche; to the abbey; and els where;
as they best myght.

In the wynnynge of the fielde such as abode hand-stroks were slayne incontinent; Edward, called Prince, was taken, fleinge to the towne wards, and
slayne, in the fielde.   Ther was also slayne Thomas, called th'Erle of Devonshire; John of Somarset, called Marqwes Dorset; Lord Wenloke; with
many othar in great nombar.

Thus this done, and with God's myght atchyved, the Kynge toke the
right way to th'abbey there, to gyve unto Almyghty God lawde and thanke
for the vyctorye, that, of his mercy, he had that day grauntyd and gyven
unto hym; where he was receyvyd with procession, and so convayed
thrwghe the churche, and the qwere, to the hy awtere, with grete devocion
praysenge God, and yeldynge unto hym convenient lawde.   And, where
there were fledd into the sayd churche many of his rebels, in great nombar
      or moo, hopynge there to have bene relevyd and savyd from bodyly
harme, he gave them all his fre pardon, albe it there ne was, ne had nat at
any tyme bene grauntyd, any fraunchise to that place for any offendars
agaynst theyr prince havynge recowrse thethar, but that it had bene lefull
to the Kynge to have commaundyd them to have bene drawne out of the
churche, and had done them to be executyd as his traytors, yf so had bene
his pleasure; but, at the reverence of the blessyd Trinitie, the moste holy
vyrgyn Mary, and the holy martir Seint George, by whos grace and helpe

he had that day atteygned so noble a victory; and, at the same reverence, he grauntyd the corpses of the sayd Edward, and othar so slayne in the field, or clls where, to be buryed there, in churche, or ells where it pleasyd the servaunts, frends, or neighbowrs, without any qwarteryng, or defoulyng theyr bodyes, by settying upe at any opne place.

This battayll thus done and atchived, and the Kyngs grace thus largly shewed, it was so that, in the abbey, and othar places of the towne, were founden Edmond, callyd Duke of Somerset, the prior of Seynt Johns, called Ser John Longestrother, Ser Thomas Tressham, Ser Gervaux of Clyfton, knyghts, squiers, and othar notable parsonnes dyvers, whiche all, dyvers tymes, were browght afore the Kyng's brothar, the Duke of Gloucestar and Constable of England, and the Duke of Norfolke, Marshall of England, theyr iudges; and so were iudged to deathe, in the mydst of the towne, Edmond Duke of Somarset, and the sayd Prior of Seint Johns, with many othar gentils that there were taken, and that of longe tyme had provoked and continuyd the great rebellyon that so long had endured in the land agaynst the Kynge, and contrye to the wele of the Realme. The sayd Duke, and othar thus iudged, were executyd in the mydste of the towne, upon a scaffolde therefore made, behedyd evereche one, and without eny othar dismembringe, or settynge up, licensyd to be buryed.

All these thyngs thus done, the Twesday, the vij. day of May, the Kynge departyd from Tewxbery, towards his citie of Worcestar, and, on the waye, he had certayne knowledge that Qwene Margarete was founden nat fer from thens, in a powre religiows place, where she had hyd hir selfe, for the surty of hir parson, the Saturdaye, erlye in the mornynge, aftar hir sonne Edward, callyd Prince, was gon to the filde, for to withdraw hir selfe from the adventure of the battayle; of whome also he was assured that she shuld be at his commaundement.

The Kynge, beinge at Worcestar, had certayne knowledge also, that certayne his rebells of the northe partyes beganne to make commocions, and assembles of people agaynst hym, in the qwarell of Henry, callyd Kynge; for whiche cawse he kept nat the ryght way to London, as he had purposyd, but, entendyng to prepare a new felashipp agaynst the sayd rebells in the north, and, to be in a good strengthe of people, whatsoevar shuld happe, he determined hym selfe to goo to Coventrye, as he so dyd the xi. day of the sayd monythe; where he refresshed well suche as were laft withe hym of his hoste, by the space of three dayes; and thethar was browght unto hym Qwene Margaret. He forgate not to send from thens his messengars, with writyngs, all abowte the contryes nere adioyninge, to suche in especiall as he trustyd best that they would do hym service. Trewth it is whiles the Kynge, in alwyse, thus preparyd a new armye, came certayne tydyngs unto hym, how they of the northe had herd the certeyntye of his great vyctories, and how that he disposyd hym to come towards them, with a great armye, and they, sore dredyng his good spede, and great fortunes; nat havynge any of the Warewyks, or Nevells, blode, whom unto they myght have restyd, as they had done afore; knowynge also, for certaynty, that th'Erle of Northumbarland was nothinge of theyr partye, but that he wowld resyste and withstand them at his uttarmoste powere, uttarly takynge parte with the Kynge, and his qwarell; the cheftaynes of them that were maliciowsly dysposed, and, for evell entent, as above, have commoned and begone to assemble the people, anon, upon thies knowledge and considerations, they withdrew them from any ferthar proceding to theyr said rebellyon, as folks not lykly to maintayne theire fals qwarell and partye. They lefte theyr bands, and compaignes, and dyvars of them made menes to th'Erle of Northumbarland, besechinge hym to be good meane to the Kynge for his grace and pardone. Some of the scowrars wer taken and put in warde. The citie of Yorke, and othar good townes, and contryes, lowly submittinge them, and [promysinge] than to the Kynge theyr dwe obedyence. And so, by the xiiij. day of May, it was knowne clerly, by suche as were sent unto the Kynge from th'Erle of Northombarland, from the citie of Yorke, and othar dyvars places in the northe, that there was no rebellyon in all the northe begon, but that it was so passyfied that it ne myght ne shwld anoy the Kynge, in any wyse. Wherefore it was to hym thowght, and to all hys counsell, that for to goo into the northe for eny pacification, or punishement of suche parsons, it was not nedefull as at that tyme; and so it was most clerly declaryd, the same daye, by th'Erle of Northombarland, who cam streyght to the Kynge to Coventrye, out of the northe contrye; as his departynge well asswred that the contrye was in good and sure tranquilitie, without any comotions, or unlawfull gatheryngs. Whiche Erle cam not accompanied greatly, but with a fewe folkes, and nat arrayed in manar of warr, for he had no mannar knowledge but that the

Kynge, aftar this his great victories acchived, shuld have good pax, every where in his realme; but it was nat so, for the Kynge had knowledge, or that he cam to Coventrye, by lettars sent hym by lords of his blode beinge at London this season, that the bastard Fawcomberge, whiche, a lytle afore that, had bene sent to the sea by th'Erle of Warwyke, and had dystressed many marchaunt-shipps of Portyngall, and taken the ships and goods to hym selfe, in breche of the amitie that of longe tyme had bene betwyxt the realmes of England and Portyngall, he had callyd unto hym, and to his fellowshipe, grete partyes and nombars of marinars, out of every party and porte of England, and many othar traytors, and misgoverned men, of every contrye of England, and also othar contries, that had great corage to atend to thefte and roberye. It was shewed the Kyng that dayly his nombar drew gretar and gretar, and that he was gone to Calays, and browght many men with hym, from thens, into Kent, where he began to gathar his people in great nombar, entendyng, by lyklyhode, to do some great myschevows dede.

Aftar the Kynge was at Coventrye, he had dayly messages from the Lords at London, how that the bastard had assembled greate people, and, bothe by lande many thowsands, and, by watar with all his shipps ful of people, he came afore London, thinkynge to robbe, and spoyle, and do almaner of myschefe; and therto many of the contrye of Kent were assentynge, and cam with theyr good wills, as people redy to be appliable to suche seditious commocions. Othar of Kentyshe people that wowld righte fayne have sytten still at home, and nat to have ronne into the dangar of suche rebellyon, by force and violence of suche riotows people as were of the sayd bastards company, for feare of deathe, and othar great manasses, and thretynynges, were compellyd, some to goo with the bastard, in theyr parsons; suche, specially, as were hable in parsons, yf they had aray, and myght not wage to such as would goo, they were compellyd, by lyke foarce, to lene them theyr araye, and harnes; and such as were unharnesyd, aged, and unhable, and of honor, they were compelled to send men waged, or to gyve mony wherewith to wage men to goo to the sayd bastards company. So that, ryght in a shorte tyme, the sayd bastard and his felowship had assembled to the nombar of xvj or xvij^M men, as they accomptyd themselves. Whiche came afore London the xij. day of May, in the qwarell of Kynge Henry, whome they sayd they wowlde have owte of the Towre of London, as they pretendyd. And, for that cawse, they desyred the citizens of London that they myght have free entrye into the citie where, first, theyr entent was to have with them the sayd Henry, and aftar, to passe pesceably thrwghe the citie, as they sayd, without any grevaunce to be done to eny parson; upon th'entent from thens to goo towards the Kynge, where so evar they myght finde hym, hym to distroy and all his partakars, in qwarell of the sayde Henry, yf they myght have of hym the ovar-hand.

But, so it was, that the Maior, Aldarmen, and othar officers and citizens of London denied them theyr entrye. As this was in doinge ovar came from London freshe tydyngs to the Kynge, from the Lords, and the citizens, which, with right grete instance, moved the Kinge, in all possible haste, to approche and com to the citie, to the defence of the Qwene, than being in the Tower of London, my Lorde Prince, and my Ladies his doghtars, and of the Lords, and of the citie, whiche, as they all wrote, was likly to stand in the grettest ioperdy that evar they stode. In consideration had for that gret nombar of the persones within the citie were rather disposyd to have helped to have suche mischiefe wroght than to defend it; some, for they were maliciowsly disposed, and were, in theyr harts perciall to th'Erle of Warwickes qwarell, and to the party of Henry, wherefore were many; some, for they were powre; some, mens servaunts, mens prentises, which would have bene right glade of a comon robery, to th'entent they might largely have put theyr hands in riche mens coffres.

Thes manar of writings moved the Kynge greatly to haste hym thetharwards; but it was behovefull, or that he came there, he were furnesshyd of as great, or gretar, hooste than he had had at any tyme sithe his comynge into the land; natheles, for that suche armye might nat be prepared so sonne as he woulde, the sayd xiiij. day of May, he apoyntyd a notable, and a well chosen, felawshipe owt of his hooste, and them sent unto the citie of London, afore his comynge, to the nombar of xv ^{c} men, well besene; for the comforte of the Quene, the Lords, and the citizens. And hymselfe departyd out of Coventrie towards London the xvj. day of May.

Here is to be remembred, that, whan the bastard and his felashipe myght not purchace of the maior and citezens of London the overtur of the sayd citie, for theyr passage thrwghe, as above, neythar for theyr promises, ne for great thretenyngs and manassyngs, they made sembland to passe ovar

Thames, by Kyngstone Brige, x myles above London, and thethar drewe them the hole hooste, levynge all theyr shipps afore Seint Katheryns, a lytle from the Towre of London; pretendyng that they shuld come and dystroy Westmynstar, and than the subarbs of London, and assay the uttarmoste agaynst the citye, revengynge that theyr entrye was denied them, and theyr passage thrwghe the citie, and so forthe, with theyr hole multitude, have passed thrwghe the contries agaynst the Kynge. But, so it was, as they were onwards in this journey, the bastard had certayne knowledge that the Kynge was greatly assistyd with all the Lords of the Realme in substaunce, great nombar of noble men and othar, in greater nombar than in eny tyme he had had afore; they, greatly fearinge his highe corage and knyghthood, and the great vyctories that God had sent hym, they delayed withe watar wyne (?) and so retowrned agayne, and came before London, and shewyd themselfe in hoole battayle in Seint Georgis filde. And that for dyvers consideracions; for ones, they dowbtyd gretly the recountar of the Kynge; also the multytud of them cam rathar for robbinge than for revengynge by way of battayle; they doubted, also, to assayle the citie on that othar syde of Thamis, for, lykly it was, that, in caas they myght not prevayle, they of London shuld lyghtly stoppe them theyr wayes homeward unto theyr contrye. And for to devide theyr hoost, some upon the one syde of London and some upon the othar syde, they thought it foly, forsomoche as, with fewe folks, they myght have broken the brydges aftar them, and, with right fewe folks, have kepte and stopped theyr passage.

Here folowethe howe the sayd bastard Faucomberge, with his felashippe, assayled the citie of London, and set fyer upon the bridge of London, and brent greate parte thereof, and upon othar two gates of the sayde citie; and how they were honorably recountred, and discomfeted, and dryven to the watar, and soo the citie delyveryd from them.

The bastard and his fellashippe, thus returnyd agayne from Kyngstonn brigge, afore London, purposynge to execute theyr greate rancowr and malice agayns the citie of London, and that in all haste, to th'entent they myght have theyr praye afore the Kyngs comynge, whiche they thowght not to abyde, and it to cary awaye in theyr shipps, whiche were ready to attend for the same entent of roberye, but a myle or two from the sayde citie. Wherefore, incontinent, they assayled the citie with greate violence, with shot of goons, suche as they had browght owt of theyr shipps, in great nombar, and layd them on length the watar syde, streight ovar agaynst the citie; where with they prevayled no thinge, for the citizens agayne-warde in dyvars placis layde ordinaunce, and made so sharp shott agaynst them, that they durst not abyde in eny place alonge the watarsyde, and so were dryven from theyr owne ordinaunce. Wherefore the bastard purveyed an othar mean to annoy and greve the sayde Citie sore, and therefore ordeynyd a great fellowshipe to set fyre upon the bridge, and to brene the howsynge upon the bridge, and, through therby, to make them an open way into the sayd citie. An othar greate felashipe he sett ovar the watar with his shipps, mo then iij ᴹ men, whiche were devided into two partes ; one partye went to Algate, wenyng to have entred the citie there, by assaulte; an othar partye went to Bysshops-gate, wenynge to have entred there by an othar assaulte; wher they shot goonns and arrows into the citie, and dyd moche harme and hurte. And, at the laste, set fiere upon the gates, for to have brent them, and so trustinge to have entred at large. Theyr brennynge at the bridge profytid them of no thynge ; albe they brent many howses to the nombar of iij ˣˣ, but the citizens hadd set suche ordenaunce in theyr ways that, thowghe all the way had been open, it had bene to harde for them to have entred by that way, but upon theyr lyves. The maior, aldarmen, and worshipfull citizens of the citie were in good array, and set to every parte, where was behovefull, greate felowshipe, welle ordered, and ordeyned, for to withstand the malice of thes forsayd rebells.

To the citizens, and defence of the citie, came th'Erle of Essex, and many knights, squiers, gentlemen, and yemen, right well arraied, which had right great diligence in orderinge the citizens, and firste to prepare and ordayne for the defence and surtye of the sayd cittie and people thereof where it was necessarye, and preparyd how and where they myght best ysswe owt upon them, and put them from theyr purpos. By which medelinge of gentlemen, and lords servauntes, with the citizens, in every parte, the citizens were greatly encoragyd to set sharply upon them with one hoole entent, where elles it had be lykely they shuld nat have willed to have done so moche therto as was donne. For, as it is afore-sayde, greate nombar of the citie were there that with right good wille woulde they have bene sofferyd to have enteryd the citie, to th'entent to have fallen to myscheffe and robberye with them. And so, aftar continu-ynge of muche shote of gonnes and arrows a greate while, upon bothe par-ties, th'Erle Ryvers, that was with the Qwene, in the Tower of London, gatheryd unto hym a felashipe right well chosen, and habiled, of iiij or v c men, and ysswyd owt at a posterne upon them, and, even upon a poynt, cam upon the Kentyshe men beinge abowte the assawltynge of Algate, and mightely laied upon them with arrows, and upon them in hands, and so killyd and toke many of them, dryvynge them from the same gate to the watar syde. Yet netheles, three placis wer fiers brennynge all at ones. The Maior, Aldarmen, and many of the sayde citie, were anone in theyr harnes, and parted theyr felashippe into divers partes, as them thowght moste behofefull, but a great parte of the citizens were at Algate, and with them many gentlemen and yemen, which all made the defence that they best myght; and shott many gouns, and arrows, amonge them; but for thy the Kentishemen spared nat to assayle at bothe the gates, so that the sayde lorde and citizens determined in themselve to arredy them in good array, and to ysswe owt upon them, in hands, and put them to flyght and discomfiture. About iij ᴍ and [mo] fell in the chas of them, and slew mo than vij ᶜ of them. Many were taken, and aftar hanged; the remenaunt went to the watarsyde, and toke theyr boates, and went to theyr shipps, and ovar to that othar syde agayn.

Thes haynows traytowrs and robbers, the bastard and his felawshyppe, seing they cowthe in nowyse profite to theyr entents, by litle and litle withdrewe them to the Blackhethe, to an hill three myle from London, the xvj., xvij., and xviij. day of Maye, there abydynge by the space of three dayes; but, theyr abydynge, they had certayne knowledge that the Kynge was comynge with great puisaunce, whereof they greatly adrad, seinge that they myght nat have theyr praye of London, ne havynge hardies to abyde the Kynge and his puisaunce, they disperbled; they of Calais, to Calais, the sonest they cowlde; suche as were of othar contrys, into theyrs; many of Kent, to theyr howses; the mariners, and myschevows robbars, rebells, and riotours with them, to theyr shipps; and drewe downe to the sea coaste with all theyr shipps.

The Kynge this season, well accompanied and mightely with great lordes, and in substaunce all the noblemen of the land, with many othar able men, well arraied for the werre, to the nombar of xxx m horsemen, cam to the citie of London, sone aftar the disperblynge of the Kentyshe hooste, the xxj. day of Maye, the Twesdaye; where he was honorably re-ceyved of all the people, the maior, aldermen, and many othar worshipfull men, citizens of the sayd citie. At the metyng of them the Kynge dubed Knyghtes the maior, the recordar, dyvars aldarmen, with othar worshipfull of the sayd citie of London, whiche as hadd mannly and honorably acquit them selfe agaynst the bastard, and his crwell hooste; honoringe, and rewardinge them with the ordar, of his good love and grace, for theyr trwe acquitaill, and as they had ryght well and trewly de-servyd that tyme.

Here it is to be remembred, that, from the tyme of Tewkesbery fielde, where Edward, called Prince, was slayne, thanne, and sonne aftar, wer taken, and slayne, and at the Kyngs wylle, all the noblemen that came from beyond the see with the sayde Edward, called Prince, and othar also theyr parte-takers as many as were of eny might or puisaunce. Qwene Margaret, hirselfe, taken, and browght to the Kynge; and, in every party of England, where any commotion was begonne for Kynge Henry's party, anone they were rebuked, so that it appered to every mann at eye the sayde partie was extincte and repressed for evar, without any mannar hope of agayne quikkening; utterly despaired of any maner of hoope or releve. The certaintie of all whiche came to the knowledge of the sayd Henry, late called Kyng, being in the Tower of London; not havynge, afore that, knowledge of the saide matars, he toke it to so great dispite, ire, and indingnation, that, of pure displeasure, and melencoly, he dyed the xxiij. day of the monithe of May. Whom the Kynge dyd to be browght to the friers prechars at London, and there, his funerall service donne, to be caried, by watar, to an Abbey upon Tha-mys syd, xvj myles from London, called Chartsey, and there honorably enteryd.

The Kynge, incontinent aftar his comynge to London, taried but one daye, and went with his hole army, aftar his sayd traytors into Kent.

them to represse, in caas they were in any place assembled, and for to let them to assemble by any comocion to be made amongs them, wher unto they, heretoforne, have often tymes bene accustomyd to doo. But, trewthe it was, that they were disperbled as afore; but the sayd bastard Faucomberge, with great nombar of mariners, and many othar mischevows men, called his sowldiours, or men of were, went streyght to Sandwyche, and there kept the towne with strengthe, and many great and small shipps, abowt xl and vij, in the haven, all undar his rule. And, as sone as they undarstode the Kynge and his hoste aprochid nere unto them, the sayd bastard sent unto hym suche meanes as best he cowthe, humbly to sew for his grace and pardon, and them of his feloshipe, and, by appoyntement, willed there to be delyveryd to the Kyngs behove all his shipps, and became his trwe liegemen, with as streight promyse of trew legiaunce as cowthe be devised for them to be made, whiche, aftar delyberation taken in that parte, for certayn great consyderations, was grauntyd. Wherefore the Kynge sent thethar his brothar Richard, Duke of Gloucestar, to receyve them in his name, and all the shipps ; as he so dyd the xxvj. day of the same monithe ; the Kynge that tyme beinge at Cantorbery.

And thus, with the helpe of Almighty God, the moaste glorious Virgin Mary his mothar, and of Seint George, and of [all] the Saynts of heven, was begon, finished, and termined, the reentrie and perfecte recover of the iuste title and right of owr sayd soveraygne Lord Kynge Edward the Fowrthe, to his realme and crowne of England, within the space of xj wekes ; in the whiche season, moienaunt the helpe and grace of Allmyghty God, by his wysdome, and polyqwe, he escaped and passyd many great perills, and daungars, and dificulties, wherin he had bene ; and, by his full noble and knyghtly cowrage, hathe optayned two right-great, crwell, and mortall battayles ; put to flight and discomfeture dyvars great assembles of his rebells, and riotows persons, in many partyes of his land ; the whiche, thowghe all they were also rygorously and maliciously disposed, as they myght be, they were, netheles, so affrayde and afferyd of the verey asswryd courage and manhod that restethe in the person of our seyd sovereigne lord, that they were, anon, as confused. Whereby it apperithe, and faythfully is belevyd, that with the helpe of Almyghty God, whiche from his begynning hitharto hathe not fayled hym, in short tyme he shall appeas his subgetes thrwghe all his royalme ; that peace and tranquillitie shall growe and multiplye in the same, from day to day, to the honour and lovynge of Almyghty God, the encreace of his singuler and famows renoume, and to the great ioye and consolation of his frinds, alies, and well-willers, and to all his people, and to the great confusion of all his enemys, and evyll wyllars.

Here endethe the arryvaile of Kynge Edward the Fowrthe. Out of Mastar Flyghtwods boke, Recordar of London.

NOTES.

P. 1, *l*. 7, *calling himself Lievetenaunte of England.*—All the knowledge we have of the parliamentary arrangements made for carrying on the government during the short repossession of the throne by Henry VI. is derived from a statement of Polydore Vergil, which seems rather at variance with the notion of Warwick alone being Lieutenant of England. The roll of the parliament which met on the 26th November 1470 is not known to be in existence; probably it was destroyed in 1477 when all the proceedings of that parliament were annulled. (*Rot. Parl. VI.* 191.) The effect of Vergil's statement is accurately given by Hall in the following words : " Besides this, the Erle of Warwycke, as one to whome the common welthe was much beholden, was made Ruler and Gouvernor of the realme, with whom as felow and compaignion was associated George Duke of Clarence his sonne-in-law." (*Hall, p* 286. *Vergil, p.* 521.) Probably the present writer is correct; but if Warwick and Clarence were, as Shakspeare expresses it,

> " Yoak'd together like a double shadow
> " To Henry's body," (*Third part of Henry VI. act IV. sc.* 7,)

the omission by the present writer, in this and several other places, of any mention of Clarence's share in the Lieutenancy may be attributed to an anxiety not to make Clarence's treachery to Henry appear the more obviously inexcusable.

—— *l*. 9, *callynge hymselfe Prynce of Wales.*—Edward was created Prince of Wales in 1454. (*Vide Rot. Parl. V.* 249.)

—— *l*. 13. *presently,* i. e. being present.

—— *l*. 17, *endynge the x. yere.*—The regnal years of Edward IV. were reckoned from the 4th day of March 1461, the day on which he took possession of the throne; (*Fabyan,* 639;) his tenth year ended therefore on the 3rd March 1471.

—— *l*. 20, *accompanied with ij thowsand Englishmen.*—Henry's government at first represented Edward's adherents as consisting wholly of foreigners, (*Fœdera, XI.* 705,) but afterwards admitted they were partly Englishmen and partly Flemings. (*Ibid.* 706.) The Chroniclers are singularly contradictory.

187

The Croyland Continuator describes them as 1500 Englishmen; (*Gale, I.* 554 ;) Fabyan as a small company of Flemings and others not exceeding 1000 in number; (*Fabyan,* 660;) Polydore Vergil as scarcely 2000 men at arms; (*Vergil, p.* 522 ;) the Chronicler in Leland as 900 Englishmen and 300 Flemings. (*Collect. II.* 503.)

P. 1, *l.* 22, *his realme of England at that tyme usurpyd and occupied by Henry, callyd Henry the VI.*—Henry's brief restoration took place in the month of October 1470 ; the day is variously stated. There are documents in the Fœdera in Henry's name dated the 9th of October. (*XI.* 661—664.)

P. 2, *l.* 18, *in especiall by th'Erle of Oxenforde.*—Preparations to resist the meditated return of Edward IV. were made as early as December 1470. On the 21st of that month a Commission was directed to the Marquis Montague, authorising him, in case of necessity, to raise the counties of Nottyngham, York, Northumberland, Cumberland and Westmerland ; (*Fœd. XI.* 676 ;) and a Commission of a similar character, but extending all over England, was directed to the Duke of Clarence, the Earl of Warwick, the Earl of Oxford and Sir John Scrope on the 28th of December. (*Ibid.* 677.) By a writ dated the 2nd January 1471, the Sheriffs and people of the counties of Cambridge, Huntingdon, Norfolk, Suffolk, Essex and Hertford, were directed to be attendant upon the last-mentioned Commissioners. (*Ibid.* 678.) The exertions of the Earl of Oxford in raising men in the Eastern Counties are manifest from two letters in the Paston Collection. (*II.* 54, 58.)

P. 3, *l.* 16, *scuringe,* i. e. assuring.

P. 4, *l.* 14, *by the ledinge and gwydynge of a priste.*—This appears to have been one John Westerdale, who was afterwards thrown into the Marshalsea prison, probably for his interference upon this occasion. (*Leland's Coll. II.* 503.)

—— *l.* 15, *Martyn of the See,* i. e. Martin de la Mere.

—— *l.* 21, *declared by the iij. astates of the land.*—The parliamentary recognition of the right of Richard, Duke of York, here referred to, took place A.D. 1460. (*Vide Rot. Parl. V.* 377.)

P. 5, *l.* 4. *gadrers,* gadres, in MS.

—— *l.* 14, *only of hardies,* hardies and, in MS.

—— *l.* 27, *he came to the gates afore the citie.*—Polydore Vergil here introduces a long account of the parleying of the citizens with Edward IV. from their walls during the whole of one day, and their ultimately insisting upon his taking an oath to be faithful to Henry VI. before they would permit him to enter; which oath he took on the following morning at the gate of the City. Vergil adds that Edward's perjury in this instance was probably the occasion of the punishment which fell upon his family in the murder of his sons. (P. 524.)

The Historian probably thought that the excellence of the moral was a sufficient justification for the invention of the incident, or, at any event, for its amplification from Fabyan, who says, that Edward confirmed with an oath his deceptive declaration that he came merely to claim his father's rights. (P. 660.) Fabyan is a poor authority for an incident which took place at York.

P. 6, l. 6, I deme ye, i. e. yea.—Although the Marquis Montague subsequently appeared in arms in the party of his brother, the Earl of Warwick, there is reason to believe that the present writer was correct in supposing that he was secretly favorable to Edward IV. (*Vide Leland's Coll. II.* 505; *Polydore Vergil,* 527.)

—— *l. 16, gret partye of the noble men and comons in thos parties, were towards th'Erle of Northumbarland, and would not stire with any lorde or noble man other than with the sayde Earle.*—The Chronicler in Leland's Collectanea asserts that " as Edward passid the Countery he shewid the Erle of Northumbrelande's lettre and seale that sent for hym," (*II.* 503)—a stratagem quite in character, but which is not mentioned by any other authority. The feudal authority of the Earl of Northumberland is exemplified in other passages, at p. 7, and p. 32. The same power is attributed in the West to the Duke of Somerset and the Earl of Devonshire, as " the old enheritors of that contrie." (P. 23.)

—— *l. 33, England had*—England and had, in MS.

—— *l. 34, a great battaile in those same parties.*—The battle of Towton, fought 29th March, 1461.

P. 7, l. 35, scorers, or, as it is in other places, *scowrers,* i. e. scouts, avant-couriers, or afore-riders.

P. 8, l. 17, disperpled,—The same as disperbled, i. e. dispersed, which occurs hereafter p. 37, and also in Fabyan, p. 31.

P. 9, l. 10, the Kynge desyred him to come owte with all his people into the filde.— The Chronicler in Leland says, that Warwick would have fought, but that " he had receyvid a lettre from the Duke of Clarence that he should not fight on til he cam." (*Coll. II.* 504.)

P. 10, l. 23, my lady, theyr mother—This was Cicely, daughter of Ralph Neville, first Earl of Westmerland, (*Dug. Bar. I.* 299, *b.*) Of her large family we here find mention, besides Edward IV. and his brothers Clarence and Gloucester, of Margaret, married to the Duke of Burgundy; Anne, the wife of Henry Holland, Duke of Exeter; and Elizabeth, wife of John de la Pole, Duke of Suffolk.

—— *l. 29, high and mighty ;* right and mighty, in MS.

—— *l. 33, so that ;* to that, in MS.

P. 11, l. 21, trew service ; trew servaunts, in MS.

P. 12, l. 16, the great promises, pacts, and othes, to the contrary, made solempnily,

and also priuately sworne, to the Frenche Kynge, Qwene Margarete, and hir sonne Edward.
There is a curious and very little known MS. upon this subject in the same
Volume of Stowe's transcripts from which the foregoing narrative has been
derived, entitled, " The Maner and Gwidynge of the Erle of Warwick at
Aungiers from the xvth day of July to the iiijth of August 1470, which day
he departed from Aungiers." It is printed in Sir Henry Ellis's Collection of Original Letters, 2d Series, I. 132.

P. 12, *l.* 22, *escape by the sea to Calais, whiche was enswryd to hym selfe in every*
caas that myght hape hym.—Warwick was Captain of Calais, and his popularity
there is very strikingly pictured by De Comines, who was an eye-witness of it.
Within a quarter of an hour after the arrival of tidings of the restoration of
Henry VI. every body in the town, high and low, rich and poor, placed the
Earl's badge, the ragged staff, in his cap. Those who could afford it had it of
gold, the poorer sort embroidered it upon the cloth. The instantaneous out-
burst of rejoicing upon this sudden change in affairs occasioned considerable
astonishment to De Comines, and called forth some of his usual sarcastic
observations. (*I.* 202.)

P. 13, *l.* 7, *barred and letted,* barred and lettynge, in MS.

—— *l.* 10, *their auctoritie,* the auctoritie, in MS.

P. 14, *l.* 23, *good hope,* good helpe, in MS.

P. 18, *l.* 31, *alnyght,* almyghe, in MS.

—— *l.* 35, *therby they,* therby he, in MS.

P. 19, *l.* 2, *there was a great miste.*—Fabyan writes in the following very prudent manner respecting this mist. " Of the mystes and other impedimentes
which fell upon the lordes partye *by reason of the incantacyons wrought by fryer*
Bungey, as the fame went, me lyst nat to wryte." (P. 661.)

—— *l.* 5. *sone they,* sone ther, in MS.

P. 20, *l.* 15—17. *The Duke of Excestar was smytten downe—and so aftar he*
escaped.—The subsequent fortunes of the Duke of Exeter are thus told by De
Comines : " J'ay veu un Duc estre allé à pied sans chausses, apres le train
dudit Duc [de Bourgongne] pour chassant sa vie de maison à maison, sans se
nommer. C'estoit le plus prochain de la lignée de Lanclastre : avoit epousé la
sœur du Roy Edoüard. Apres fu connu : et eut une petite pension pour s'en-
tretenir." (*I.* 185.)

P. 21, *l.* 10. *My Lord Cardinall of England.*—Thomas Bourchier, Archbishop
of Canterbury.

P. 22, *l.* 31. *Beawlew.*—Beaulieu Abbey, founded by King John. (*Vide*
Monasticon, V. 680.)

P. 23, *l.* 1. *Seern,* i. e. Cerne Abbey.

P. 24, *l.* 20. *Jasper, called Erle of Penbroke, had been afore sent into the contrie of Wales to arays them.*—A Commission to array the Welsh in the cause of Henry VI. and directed to the Duke of Clarence and the Earls of Pembroke and Warwick, was issued as early as the 30th January 1471. (*Fœdera, XI.* 680.)

P. 24, *l.* 37, *algates*, i. e. always.

P. 27, *l.* 5, *ether have kept*, othar have kept, in MS.

P. 29, *l.* 21, *one of;* on in, in MS.

P. 30, *l.* 14, *mylene* ; i. e. a mill.

—— *l.* 18. *Edward, called Prince, was taken fleinge to the towne wards and slayne in the fielde.*—The authorities are greatly at variance upon the long disputed subject of the death of this young Prince ; but much matter, that is really of no weight at all, has been very unnecessarily introduced into what has been written on both sides. The following, with the addition of the author now printed, may be considered as the statements of the contemporary writers.

The *Croyland Continuator* writes with what seems to be a studious ambiguity.

" Potitus est Rex Edwardus præclara victoria, interfectis de parte Reginæ, tum in campo tum postea ultricibus quorundam manibus, ipso Principe Edwardo, unigenito Regis Henrici, victo Duce Somersetiæ, Comiteque Devoniæ, ac aliis dominis omnibus et singulis memoratis." (*Gale, I.* 555.) Here it is uncertain whether the Prince died in the field, or afterwards " ultricibus quorundam manibus ;" and whether those words allude to the decapitation of the Duke of Somerset and the others on the day after the battle, which is admitted, or to the assassination of Edward in the manner related by other historians, which is controverted.

Fabyan says,

" In the which batayll she [Queen Margaret] was taken and Sir Edwarde her sone, and so brought unto the Kynge. But after the Kinge hadde questyoned with the sayd Sir Edwarde, and he had answeryd unto hym contrarye his pleasure, he thenne strake hym with his gauntelet upon the face; after whiche stroke so by him receyved, he was by the Kynges seruantes incontynently slayne upon the iiij. day of the moneth of May." (P. 662.) Fabyan's statement, that Queen Margaret was taken in the battle, is certainly not accurate.

The *Chronicler in Leland* says,

" There [at Tewkesbury] was slayn Prince Edwarde crying on the Duke of Clarence, his brother in law, for help. There was slayne also Curtney, Erle of Devonshir," and various others, all of whom are agreed to have been killed in the battle. (*Leland's Coll. II.* 506.)

Polydore Vergil writes thus :

" Edouardus princeps adolescens præstantissimus, aliquanto post ductus ad colloquium cum Edouardo, interrogatur ab eo, cur ejus regnum ingressus

ausus esset id armis divexare? Cui præsenti animo respondit se avitum regnum recuperatum venisse. Ad ea Edouardus nihil respondens, tantum manu
adolescentem procul submovit, quem in vestigio qui circumstabant (circumstabant autem Georgius Clarentiæ, Ricardus Glocestriæ duces, et Gulielmus
Hastyngius,) crudeliter trucidarunt, ejusque corpus cum reliquis interfectorum
cadaveribus in proximo cænobio monachorum ordinis divi Benedicti huma-
tur."* (P. 530.)

De Comines simply remarks,

" Le dit Roy Edoüard en eut la victoire et fut le Prince des Galles tué sur
le champ." (*I.* 210.)

P. 31, *l.* 10, *Clyfton*, Clyston, in MS.

—— *l.* 23, *founden nat fer*, nat founden far, in MS.

P. 38, *l.* 9, *the Kynge dubed Knyghtes the maior, the recordar, dyvars aldermen,
with othar worshipfull of the sayd Citie of London.*—The Chronicler in Leland,
supplying information which we might have expected to find in Fabyan, in-
forms us, that "Syr John Stokton [the Mayor], Syr Rafe Verney, Syr
Richard Lee, Syr John Young, Syr William Taylor, Syr George Ireland,
Syr John Stoker, Syr Matthieu Philip, Syr William Hampton, Syr Thomas
Stalbroke, Syr John Crosby [one of the Sheriffs], and Syr Thomas Ursewike,
Recorder of London," were the persons thus honored. (*Lel. Coll. II.* 507.)

—— *l.* 29, *he dyed the xxiij. day of the monithe of May.*—Some one has added
here in the margin of the MS. with a reference after the word " dyed," " or was
mordered." The death of Henry VI. is one of those dark events, the truth
respecting which cannot fail to become matter of dispute. The present
author states, it will be perceived, that he died " of pure displeasure and
melencoly" on the 23rd May, which was the day of the Ascension, or Holy
Thursday. The other authorities are as follow :

The Croyland Continuator tells all that was certainly known—perhaps all that
ever will be known—in the following significant words :

" Taceo, hoc temporum interstitio [i. e. during Edward's absence in Kent]
inventum esse corpus Regis Henrici in Turri Londinensi exanime : Parcat
Deus, et spatium pœnitentiæ ei donet, quicunque tam sacrilegas manus in Chris-
tum Domini ausus est immittere." (*Gale, I.* 556.)

---

* Hall, as usual, translates Polydore Vergil ; but adds, that Prince Edward was taken on the
field by Sir Richard Croftes, and by him delivered up after the battle, in consequence of a proclamation offering a reward of £100 per annum for life to any one who would find the Prince, dead
or alive, and also declaring that the Prince's life should be spared. Hall is a very poor authority
in his additions to Vergil ; but it is worthy of investigation whether Sir Richard Crofts ever received any annuity of £100 per annum.

Fabyan, after stating that on " Ascension Euyn," that is, on the 22nd May, the late King's corpse was brought " unreverently " from the Tower to St. Paul's, and thence conveyed, on the morrow, to Chertsey, adds :

" Of the death of this Prynce dyuerse tales were tolde : but the most common fame wente, that he was stykked with a dagger by the handes of the Duke of Gloucester." (P. 662.)

The Chronicler in Leland writes as if he had known " the very heart of the mystery."

" The same night, beyng the 21. day of May, and Tuesday, at night, betwixt a xi. and xii. of the Clok, was King Henry, being Prisoner yn the Toure, put to Deth : the Duke of Glocestre and dyverse other beyng there that night." (*Coll. II.* 507.)

The same author agrees with Fabyan that the corpse was removed to St. Paul's on the 22nd May.

Polydore Vergil relates the common rumour ;

" Henricus Sextus, paulo ante regno dejectus, in Turri morte affectus est ; hunc, ut fama constans est, Ricardus Glocestriæ dux gladio percussit, quo ita Edouardus rex ejus frater omni hostili metu liberaretur." (P. 532.)

De Comines places the death after the battle of Barnet instead of Tewkesbury, and says,

" Si je n'en ai oüi mentir, incontinent apres cette battaille le Duc de Glocestre....tua de sa main, ou fit tuer en sa presence, en quelque lieu à part, ce bon homme le Roy Henry."—(*Id.* 209.)

The contradiction between the date of the exhibition of the corpse as stated by the Leland Chronicler, who is a very good authority—and by Fabyan, who is generally pretty accurate respecting matters which took place in London—and the date of the death as given by the author now published, if considered with reference to the position of the various persons interested in Henry's death on those days, and the circumstances of his hurried interment, will be found to be destructive of the credit of our author's version of what was in all probability an infamous murder.

INDEX.